YOUR ALL-IN-ONE DICTIONARY OF
GOOD HEALTH AND NUTRITION

Many thousands across the country can attest to the
great value of having *The All-in-One Carbohydrate
Gram Counter* at their fingertips. Now, renowned
nutrition expert Jean Carper has completely revised
and updated this book with the latest information
available from food manufacturers and from the U.S.
Department of Agriculture. She has also included
the latest research on the health benefits of complex
carbohydrates. This convenient and important book
contains entries on virtually every food imaginable—
from fast foods, to brand-names, to fresh foods and
vegetables, to many foods most of us overlook in our
pursuit of good health and nutrition.

The All-In-One Carbohydrate Gram Counter

By Jean Carper

2nd Revised Edition

BANTAM BOOKS

TORONTO · NEW YORK · LONDON · SYDNEY · AUCKLAND

THE ALL-IN-ONE CARBOHYDRATE GRAM COUNTER
*A Bantam Book / published by arrangement with
Workman Publishing Co., Inc.*

PRINTING HISTORY
Bantam edition / November 1973

2nd printing..........April 1974	6th printing...........June 1976
3rd printing....December 1974	7th printing......January 1977
4th printing ....May 1975	8th printing....September 1977
5th printing ....March 1976	9th printing......January 1978
10th printing........January 1979	

Revised Bantam edition / August 1980

2nd printing ...January 1981	4th printing ....March 1983
3rd printing............May 1982	5th printing......January 1984
6th printing........January 1986	

2nd Bantam revised edition........March 1987

ISBN 0-553-26405-2

Published simultaneously in the United States and Canada

Bantam Books are published by Bantam Books, Inc. Its trademark, consisting of the words "Bantam Books" and the por-
trayal of a rooster, is Registered in U.S. Patent and Trademark
Office and in other countries. Marca Registrada. Bantam
Books, Inc., 666 Fifth Avenue, New York, New York 10103.

PRINTED IN THE UNITED STATES OF AMERICA
O   0 9 8 7 6 5 4 3 2 1

Contents

Introduction

There are any number of reasons why you might want to know how much carbohydrate you are consuming. There are two types of carbohydrates: simple carbohydrates or sugars and complex carbohydrates or starches found in foods such as grains and vegetables.

When I wrote those lines for the very first edition of this book in 1973, millions of Americans were united in a passion to avoid carbohydrates; they were following one of the most popular diets of all time—the low-carbohydrate weight-loss diet formulated by Dr. Robert Atkins and explained in his book, *Dr. Atkins' Diet Revolution*. The *All-In-One Carbohydrate Counter* was conceived as "the perfect companion" to Dr. Atkins' book. Obviously, to cut down on carbohydrates, you must know which foods contain them. Now, years later, many Americans still follow Dr. Atkins' diet revolution; his books, advising people to restrict carbohydrates, are sensationally popular year after year. And *The All-In-One Carbohydrate Counter* is still an essential companion if you are following a low-carbohydrate diet.

There is no question that some persons who never seem to lose weight by counting calories achieve amazing success on a low-carbohydrate diet. Undeniably, some dieters simply find low-carbohydrate diets in which they can eat certain calorie-laden foods, such as high-fat dairy foods, more pleasant, filling and effective than counting calories. You may be one of these dieters.

Although Dr. Atkins' diet is perhaps the best known, carbohydrate-sparing diets are not really new. The first one appeared in the 1880s. And there have been numerous popular variations, such as *The Drinking Man's Diet* and Dr. Stillman's *Doctor's Quick Weight Loss Diet*. More recently, Dr. Judith Wurtman's *The Carbohydrate Craver's Diet Book* details scientifically how too much carbohydrate can do you in, creating a blood chemistry that causes you to want more carbohydrates. Dr. Wurtman also notes that a person who craves carbohydrates may have a special type of metabolic makeup that needs restrictive carbohydrate feedings to keep his or her blood chemistry stable.

There are the other negative features of sugary carbohydrates. It has been known for years that sugar rots your teeth. There have also been periodic suggestions that sugar plays a role in heart disease, although the evidence is far from conclusive. Some persons have an inborn metabolic intolerance to sugar; some develop diabetes. And even perfectly normal people can experience attacks of trembling and headaches after eating too much sugar. It seems medically certain that people vary in their response to sugar. As Dr. Jesse Roth of the National Institute of Arthritis and Metabolic Diseases has said, a person should learn his or her individual capacity for simple carbohydrates just as a person learns his or her capacity for alcohol. Some people simply can tolerate sugar better than others.

At the same time, complex carbohydrates (the starchy types) have achieved a remarkable new status in the nutritional arena. Many people are now trying to increase their intake of carbohydrates. Cancer experts proclaim that the nutritional elements in a variety of carbohydrate foods, including certain vegetables and grains, are extremely good for you—as a possible preventive for various cancers, namely colon and lung cancer. Studies show that when people eat more carbohydrates, they automatically eat less fat, and fat is believed to contribute to the progression of some cancers, notably breast cancer. Carbohydrate foods such as oat bran and dried beans, very high in insoluble dietary fiber, have been shown to lower blood cholesterol, thus helping ward off heart disease.

Athletes have shifted their preference for energy generators from protein to carbohydrate foods. Tennis star Martina Navratilova has led the way, crediting much of her high performance to a high-carbohydrate diet, as noted in Robert Haas's bestselling book, *Eat to Win*.

Thus, while many readers will consult this carbohydrate counter to avoid carbohydrates, others will use it to increase their intake of complex carbohydrates.

Presumably, if you are following a low-carbohydrate diet, you already know the rules of your specific diet and are committed to losing weight. So there is no use wasting your time by telling you all the horrible things that can happen to you if you don't keep your weight in check. If you are embarked on or contemplating a low-carbohydrate diet, all you need to know now are the foods you can safely eat so as not to exceed the carbohydrate limit you have set for yourself. And that is where this book will help you. Conversely, if you desire to increase your consumption of complex carbohydrate foods, this book will also help you by steering you to grains, fruits and vegetables that are high in carbohydrates. Remember that the type of carbohydrate in candy, cake, pastry and other sweets is sugar, not starch; you will undoubtedly want to limit sugary carbohydrates in any case.

In this book you will find the latest information on how many grams of carbohydrate there are in all kinds of foods— both fresh and processed (the latter by brand name, of course) —from A to Z. And there's a special section on fast foods, everything from Big Mac's to Dairy Queen sundaes.

A word about the figures in the book. This book was first published in 1973 and has been an enormous success. Numerous readers have written to say how much it helped them. Since the last revision in 1980, some of the carbohydrate counts have changed because of new analyses or reformulation of products, and new products have been introduced. Thus, new figures were gathered for this complete revision. We simply did the book over from start to finish. Of course, some of the gram counts are the same or similar, since the carbohydrate content in many basic foods, such as bread, cereals, milk, as well as alcoholic drinks, don't change much. A few companies we contacted did not have new information; thus we used their previous figures.

The figures bearing brand names in this book were provided by food companies and are the latest the company advised us were available. Only a few companies we contacted declined to send available information.

In virtually all cases we used the serving sizes indicated by the companies; in a few instances we changed the serving size and corresponding carbohydrate counts. For example, we converted a "serving size" of two slices of bread to one slice.

We used the carbohydrate figures as provided by the companies. Many companies, notably those using nutritional labeling, provide carbohydrate gram counts that are rounded off. For example, a count of 5.9 grams may be rounded up to 6 grams. On the other hand, many companies still report figures without rounding off, which accounts for the more precise counts. Since foods may vary slightly, such rounding off is insignificant. Some companies have asked us to point out that their figures are the best average calculations or analyses they have on specific products, but because of normal variations beyond their control, there may be ever-so-slight variations from batch to batch for the same manufacturer. Even such factors as seasonal conditions or soil composition may influence final food nutritional values.

More companies are now putting nutritional labels on their foods. Still, it is difficult to make comparisions among various brand name foods without running all around the supermarket. Thus a primary benefit of this book: You can pick out the foods with carbohydrate counts to your liking *before* you go shopping.

Most carbohydrate counts remain exceedingly stable over the years. However, occasionally a food maker will change the composition of a product, changing the carbohydrate content. In that case, if the food is labeled, the carbohydrate count on the label will differ from that in this book. To avoid confusion, if such contradictions exist, you should assume the food composition has changed and the label is correct. The accuracy of a food company's labeling is regulated by the federal Food and Drug Administration, and a company would be subject to severe penalties for putting out a food label that is grossly inaccurate.

All the carbohydrate gram counts without a brand name or company attribution are from the U.S. Department of Agriculture. Here, too, some calculations were done to make sure the figures were in the most convenient form.

To sum up, the new revised *All-In-One Carbohydrate Gram Counter* will provide you with the latest, most accurate, comprehensive data available on fresh foods, processed foods and restaurant chain fast foods.

JEAN CARPER

How to Use This Book

The most important organizational fact about the All-In-One Carbohydrate Gram Counter, as you will quickly see, is that it is alphabetized for easy use according to food categories. That is, you don't have to look in the front of the book under B for bean soup and then flip to the T's to find out if tomato soup is lower in carbohydrates. The supermarket portion of the book runs through the alphabet, starting with baby food and ending with yogurt. After that, you will find a special section on fast-food chains.

All the breads are listed together in the B section, all the fruits are grouped together under F, the vegetables under V and so on. Simply by looking at the Contents in the front of the book, you can quickly spot which category a food is in and turn directly to that section. You will then find the foods alphabetized within the sections. Some foods, to be sure, just don't fit easily into categories, and rather than force them into some artificial grouping, we have listed them alphabetically too, even though there may be only one or two of a kind; for example, baking powder and thickeners have listings of their own.

In other words, the book is akin to a dictionary—with headings at the top of each page, too, to help you out. If you get stuck and can't decide where a food might be, just consult the index.

We have tried to standardize the language and the serving sizes as much as possible to make them useful, but here again we haven't strained the point. We have tried to be practical. For example, under cereals you won't find all of them in either 1-cup or ½-cup portions. The reason: Cereals vary greatly in their density and weight. Thus, the typical 1-ounce serving size for cereals varies in cup measurements, depending on the type of cereal. An ounce of puffed rice will fill a 1-cup measuring cup, but an ounce of heavier All-Bran fills about ⅓ of a measuring cup. In all cases, we have followed the manufacturers' recommendations and provided single serving sizes they believe appropriate.

For listings using the word "prepared," the carbohydrate counts are based on the assumption that the food has been prepared according to the manufacturer's directions. If you alter the preparation, for example, by adding sugar to a sauce, or adding other embellishments of your own, you must figure in these extras.

In most cases, companies prefer to tell you how many carbohydrates are in the finished prepared product—for example, a cup of mashed potatoes from the dry flakes—because it is rare that the powder would be used in any other way. But in some instances you will find the carbohydrate count for the dry mix only—*before* preparation. That way, if you want to add another ingredient to your mix, you can do so and add up the extra carbohydrate. Also on this note: Whenever you merely add water to a mix, you are not adding any carbohydrate—for example when you prepare a Lipton's dry soup mix. If you use the dry soup mix in any other fashion, say as a dip mix, there are the same number of carbohydrate grams in the dry mix as in the cup of prepared soup.

In keeping with our determination to make this book easy to use, we have taken due note of the power of identity of brand names. Whenever possible, without interfering with the organization, we have used brand names for quick identification. Thus, when you look up a certain cookie, cracker or cereal, you don't have to peruse the whole list searching for a description of your cookie. We don't have Cheez-Its listed under "crackers, cheese"; it is alphabetized simply under Cheez-Its. Similarly, we have Oreo cookies under O and not under "Chocolate creme sandwiches." The same goes for Froot Loops (under F in the cereal section). At the same time, it was not always possible to do this without creating a chaotic organization, and in many cases the only identifying factor is a description of the product (chocolate chip cookies, for example) and the name of the manufacturer.

Within the listings, we repeat the measurements frequently. However, on items such as cookies, crackers and frozen dinners, where the portion size is almost always one cracker, cookie or complete dinner, we have simply noted the portion at the head of the section. This has also been done on fairly short listings.

To avoid confusion, whenever possible, we have stated the measurement in the most easily used terms: cups, tablespoons and fluid ounces for liquids and items such as canned fruits and vegetables; and weight ounces for items such as cheese and frozen fish filets. On some of the candy bars, we have noted the grams of carbohydrate per ounce, so you can figure total amounts if the sizes of the candy bars change. Since many candy companies report carbohydrate content for their current-size bars, we urge you to check the weight of the candy bar on the wrapper to be sure it corresponds with the weight noted in this book.

In this revision, we have retained our "health foods" section, even though such foods have become increasingly popular and widely purchased. The line between such "health and natural" foods and general foods is growing less clear, as Americans become more nutrition-conscious and many food companies respond by formulating and promoting so-called "health foods." Even so, some companies and some ingredients, such as carob, are still closely associated in the public's mind with "health and natural" foods and we think it is easier for readers who want to find those products to look them up in a special section. Some of the products are still sold only in specialty or "health food" stores. However, we have to admit that some such foods may have slipped over into other sections. So if you don't find them one place, check elsewhere.

For our readers who have used the previous edition, here is what's new about this revision. It has many more items both by brand name and generic. We are listing nearly 7500 items compared with 5500 in our last edition. The sections on candy, beer and wine, snacks of all types, doughnuts and "health and natural" foods have been especially expanded.

Despite our best efforts, there is no way we can save you from doing some figuring on your own, simply because no one, including yourself, wants to eat the food company's designated serving size all the time. And obviously, when you use your own recipes, you can obtain the gram counts for only the basic ingredients. You have to take it from there.

For doing your own conversions, here is an equivalency table that may help:

1 tablespoon = 3 teaspoons
2 tablespoons = 1 fluid ounce

4 tablespoons = ¼ cup
5⅓ tablespoons = ⅓ cup
16 tablespoons = 1 cup
1 cup = 8 fluid ounces
= 1 pint
2 pints = 1 quart
1 pound = 16 ounces

Happy gram counting!

Abbreviations

art	artificial
diam	diameter
fl	fluid
in	inch
lb	pound
med	medium
oz	ounce
pkg	package
swt	sweetened
tbsp	tablespoon
tsp	teaspoon
unswt	unsweetened
w	with
wo	without

Baby Food

BAKED GOODS

1 piece

Biscuits / **Gerber**	9
Cookie, animal shaped / **Gerber**	4.5
Cookie, arrowroot / **Gerber**	4
Pretzel / **Gerber**	5
Zwieback toast / **Gerber**	5

STRAINED BABY FOODS

Cereal: 1 jar

Mixed w apples and bananas / **Heinz**	22
Mixed w applesauce and bananas / **Beechnut** Stage 2	18
Mixed w applesauce and bananas / **Gerber**	18
Oatmeal w applesauce and bananas / **Beechnut** Stage 2	17
Oatmeal w applesauce and bananas / **Gerber**	15
Rice w applesauce and bananas / **Beechnut** Stage 2	20
Rice w apples and bananas / **Heinz**	24
Rice w applesauce and bananas / **Gerber**	22

Cereal, dry: ½ ounce unless noted: (½ ounce is about 6 tablespoons dry)

Barley / **Beechnut** Stage 1	10
Barley: 4 tbsp / **Gerber**	11
Barley / **Heinz**	10
Brown rice / **Health Valley**	10
Hi-Protein / **Beechnut** Stage 2	7

1

	GRAMS
High Protein: 4 tbsp / **Gerber**	6
Hi-Protein / **Heinz**	6
High Protein w apple and orange: 4 tbsp / **Gerber**	8
Mixed / **Beechnut** Stage 2	10
Mixed: 4 tbsp / **Gerber**	10
Mixed / **Heinz**	10
Mixed w banana: 4 tbsp / **Gerber**	11
Oatmeal / **Beechnut** Stage 1	9
Oatmeal: 4 tbsp / **Gerber**	9
Oatmeal / **Heinz**	9
Oatmeal w banana: 4 tbsp / **Gerber**	10
Rice / **Beechnut** Stage I	11
Rice: 4 tbsp / **Gerber**	11
Rice / **Heinz**	11
Rice w banana / **Gerber**	11
Sprouted baby cereal / **Health Valley**	11

Desserts: 1 jar

Apple Betty / **Beechnut** Stage 2	22
Banana apple dessert / **Gerber**	23
Cottage cheese w pineapple / **Beechnut** Stage 2	21
Dutch apple dessert / **Gerber**	22
Dutch apple dessert / **Heinz**	23
Fruit dessert / **Beechnut** Stage 2	24
Fruit dessert / **Gerber**	23
Fruit dessert / **Heinz**	22
Hawaiian Delight / **Gerber**	25
Mixed fruit yogurt / **Beechnut** Stage 2	25
Peach cobbler / **Gerber**	23
Peach cobbler / **Heinz**	21
Peaches and yogurt / **Beechnut** Stage 2	22
Pineapple dessert / **Beechnut** Stage 2	25
Pineapple-orange / **Heinz**	23
Pudding	
Apple custard / **Beechnut** Stage 2	20
Banana / **Heinz**	23
Banana custard / **Beechnut** Stage 2	18
Cherry vanilla / **Gerber**	22

	GRAMS
Chocolate custard / **Gerber**	20
Custard / **Heinz**	17
Orange / **Gerber**	24
Vanilla custard / **Beechnut** Stage 2	20
Vanilla custard / **Gerber**	21
Raspberry dessert w nonfat yogurt / **Gerber**	20
Tutti-frutti / **Heinz**	22

Fruit: 1 jar

Apples and apricots / **Heinz**	15
Apple blueberry / **Gerber**	17
Apples and cranberries / **Heinz**	20
Apples and grapes / **Beechnut** Stage 2	27
Apples, oranges and bananas / **Beechnut** Stage 2	22
Apples, peaches and strawberries / **Beechnut** Stage 2	24
Apples and pears / **Heinz**	18
Apples, pears and bananas / **Beechnut** Stage 2	24
Apples, pears and pineapples / **Beechnut** Stage 2	24
Apples and strawberries / **Beechnut** Stage 2	24
Applesauce	
Gerber	15
Heinz	16
Beechnut Stage 1	14
and apricots / **Beechnut** Stage 2	14
and apricots / **Gerber**	17
and bananas / **Beechnut** Stage 2	15
and cherries / **Beechnut** Stage 2	17
w pineapple / **Gerber**	16
Apricots w tapioca / **Beechnut** Stage 2	20
Apricots w tapioca / **Gerber**	22
Apricots w tapioca / **Heinz**	19
Bananas	
Beechnut Stage 1	24
w tapioca / **Gerber**	21
w tapioca / **Heinz**	24

GRAMS

w tapioca and pineapple / **Beechnut** Stage 2	19
w pineapple and tapioca / **Gerber**	15
w pineapple and tapioca / **Heinz**	22
Guava w tapioca / **Beechnut** Stage 2	25
Island Fruits / **Beechnut** Stage 2	22
Mango w tapioca / **Beechnut** Stage 2	22
Peaches	
Gerber	23
Heinz	12
Beechnut Stage 1	14
Pears	
Gerber	15
Heinz	17
Beechnut Stage 1	16
and pineapple / **Beechnut** Stage 2	25
and pineapple / **Gerber**	16
and pineapple / **Heinz**	18
Plums w tapioca	
Beechnut Stage 2	25
Gerber	22
Heinz	20
Prunes w tapioca	
Beechnut Stage 2	24
Gerber	24
Heinz	27

Juices: 1 jar or can unless noted

Apple	
Beechnut Stage 1	14
4 fl oz / **Beechnut** Stage 2	14
Gerber	16
Heinz	15
Apple-apricot: 4.2 oz / **Heinz**	16
Apple-banana / **Gerber**	15
Apple-cherry / **Beechnut** Stage 2	12
Apple-cherry / **Gerber**	16
Apple-cherry: 4.2 fl oz / **Heinz**	15
Apple-cranberry / **Beechnut** Stage 2	14
Apple-grape / **Beechnut** Stage 2	14

GRAMS

Apple-grape / **Gerber**	16
Apple-grape: 4.2 fl oz / **Heinz**	16
Apple-peach / **Beechnut** Stage 2	15
Apple-peach / **Gerber**	15
Apple-peach: 4.2 fl oz / **Heinz**	15
Apple-pineapple: 4.2 fl oz / **Heinz**	15
Apple-plum / **Gerber**	16
Apple-prune / **Gerber**	16
Apple-prune: 4.2 fl oz / **Heinz**	16
Grape / **Beechnut** Stage 1	19
Juice Plus / **Beechnut** Stage 2	15
Mixed fruit / **Beechnut** Stage 2	15
Mixed fruit / **Gerber**	16
Mixed fruit: 4.2 fl oz / **Heinz**	17
Orange / **Beechnut** Stage 2	14
Orange / **Gerber**	14
Orange: 4.2 fl oz / **Heinz**	14
Orange-apple / **Gerber**	15
Orange-apple-banana: 4.2 fl oz / **Heinz**	16
Orange-apricot / **Gerber**	15
Orange-pineapple / **Gerber**	17
Pear / **Beechnut** Stage 1	14
Tropical blend / **Beechnut** Stage 2	15

Main Dishes: 1 jar

Beef Dinner Supreme / **Beechnut** Stage 2	12
Beef and egg noodles / **Heinz**	10
Beef noodle w vegetables / **Beechnut** Stage 2	10
Beef and noodles w vegetables / **Gerber**	12
Beef w vegetables / **Gerber** High Meat Dinner	8
Beef w vegetables / **Heinz** High Meat Dinner	6
Cereal and egg yolk / **Gerber**	10
Chicken and noodles / **Gerber**	12
Chicken-noodle / **Heinz**	10
Chicken-noodle w vegetables / **Beechnut** Stage 2	12
Chicken-rice w vegetables / **Beechnut** Stage 2	12
Chicken w vegetables / **Gerber** High Meat Dinner	8

GRAMS

Chicken w vegetables / **Heinz** High Meat Dinner	7
Chicken soup / **Heinz**	10
Chicken soup, cream of / **Gerber**	11
Cottage cheese w pineapple / **Gerber** High Meat Dinner	19
Ham w vegetables / **Gerber** High Meat Dinner	9
Macaroni and cheese / **Gerber**	11
Macaroni, tomato and beef / **Beechnut** Stage 2	13
Macaroni-tomato w beef / **Gerber**	13
Macaroni, tomatoes and beef / **Heinz**	11
Turkey	
Beechnut Stage 2	10
and rice w vegetables / **Gerber**	10
and rice w vegetables / **Beechnut** Stage 2	11
and rice w vegetables / **Heinz**	10
w vegetables / **Gerber** High Meat Dinner	8
w vegetables / **Heinz** High Meat Dinner	9
Veal w vegetables / **Gerber** High Meat Dinner	8
Vegetables	
and bacon / **Gerber**	11
and bacon / **Heinz**	10
and beef / **Beechnut** Stage 2	12
and beef / **Gerber**	11
and beef / **Heinz**	8
and chicken / **Beechnut** Stage 2	13
and chicken / **Gerber**	9
dumplings and beef / **Heinz**	11
and ham / **Beechnut** Stage 2	13
and ham / **Gerber**	11
and ham / **Heinz**	9
w noodles and chicken / **Heinz**	13
w noodles and turkey / **Heinz**	10
and lamb / **Beechnut** Stage 2	12
and lamb / **Gerber**	10
and lamb / **Heinz**	9
and liver / **Gerber**	10
and turkey / **Gerber**	10

GRAMS

Meat and Eggs: 1 jar

Beef / **Gerber**	1
Beef and beef broth / **Beechnut** Stage 1	1
Beef and beef broth / **Heinz**	0
Beef w beef heart / **Gerber**	1
Beef liver / **Gerber**	3
Chicken / **Gerber**	1
Chicken and chicken broth / **Beechnut** Stage 1	1
Chicken and chicken broth / **Heinz**	0
Egg yolks / **Gerber**	1
Ham / **Gerber**	1
Lamb / **Gerber**	1
Lamb and lamb broth / **Beechnut** Stage 1	1
Lamb and lamb broth / **Heinz**	0
Liver and liver broth / **Heinz**	2
Pork / **Gerber**	1
Turkey / **Gerber**	1
Turkey and turkey broth / **Beechnut** Stage 1	1
Turkey and turkey broth / **Heinz**	0
Veal / **Gerber**	0
Veal and veal broth / **Beechnut** Stage 1	1
Veal and veal broth / **Heinz**	0

Vegetables: 1 jar

Beets / **Gerber**	11
Beets / **Heinz**	10
Carrots / **Gerber**	7
Carrots / **Heinz**	6
Carrots / **Beechnut** Stage 1	8
Corn, creamed / **Beechnut** Stage 2	15
Corn, creamed / **Gerber**	17
Corn, creamed / **Heinz**	
Garden / **Beechnut** Stage 2	
Garden / **Gerber**	
Green beans / **Beechnut** Stage 1	
Green beans / **Gerber**	
Green beans / **Heinz**	
Mixed / **Beechnut** Stage 2	
Mixed / **Gerber**	

GRAMS

Mixed / **Heinz**	10
Peas / **Beechnut** Stage 1	12
Peas / **Gerber**	10
Peas, creamed / **Heinz**	12
Peas and carrots / **Beechnut** Stage 2	11
Spinach, creamed / **Gerber**	7
Squash / **Beechnut** Stage 1	7
Squash / **Gerber**	8
Squash / **Heinz**	9
Sweet potatoes / **Beechnut** Stage 1	16
Sweet potatoes / **Gerber**	19
Sweet potatoes / **Heinz**	21

JUNIOR BABY FOODS

Cereal, 1 jar

Mixed w applesauce and bananas / **Gerber**	28
Oatmeal w applesauce and bananas / **Gerber**	24
Rice w mixed fruit / **Gerber**	37

Desserts: 1 jar

Banana / **Beechnut** Stage 3	40
Banana-apple / **Gerber**	39
Cottage cheese w pineapple / **Beechnut** Stage 3	31
Dutch apple / **Gerber**	36
Dutch apple / **Gerber** Chunky	30
Dutch apple / **Heinz**	37
/ **Beechnut** Stage 3	42
/ **Gerber**	39
/ **Heinz**	38
Delight / **Gerber**	42
yogurt / **Beechnut** Stage 3	41
/ **Gerber**	38
/ **Gerber** Chunky	31
/ **Heinz**	34
stard / **Beechnut** Stage 3	38
nilla / **Gerber**	36
Heinz	30

GRAMS

Vanilla custard / **Beechnut** Stage 3	29
Vanilla custard / **Gerber**	35
Raspberry w nonfat yogurt / **Gerber**	34
Tutti-Frutti / **Heinz**	35

Fruit: 1 jar

Apples
and apricots / **Heinz**	25
and blueberries / **Gerber**	28
and cranberries w tapioca / **Heinz**	33
and grapes / **Beechnut** Stage 3	44
Mandarin oranges and bananas / **Beechnut** Stage 3	37
Peaches and strawberries / **Beechnut** Stage 3	40
and pears / **Heinz**	30
Pears and bananas / **Beechnut** Stage 3	40
Pears and pineapples / **Beechnut** Stage 3	40
and strawberries / **Beechnut** Stage 3	40

Applesauce
Gerber	24
Heinz	26
and apple bits / **Beechnut** Stage 3	24
and apricots / **Beechnut** Stage 3	23
and apricots / **Gerber**	24
and bananas / **Beechnut** Stage 3	26
and cherries / **Beechnut** Stage 3	28
Apricots w tapioca / **Beechnut** Stage 3	33
Apricots w tapioca / **Gerber**	38
Apricots w tapioca / **Heinz**	36

Bananas
w tapioca / **Beechnut** Stage 3	32
w tapioca / **Gerber**	35
w tapioca / **Gerber** Chunky	29
w tapioca / **Heinz**	39
w pineapple and tapioca / **Gerber**	27
w pineapple and tapioca / **Heinz**	36
Island fruits / **Beechnut** Stage 3	37
Peaches / **Beechnut** Stage 3	37
Peaches / **Gerber**	37

GRAMS

Peaches / **Heinz**	21
Pears	
Beechnut Stage 3	35
Gerber	26
Heinz	30
and pineapple / **Beechnut** Stage 3	40
and pineapple / **Gerber**	26
Plums w tapioca / **Gerber**	39
Prunes w tapioca / **Gerber**	42

Fruit Juices: 4 fluid ounces

Apple / **Gerber** Toddler	15
Apple-cherry / **Gerber** Toddler	14
Apple-grape / **Gerber** Toddler	15
Mixed fruit / **Gerber** Toddler	15

Main Dishes: 1 jar

Beef	
Beechnut Stage 3	20
w noodles and vegetables / **Gerber**	20
w noodles and vegetables / **Gerber** Chunky	15
w noodles and vegetables / **Beechnut** Stage 3	21
Stew / **Beechnut** Table Time	15
w vegetables / **Gerber** High Meat Dinner	9
w vegetables and cereal / **Heinz** High Meat Dinner	7
Cereal and egg yolk / **Gerber**	15
Chicken	
and noodles / **Gerber**	19
and noodles / **Heinz**	23
and noodles w vegetables / **Beechnut** Stage 3	21
w vegetables / **Gerber** High Meat Dinner	8
w vegetables / **Heinz** High Meat Dinner	10
Soup w stars / **Beechnut** Table Time	17
Egg noodles and beef / **Heinz**	18
Ham w vegetables / **Gerber** High Meat Dinner	10

GRAMS

Macaroni
and cheese / **Gerber**	19
w tomatoes and beef / **Beechnut** Stage 3	24
w tomatoes and beef / **Gerber**	22
w tomatoes and beef / **Heinz**	16
Noodles and chicken / **Gerber** Chunky	14
Pasta squares in meat sauce / **Beechnut** Table Time	22

Spaghetti
Rings in meat sauce / **Beechnut** Table Time	22
Tomato and beef / **Beechnut** Stage 3	22
Tomato sauce and beef / **Gerber**	25
Tomato sauce and meat / **Heinz**	22
Split peas with ham / **Gerber**	24

Turkey
Beechnut Stage 3	24
and rice w vegetables / **Gerber**	18
and rice w vegetables / **Beechnut** Stage 3	20
and rice with vegetables / **Heinz**	18
w vegetables / **Gerber** High Meat Dinner	8
w vegetables / **Heinz** High Meat Dinner	9
Veal w vegetables / **Gerber** High Meat Dinner	10

Vegetables
and bacon / **Beechnut** Stage 3	21
and bacon / **Gerber**	20
and bacon / **Heinz**	17
and beef / **Beechnut** Stage 3	20
and beef / **Gerber**	21
and beef / **Gerber** Chunky	15
and beef / **Heinz**	18
and chicken / **Beechnut** Stage 3	20
and chicken / **Gerber**	17
and chicken / **Gerber** Chunky	16
dumplings and beef / **Heinz**	17
and ham / **Gerber**	20
and ham / **Gerber** Chunky	15
and ham / **Heinz**	19
and lamb / **Gerber**	18
and lamb / **Beechnut** Stage 3	21
and liver / **Gerber**	17

GRAMS

w noodles and chicken / **Heinz**	20
w noodles and turkey / **Heinz**	16
Soup / **Beechnut** Table Time	16
Stew w chicken / **Beechnut** Table Time	21
and turkey / **Gerber**	19
and turkey / **Gerber** Chunky	16

Meat: 1 jar

Beef / **Gerber**	1
Beef and beef broth / **Heinz**	0
Chicken	
Gerber	0
and chicken broth / **Heinz**	0
Sticks / **Gerber**	1
Ham / **Gerber**	1
Lamb / **Gerber**	1
Lamb and lamb broth / **Heinz**	0
Meat sticks / **Gerber**	1
Turkey / **Gerber**	0
Turkey sticks / **Gerber**	1
Veal / **Gerber**	0
Veal and veal broth / **Heinz**	0

Vegetables: 1 jar

Carrots / **Beechnut** Stage 3	14
Carrots / **Gerber**	12
Carrots / **Heinz**	11
Corn, creamed / **Gerber**	27
Corn, creamed / **Heinz**	37
Garden / **Beechnut** Stage 3	19
Green beans / **Beechnut** Stage 3	13
Green beans, creamed / **Gerber**	20
Green beans, creamed / **Heinz**	12
Mixed / **Beechnut** Stage 3	20
Mixed / **Gerber**	18
Peas / **Gerber**	24
Peas, creamed / **Heinz**	21
Potatoes, scalloped / **Beechnut** Stage 3	25
Squash / **Gerber**	13
Sweet potatoes / **Beechnut** Stage 3	27

	GRAMS
Sweet potatoes / **Gerber**	31
Sweet potatoes / **Heinz**	30

Baking Powder

	GRAMS
Canned: 1 tsp / most brands	1.3

Beer, Ale, Malt Liquor

12 fluid ounces   GRAMS

ALE

Duke	12
Koehler	12
McSorley's Cream Ale	15
Red Cap	12
Scheidt 20th Century	15
Tiger Head	15

BEER

Amstel Light	5
Andeker	15
Bavarian	12
Bavarian Light	3
Bergheim	12
Black Label	12
Break L.A.	16

GRAMS

Budweiser	12
Budweiser Light	9
Busch	12
Christian Schmidt Classic	12
Christian Schmidt Select	12
Coors	12
Duke	12
Erlanger	14
Gablinger's Light	3
Goebel	13
Heileman	13
Heileman Light	4
Heileman Near Beer	4
Heileman Premium	14
Kaier's	12
Knickerbocker	12
Koehler	12
L.A. (Annheuser Busch)	16
L.A. (Miller)	10
Meisterbrau	13
Meisterbrau Light	8
Michelob	15
Michelob Light	12
Miller High Life	14
Miller Lite	3
Milwaukee's Best	11
Natural Light	6
Old Milwaukee	13
Old Milwaukee Light	9
Olde Pub	12
Otlieb's	12
Pabst Blue Ribbon	13
Piels Draft Style	13
Plank Road	14
P.O.C.	12
Primo	13
Prior Double Dark	16
Reading	12
Rheingold	13
Rheingold Extra Light	3
Rock & Roll	12

	GRAMS
Schaefer	13
Schaefer Light	9
Schaefer Low Alcohol	11
Scheidt	12
Schlitz	13
Schlitz Light	4
Schmidt's	13
Schmidt's Light	3
Schmidt's Bock	15
Signature	16
Silver Thunder	18
Stroh Light	8
Stroh Premium	13
U Save A Lot (USA)	12
Valley Forge	12

MALT LIQUOR

Coqui 900	10
Golden Hawk	11
Heileman	14
Schlitz	15

Biscuits

	GRAMS
Mix: 2 oz / **Arrowhead Mills**	19
Mix: 2 oz / **Bisquick**	38

BISCUITS, REFRIGERATED

1 biscuit

Ballard Oven Ready	10
Hungry Jack Butter Tastin' Flaky	11
Hungry Jack Flaky	12

	GRAMS
Merico Butter Flavored	12
Merico Butter-Me-Not	11
Merico Homestyle	9
Merico Mountain Man	12
Merico Texas Style	16
Merico Texas Style Butter Flavored	14
Merico Texas Style Flaky	15
1869 Brand	13
Pillsbury Country Style	10
Pillsbury Good 'n Buttery Big Country	13
Baking Powder / **1869 Brand**	13
Baking Powder / **Pillsbury** Tenderflake	7
Butter / **Pillsbury**	10
Buttermilk	
Ballard Oven Ready	10
1869 Brand	13
Hungry Jack Extra Rich	9
Hungry Jack Flaky	12
Hungry Jack Fluffy	12
Merico Weight Watchers	9
Pillsbury	10
Pillsbury Big Country	14
Pillsbury Big Premium Heat 'n Eat	16
Pillsbury Extra Lights	9
Pillsbury Heat 'n Eat	13
Pillsbury Tenderflake	7
Weight Watchers	8
Wheat / **Merico** Weight Watchers	9
Wheat / **Weight Watchers**	8

Bread

GRAMS

1 slice unless noted

Apple w cinnamon / **Pepperidge Farm**	13
Barley bran / **Earth Grains**	14
Bran w diced raisins / **Pepperidge Farm**	13.5
Bran 'N honey / **Country Hearth**	13
Bran'nola / **Arnold**	15.5
Bran'nola Hearty / **Arnold**	17.5
Brown, canned: ½-in slice / **B & M**	18
Brown, canned w raisins: ½-in slice / **B & M**	18
Buckwheat	
Butternut	12
Weber's	12
Buttermilk	
Butternut	12
Country Hearth	12
Country Hearth Old Fashioned	13
Eddy's	12
Millbrook	12
Sweetheart	12
Weber's	12
Cinnamon / **Pepperidge Farm**	12.5
Cinnamon apple and walnut / **Pepperidge Farm**	13
Cinnamon-raisin / **Butternut**	14
Corn and molasses / **Pepperidge Farm** Thin Sliced	14.5
Dark / **Hollywood**	12.5
Date and nut loaf: 1 oz **Crosse & Blackwell**	13
Date walnut / **Pepperidge Farm**	11.5
Earth bread / **Earth Grains**	11
European butter sesame / **Country Hearth**	12
French / **Earth Grains**	14
French: 2 oz / **Pepperidge Farm**	25
French: 2 oz / **Pepperidge Farm** Brown & Serve	26
French / **Wonder**	13.5
French style: 2 oz / **Arnold Francisco**	29
French style: 2 oz **Pepperidge Farm**	28

GRAMS

Grainola / **Country Hearth**	12
Honey bran 1½-lb loaf / **Pepperidge Farm**	18
Honey and buttermilk / **Earth Grains**	14
Honey grain	
Colonial	13
Kilpatrick's	13
Rainbo	13
Honey and oat / **Country Hearth**	13
Honey oatberry / **Earth Grains**	14
Honey wheatberry / **Arnold**	16
Honey wheatberry / **Earth Grains**	12
Honey wheatberry / **Home Pride**	13
Honey wheatberry / **Pepperidge Farm**	13.5
Honey whole grain	
Butternut	13
Eddy's	13
Millbrook	13
Sweetheart	13
Weber's	13
Italian: 2 oz / **Pepperidge Farm** Brown & Serve	27
Low protein: about 1.1 ounces / **Nutri-Dyne**	
Aproten	15
Multigrain	
A&P	14
Earth Grains	13
Pepperidge Farm Very Thin Sliced	7
Oat / **Bran'nola** Country	19
Oatmeal	
Pepperidge Farm 1½-lb loaf	12.5
Pepperidge Farm Thin Sliced	12.5
Onion / **Pepperidge Farm** Party Slices	3
Orange and raisin / **Pepperidge Farm**	13.5
Potato	
Eddy's	14
Sweetheart	14
Protein / **Thomas**	7.5
Pumpernickel	
Arnold	14
Levy Real	15.5
Pepperidge Farm Family	15

GRAMS

Pepperidge Farm Party Slices	3
Raisin / **Earth Grains**	16
Raisin w cinnamon / **Pepperidge Farm**	14
Raisin tea / **Arnold**	13
Rye	
Butternut	13
Country Hearth Deli	14
Earth Grains Light	13
Earth Grains Light, Very Thin	14
Earth Grains Party: 1 oz	14
Earth Grains Pumpernickel Rye	14
Eddy's	13
Millbrook	13
Pepperidge Farm Family	15.5
Pepperidge Farm Party	3
Pepperidge Farm Sandwich 1½-lb loaf	16
Pepperidge Farm Very Thin Sliced	8
Sweetheart	13
Dijon mustard / **Pepperidge Farm**	9
Dill, seeded / **Arnold**	13.5
Jewish / **Pepperidge Farm**	16.5
Jewish, seeded / **Arnold**	14
Jewish, seeded / **Levy Real**	14.5
Jewish, unseeded / **Arnold**	14
Jewish, unseeded / **Levy Real**	15
Melba thin / **Arnold**	9.5
Seedless / **Pepperidge Farm**	15.5
Weight Watchers	7.5
Seven grain / **Home Pride**	12.5
Sour dough	
DiCarlo	13.5
Earth Grains Mini Loaf	7
Sour dough French / **Earth Grains**	14
Vienna / **Pepperidge Farm**	13.5
Vienna French: 2 oz / **Arnold** Francisco	29
Wheat	
Arnold Brick Oven 1-lb loaf	9.5
Arnold Brick Oven 2-lb loaf	13
Arnold Brick Oven Small Family	9.5
Arnold Measure Up Whole Wheat	6.5

	GRAMS
Butternut	14
Colonial	13
Colonial Whole Wheat	12
Country Hearth Butter Split Top	13
Country Hearth Nature's Wheat	13
Country Hearth Sandwich	13
Country Hearth 7 Whole Grain	14
Earth Grains Gold 'N Bran	12
Earth Grains Lite 35	12
Earth Grains 100% Whole Wheat	11
Earth Grains Very Thin	13
Eddy's	14
Fresh Horizons	9.5
Fresh & Natural	13.5
Home Pride Butter Top	13
Home Pride 100% Whole Wheat	12
Kilpatrick's	13
Kilpatrick's Whole Wheat	12
Pepperidge Farm 1½-lb loaf	17.5
Pepperidge Farm 2-lb loaf	13
Pepperidge Farm Sandwich	10
Pepperidge Farm Thin Sliced Whole Wheat	12
Pepperidge Farm Very Thin Sliced Whole Wheat	7.5
Rainbo	13
Rainbo Whole Wheat	12
Roman Meal	12.5
Sweetheart	14
Weber's	14
Weight Watchers Thin Sliced	7.5
Wonder Family	13.5
Wonder 100% Whole Wheat	12
Wheat, cracked	
Butternut	13
Earth Grains	12
Earth Grains Mini Loaf	14
Eddy's	13
Pepperidge Farm Thin Sliced	13
Sweetheart	13
Weber's	13

	GRAMS
Wonder	13.5
Wheat, honey	
Home Pride	13
Wheat, light fiber	
Butternut	11
Millbrook	11
Sweetheart	11
Wheat, sprouted	
Arnold	12
Pepperidge Farm Sliced	11.5
Wheat, stoneground	
Earth Grains	13
100% Whole Wheat / **Arnold**	9.5
100% Whole Wheat / **Country Hearth**	12
Wheatberry	
Country Hearth	13
Home Pride	12.5
Wheat germ / **Pepperidge Farm** Thin Sliced	12.5
White	
Arnold Brick Oven 1-lb loaf	11
Arnold Brick Oven 2-lb loaf	14.5
Arnold Brick Oven Small Family 8 oz	11
Arnold Country White	17
Arnold Hearthstone	15
Arnold Measure Up	7
Bran'nola Old Style / **Arnold**	19
Butternut	14
Colonial	13
Colonial Country Meal	14
Country Hearth Butter Split Top	13
Country Hearth D'Italia	13
Country Hearth Old Fashioned	13
Earth Grains Country White Mini	14
Earth Grains Lite 35	12
Earth Grains Salt Free Sandwich	14
Earth Grains Very Thin	14
Fresh Horizons	9.5
Hillbilly	13
Hollywood Light	13
Home Pride Butter Top	13

	GRAMS
Kilpatrick's	14
Kilpatrick's Country Meal	14
Pepperidge Farm 1½-lb loaf	17
Pepperidge Farm Large Family	13.5
Pepperidge Farm Sandwich	11.5
Pepperidge Farm Thin Sliced	12.5
Pepperidge Farm Very Thin Sliced	8
Pepperidge Farm Toasting White	16
Rainbo	14
Rainbo Country Meal	14
Sweetheart	14
Weber's	14
Wonder	13.5
w buttermilk / **Wonder**	13.5
w cracked wheat / **Pepperidge Farm**	17.5
Light, fiber / **Butternut**	11
Low sodium	
Butternut	13
Eddy's	13
Wonder	13.5
Weight Watchers Thin Sliced	7.5
Yogurt bran / **Earth Grains**	11

BREAD AND CRACKER CRUMBS

Pepperidge Farm Premium: 1 oz	22
Pepperidge Farm Premium Herb Seasoned: 1 oz	22
Seasoned: 1 rounded tsp / **Contadina**	7
Toasted: 2 oz / **Old London** Regular Style	40
Corn flake crumbs: ¼ cup / **Kellogg's**	25
Cracker meal: 1 cup / **Nabisco**	95

BREAD MIXES

Applesauce spice: ⅟₁₂ loaf / **Pillsbury**	28
Blueberry nut: ⅟₁₂ loaf / **Pillsbury**	26
Carrot nut: ⅟₁₂ loaf / **Pillsbury**	27
Cherry nut: ⅟₁₂ loaf / **Pillsbury**	30
Corn	
Arrowhead Mills: 1 oz baked	19
Aunt Jemima Easy Mix: 1.7 oz baked	34

	GRAMS
Dromedary: 2 x 2 in sq	19
Fearn: 1.6 oz dry	27
Date: ¹⁄₁₂ loaf / **Pillsbury**	31
Multigrain: 2 oz baked / **Arrowhead Mills**	29
Nut: ¹⁄₁₂ loaf / **Pillsbury**	31
Rye: ½-in slice / **Pillsbury** Poppin' Fresh	21
Wheat: ½-in slice / **Pillsbury** Poppin' Fresh	20
Wheat: 1-in slice / **Pillsbury** Pipin' Hot	12
White: ½-in slice / **Pillsbury** Poppin' Fresh	21
White: 1-in slice / **Pillsbury** Pipin' Hot	13
Whole wheat: 2 oz baked / **Arrowhead Mills**	27
Whole wheat, stone ground: 2 oz (½ cup) / **Elam's**	40

BREAD STICKS

1 stick

Stella D'Oro	7
Stella D'Oro Dietetic	7
Onion / **Stella D'Oro**	6
Sesame / **Stella D'Oro**	7
Sesame / **Stella D'Oro** Dietetic	7
Soft / **Pillsbury**	18
Whole wheat / **Stella D'Oro**	6

STUFFING MIXES

½ cup prepared unless noted

Bells Ready Mix Stuffing	24
Kellogg's Croutettes	14
Stove Top Americana New England, prepared w butter	21
Stove Top Americana San Francisco, prepared w butter	20
Beef, prepared w butter / **Stove Top**	21
Chicken, pan style: 1 oz dry **Pepperidge Farm** 6-oz pkg	22
Chicken-flavored / **Bells**	24
Chicken, prepared w butter / **Stove Top**	20
Chicken-flavored w cornbread / **Uncle Ben's**	24

GRAMS

Corn bread: 1 oz dry / **Pepperidge Farm** 8-oz or 16-oz pkg	22
Corn bread, prepared w butter / **Stove Top**	21
Cube: 1 oz dry **Pepperidge Farm** 7-oz or 14-oz pkg	22
Cube, unseasoned: 1 oz dry **Pepperidge Farm** 7-oz or 14-oz pkg	22
Herb-seasoned: 1 oz dry **Pepperidge Farm** 8-oz or 16-oz pkg	22
Pork, prepared w butter / **Stove Top**	20
Seasoned, pan style: 1 oz dry **Pepperidge Farm** 6-oz pkg	22
Turkey, prepared w butter / **Stove Top**	20
w rice, prepared w butter / **Stove Top**	23

CROUTONS

½ oz

Bacon and cheese / **Pepperidge Farm**	8
Blue cheese / **Pepperidge Farm**	7
Cheddar and Romano cheese / **Pepperidge Farm**	9
Cheese and garlic / **Pepperidge Farm**	9
Dijon mustard rye and cheese / **Pepperidge Farm**	7
Onion and garlic / **Pepperidge Farm**	9
Seasoned / **Pepperidge Farm**	9
Sour cream and chive / **Pepperidge Farm**	9

Butter, Margarine and Oils

GRAMS

BUTTER

Any quantity, all Brands	0

GRAMS

MARGARINE
Any quantity, all Brands   0

OILS
(Corn, olive, peanut, safflower, vegetable): any
   quantity, all brands   0

Cakes

	GRAMS
Apple walnut: ⅛ cake (1⅜ oz) / **Pepperidge Farm** Old Fashion	18
Black forest: ⅛ cake / **Sara Lee**	28
Boston cream: ¼ cake (2⅞ oz) / **Pepperidge Farm** Supreme	39
Butter pound: ¹⁄₁₀ cake (1 oz) / **Pepperidge Farm** Old Fashion	16
Butterscotch pecan layer: ¹⁄₁₀ cake (1⅝ oz) / **Pepperidge Farm**	23
Carrot: ⅛ cake (1⅜ oz) **Pepperidge Farm** Old Fashion	17
Carrot: 2.6 oz / **Weight Watchers**	26
Cheesecake	
Sara Lee: ⅙ cake	29
Weight Watchers: 4 oz	27
Black cherry: 4 oz / **Weight Watchers**	26
Cherry, individual: 1 (6 oz) / **Morton's** Great Little Desserts	47
Chocolate chip: ⅙ cake / **Sara Lee**	38
Cream, individual: 1 (6 oz) / **Morton's** Great Little Desserts	42
French cream: ⅛ cake / **Sara Lee**	23
Pecan praline: ⅙ cake / **Sara Lee**	32
Pineapple, individual: 1 (6 oz) / **Morton's** Great Little Desserts	48
Strawberry: 4 oz / **Weight Watchers**	22
Strawberry French: ⅛ cake / **Sara Lee**	29
Strawberry, individual: 1 (6 oz) / **Morton's** Great Little Desserts	50

	GRAMS
Chocolate: 1/4 cake (2 7/8 oz) / **Pepperidge Farm Supreme**	37
Chocolate chip pound: 1/10 cake / **Sara Lee**	19
Chocolate fudge layer: 1/10 cake (1 5/8 oz) / **Pepperidge Farm**	23
Chocolate mint layer: 1/10 cake (1 5/8 oz) / **Pepperidge Farm**	22
Chocolate mousse Bavarian: 1/8 cake / **Sara Lee**	23
Coconut layer: 1/10 cake (1 5/8 oz)/ **Pepperidge Farm**	25
Coffee cake, pecan: 1/8 cake / **Sara Lee**	19
Coffee cake, walnut: 1/8 cake / **Sara Lee**	18
Devil's food layer 1/10 cake (1 5/8 oz) / **Pepperidge Farm**	24
German chocolate layer: 1/10 cake (1 5/8 oz) / **Pepperidge Farm**	23
Golden layer: 1/10 cake (1 5/8 oz) / **Pepperidge Farm**	24
Lemon coconut: 1/4 cake (3 oz) **Pepperidge Farm Supreme**	38
Pineapple cream: 1/12 cake (2 oz) / **Pepperidge Farm** Supreme	27
Raisin walnut pound: 1/10 cake / **Sara Lee**	20
Spice: 2.6 oz / **Weight Watchers**	27
Strawberry cream: 1/12 cake (2 oz) / **Pepperidge Farm** Supreme	27
Strawberry shortcake: 1/8 cake / **Sara Lee**	26
Vanilla layer: 1 5/8 oz / **Pepperidge Farm**	25
Walnut: 1/10 cake (2 1/2 oz) / **Pepperidge Farm**	33

MIXES

1/12 cake unless noted

Angel food	
Duncan Hines	30
Chocolate / **Betty Crocker**	35
Confetti / **Betty Crocker**	36
Lemon chiffon / **Betty Crocker**	35
Lemon custard / **Betty Crocker**	35
Raspberry / **Pillsbury**	32
Strawberry / **Betty Crocker**	35
White, traditional / **Betty Crocker**	31
White / **Betty Crocker**	35

GRAMS

White / **Pillsbury**	33
Apple / **Duncan Hines**	34
Apple cinnamon / **Betty Crocker** SuperMoist	36
Applesauce raisin: ⅑ cake / **Betty Crocker** Snackin' Cake	33
Applesauce spice / **Pillsbury** Plus	36
Banana / **Betty Crocker** SuperMoist	36
Banana / **Duncan Hines**	36
Banana / **Pillsbury** Plus	36
Banana walnut: ⅑ cake / **Betty Crocker** Snackin' Cake	31
Bundt: ⅟₁₆ cake	
Boston cream / **Pillsbury**	43
Chocolate macaroon / **Pillsbury**	37
Fudge / **Pillsbury** Tunnel of Fudge	37
Fudge nut crown / **Pillsbury**	31
Lemon / **Pillsbury** Tunnel of Lemon	45
Lemon blueberry / **Pillsbury**	28
Marble / **Pillsbury**	38
Pound / **Pillsbury**	33
Butter recipe / **Pillsbury**	36
Butter brickle / **Betty Crocker** SuperMoist	38
Butter pecan: ⅑ cake / **Betty Crocker** Snackin' Cake	31
Butter pecan / **Betty Crocker** SuperMoist	35
Butter recipe / **Betty Crocker** SuperMoist	37
Carrot / **Betty Crocker** SuperMoist	34
Carrot / **Duncan Hines**	34
Carrot nut: ⅑ cake / **Betty Crocker** Snackin' Cake	30
Carrot w cream cheese frosting: ⅙ cake / **Betty Crocker** Stir n' Frost	43
Carrot and spice / **Pillsbury** Plus	36
Cheesecake: ⅛ cake / **Jello**	38
Cherry chip / **Betty Crocker** SuperMoist	36
Cherry / **Duncan Hines**	36
Chocolate: ⅟₁₀ cake / **Dia-Mel**	17
Chocolate: ⅟₁₀ cake / **Estee**	17
Chocolate chip / **Betty Crocker** SuperMoist	35
Chocolate chip / **Duncan Hines**	34
Chocolate chip w chocolate frosting: ⅙ cake / **Betty Crocker** Stir 'n Frost	41

GRAMS

Chocolate chocolate chip / **Betty Crocker** SuperMoist	33
Chocolate chocolate chip w chocolate chocolate chip frosting: ⅙ cake / **Betty Crocker** Stir 'n Frost	41
Chocolate devil's food w chocolate frosting: ⅙ cake / **Betty Crocker** Stir n' Frost	41
Chocolate fudge / **Betty Crocker** SuperMoist	35
Chocolate fudge chip: ⅑ cake / **Betty Crocker** Snackin' Cake	32
Chocolate fudge w vanilla frosting: ⅙ cake / **Betty Crocker** Stir 'n Frost	43
Chocolate mint / **Pillsbury** Plus	35
Coconut pecan: ⅑ cake / **Betty Crocker** Snackin' Cake	30
Coffee cake	
Aunt Jemima / 1.3 oz	29
Apple cinnamon: ⅛ cake / **Pillsbury**	40
Butter pecan: ⅛ cake / **Pillsbury**	39
Cinnamon streusel: ⅛ cake / **Pillsbury**	41
Sour cream: ⅛ cake / **Pillsbury**	35
Cupcake: 1 piece / **Flako**	21
Dark chocolate / **Pillsbury** Plus	35
Deep chocolate / **Duncan Hines**	33
Devil's food / **Betty Crocker** SuperMoist	35
Devil's food / **Duncan Hines**	33
Devil's food / **Pillsbury** Plus	35
Fudge / **Duncan Hines** Butter Recipe	34
Fudge marble / **Duncan Hines** Deluxe	36
Fudge marble / **Pillsbury** Plus	36
Fudge peanut butter chip: ⅑ cake / **Betty Crocker** Snackin' Cake	32
German Black Forest / **Betty Crocker**	28
German chocolate / **Betty Crocker** SuperMoist	36
German chocolate / **Pillsbury** Plus	36
German chocolate coconut pecan: ⅑ cake / **Betty Crocker** Snackin' Cake	32
Gingerbread: ⅑ cake / **Betty Crocker**	35
Gingerbread: 2 x 2-in square / **Dromedary**	20
Gingerbread: 3-in square / **Pillsbury**	36
Golden / **Duncan Hines**	36

GRAMS

Golden chocolate chip: ⅑ cake / **Betty Crocker** Snackin' Cake	34
Golden vanilla / **Duncan Hines**	36
Lemon / **Betty Crocker** SuperMoist	36
Lemon: ⅒ cake / **Dia-Mel**	18
Lemon: ⅒ cake / **Estee**	18
Lemon / **Pillsbury** Plus	36
Lemon / **Duncan Hines** Deluxe	36
Marble / **Betty Crocker** SuperMoist	36
Milk chocolate / **Betty Crocker** SuperMoist	35
Mint fudge chip: ⅑ cake / **Betty Crocker** Snackin' Cake	32
Oats and brown sugar / **Pillsbury** Plus	35
Orange / **Betty Crocker** SuperMoist	36
Orange / **Duncan Hines** Deluxe	36
Pineapple / **Duncan Hines** Deluxe	36
Pineapple upside-down: ⅑ cake / **Betty Crocker**	43
Pound: ⅒ cake / **Dia-Mel**	18
Pound: ¾-in slice / **Dromedary**	29
Pound, golden / **Betty Crocker**	27
Pudding, chocolate: ⅙ cake / **Betty Crocker**	45
Pudding, lemon: ⅙ cake / **Betty Crocker**	45
Sour cream chocolate / **Betty Crocker** SuperMoist	36
Sour cream chocolate / **Duncan Hines**	33
Sour cream white / **Betty Crocker**	36
Spice / **Betty Crocker** SuperMoist	37
Spice: ⅒ cake / **Dia-Mel**	18
Spice / **Duncan Hines** Deluxe	36
Spice w vanilla frosting: ⅙ cake / **Betty Crocker** Stir n' Frost	48
Strawberry / **Betty Crocker** SuperMoist	36
Strawberry / **Pillsbury** Plus	37
Strawberry / **Duncan Hines** Deluxe	36
Streusel: ⅟₁₆ cake	
Banana / **Pillsbury**	38
Butter, rich / **Pillsbury**	38
Cinnamon / **Pillsbury**	38
Dutch apple / **Pillsbury**	38
Fudge marble / **Pillsbury**	38
German chocolate / **Betty Crocker**	42

	GRAMS
German chocolate / **Pillsbury**	36
Lemon / **Pillsbury**:	39
Pecan, brown sugar / **Pillsbury**	37
Swiss chocolate / **Duncan Hines** Deluxe	33
White / **Betty Crocker** SuperMoist	37
White / **Duncan Hines** Deluxe	36
White: ⅒ cake / **Estee**	18
White / **Pillsbury** Plus	35
Yellow / **Betty Crocker** SuperMoist	36
Yellow / **Duncan Hines** Deluxe	36
Yellow / **Pillsbury** Plus	36
Yellow w chocolate frosting: ⅙ cake / **Betty Crocker** Stir n' Frost	37

SNACK CAKES

1 piece

Chip Flips / **Hostess**	47
Coffee cake / **Drake's**	32
Creamie, chocolate / **Tastykake**	25
Crumb cakes / **Hostess**	22
Cupcakes	
Buttercream, cream-filled / **Tastykake**	23
Chocolate / **Dolly Madison**	29
Chocolate / **Hostess**	29
Chocolate / **Tastykake**	20
Chocolate, cream-filled / **Tastykake**	21
Orange / **Hostess**	28
Dessert cups / **Hostess**	14
Devil Dogs / **Drake's**	22
Ding Dongs / **Big Wheels**	21
Fruit Loaf / **Hostess**	77
Funny Bones / **Drake's**	18
Ho-Ho's / **Hostess**	17
Hostess-O's / **Hostess**	33
Junior chocolate / **Tastykake**	56
Junior coconut / **Tastykake**	60
Kandy Kake, chocolate / **Tastykake**	12
Kandy Kake, coconut / **Tastykake**	14
Kandy Kake, mint / **Tastykake**	14

	GRAMS
Kandy Kake, peanut butter / **Tastykake**	11
Koffee Kake / **Tastykake**	49
Koffee Kake, cream-filled / **Tastykake**	21
Krimpet, butterscotch / **Tastykake**	20
Krimpet, cream-filled, chocolate / **Tastykake**	25
Krimpet, cream-filled, vanilla / **Tastykake**	24
Krimpet, jelly / **Tastykake**	19
Krumb Kake, apple-filled / **Tastykake**	27
Lil' Angels	14
Peanut Putters, filled	46
Peanut Putters, unfilled	43
Ring Ding Jr. / **Drake's**	20
Sno Balls / **Hostess**	28
Suzy Q banana / **Hostess**	38
Suzy Q, chocolate / **Hostess**	37
Teen, chocolate / **Tastykake**	44
Tempty, chocolate / **Tastykake**	17
Tiger Tail / **Hostess**	38
Twinkies / **Hostess**	26
Yankee Doodles / **Drake's**	15

Candy

	GRAMS
Almond Joy, bar: 1.6 oz	26
Breath candy: 1 piece	
Breath Savers, sugar free / **Life Savers**	2
Certs, clear	2
Certs, pressed	1.5
Clorets Mints	1.6
Dentyne Dynamints	.3
Trident Mints	2
Baby Ruth: 1 oz	20
Bonkers!: 1 piece	5
Bridge mix, chocolate: 1 oz / **Deran**	20

GRAMS

Butterfinger: 1 oz	20
Butter toffee peanuts: 1 oz / **Harmony**	17
Candy corn: 1 piece / **Curtiss**	1
Caramello bar: 2 oz / **Cadbury**	37
Caramel Nip: 1¾ oz / **Pearson**	43
Charleston Chew: 1¾-oz bar	40
Chocolate bars	
Cadbury Dairy Milk: 2 oz	34
Ghirardelli Milk: 1⅛ oz	18
Ghirardelli Dark: 1⅛ oz	19
Hershey's: 1.45 oz	23
Hershey's: miniature bar	6
Nestlé's: 1¹⁄₁₆-oz	19
Nestlé's: miniature	6
Hershey's Special Dark: 1.05 oz	18
Hershey's Special Dark: 4 oz	70
w almonds: 1⅛ oz / **Ghirardelli**	18
w almonds: 1.45 oz bar / **Hershey's**	22
w almonds: miniature bar / **Hershey's**	5
w almonds: 1 oz / **Nestlé's**	16
w brazil nuts: 2 oz / **Cadbury**	32
w fruit and nuts: 2 oz / **Cadbury**	33
w hazel nuts, 2 oz / **Cadbury**	32
w munchy malt: 1⅛ oz / **Ghirardelli**	18
w raisins: 1⅛ oz / **Ghirardelli**	18
Chocolate-covered nuts and fruit	
Almonds, dark chocolate: 1 oz / **Harmony**	13
Almonds, milk chocolate: 1 oz / **Harmony**	13
Apricots: 1 oz / **Harmony**	18
Bridge mix: 1 oz (about 14 pieces) / **Nabisco**	20
Cashews: 1 oz / **Harmony**	14
Cherries: 4 pieces / **Nabisco**	54
Macadamias: 1 oz / **Harmony**	12
Peanuts: 1 oz / **Brach**	13
Peanuts: 1 oz / **Harmony**	12
Peanut Snackums: 1 oz / **Harmony**	17
Pecans: 1 oz / **Harmony**	12
Pistachios: 1 oz / **Harmony**	13
Raisins, dark chocolate: 1 oz / **Harmony**	19
Raisins, milk chocolate: 1 oz **Harmony**	19

GRAMS

Raisins: 1 oz / **Deran**	20
Raisins: 1 box (2½ oz) / **Nabisco**	52
Walnuts: 1 oz / **Harmony**	12
Chocolate crisp: 1⅛ oz / **Ghirardelli**	18
Chocolate mint: 1⅛ oz / **Ghirardelli**	18
Chocolate mint square: ⅜ oz / **Ghirardelli**	6
Chocolate parfait: 1¾ oz / **Pearson**	40
Chocolate stars: 1 box (2¼ oz) / **Nabisco**	41
Chuckles:	
Cherry: 7 pieces (1⅞ oz)	44
Cinnamon softee: 1 box (1⅞ oz)	49
Coconut squares: 4 pieces (2 oz)	37
Jelly beans: 1 box (1¾ oz)	45
Jelly candy: 5 pieces (2 oz)	50
Jelly mint softees: 11 pieces (1⅞ oz)	43
Jelly rings: 6 pieces (2 ¼ oz)	50
Ju Ju Softees: 1 box (1½ oz)	38
Licorice jellies: 6 pieces (2 oz)	46
Licorice softees: 1 pkg (1⅞ oz)	49
Orange slices: 1 pkg (2 oz)	47
Spearmint leaves: 1 pkg (1½ oz)	38
Spice drops: 1 pkg (1½ oz)	36
Spice sticks: 18 pieces (2¹⁄₁₆ oz)	48
Clark, bar: 1 oz	20
Coffee Nip: 1¾ oz / **Pearson**	43
Coffioca: 1¾ oz / **Pearson**	40
Cough drops: 1 drop / **Beech-Nut**	3
Cough drops: 1 drop / **Pine Bros.**	2
Crispy / **Switzer Clark:** 1 oz	17
Crows: 1 piece	2.7
Crunch / **Nestlé's:** 1¹⁄₁₆ oz	19
1 oz	18
Dots: 1 piece	2.7
Golden Almond, bar / **Hershey's:** 1 oz	12
Good & Plenty: 1 box	34
Good 'n Fruity: 1 box	34
Hard candies	
Butterscotch disc: 1 piece	6
Red Hot dollars: 1 oz	27
Sour bites: 1 piece	9

GRAMS

Sweet Tarts: 1 piece	1
Red Hots: 1 ball	7
Root beer barrel: 1 piece	10
Candy cane: 1 cane (½ oz)	14
Candy hearts: 1 piece	6
Christmas candy: 1 cup	197
Jawbreakers: 1 piece	2
Fudge bar / **Nabisco:** 2 bars (1⅜ oz)	29
Heath bar, English toffee: 1¹⁄₁₆ oz	19
Junior Mints / **Nabisco:** 1 pkg (1.43 oz)	33
Jumbo Block / **Nabisco:** 1 oz	13
Kisses / **Hershey:** 1 oz (6 pieces)	16
Kit Kat, bar: 1.5 oz	25
Krackel, bar: 1.45 oz	25
Krackel, bar, miniature	6
Licorice Nip / **Pearson:** 1¾ oz	43
Life Savers roll candy, fruit flavors: 1 drop	3
Life Savers, mint: 1 piece	2
Life Savers, sours: 1 piece	3
Lollipop: **Life Savers,** fruit, swirled: 1 lollipop	11
M & M's, plain: 1.7 oz	33
M & M's, peanut: 1.7 oz	28
Mallo Cup: 1.2 oz cup	24
Maltballs / **Harmony:** 1 oz	20
Malted milk balls: 1 oz / **Deran**	20
Mars, bar: 1.9 oz	32
Marshmallows: 2 large or 24 mini / **Campfire**	10
Marzipan paste: 1 oz	36
Milk chocolate, bar / **Switzer Clark**	16
Milk Duds: 1 oz	23
Milk Maid caramels / **Brach:** 1 oz	22
Milky Way, bar: 2 oz	41
Mint parfait / **Pearson:** 1¾ oz	40
Mounds, bar: 1.65 oz	28
Mr. Goodbar, bar: 1.65 oz	23
Mr. Goodbar, miniature	5
Nut fudge squares / **Nabisco:** 4 pieces (2 oz)	42
Nutcracker / **Switzer Clark:** 1 oz	15
$100,000; bar: 1½ oz	31
$100,000; bar: ¾ oz	15
Payday, bar	38

GRAMS

Peanut candy: 1 oz / **Planters** Old Fashioned (vacuum can)	15
Peanut caramel clusters, chocolate: 1 oz	14
Peanut clusters, chocolate: 1 oz / **Brach**	14
Peanut clusters, chocolate: 1 oz / **Deran**	13
Pecan nut cluster: 1 piece (1 oz) / **Heath**	18
Peppermint patties: 4 pieces (2 oz) / **Nabisco**	50
Pom Poms: 1 box (1.48 oz)	31
Powerhouse, bar: 2.2 oz	42
Reese's Peanut Butter Cup, plain or crunchy: 2 pieces (1.6 oz)	23
Reese's peanut butter–flavored chips: ¼ cup	19
Reese's Pieces: 35 pieces (1 oz)	17
Reggie: 2-oz bar	29
Rolo: 5 pieces (1 oz)	19
Royals: 1 oz / **Brach**	21
Rum wafers: 1 oz / **Deran**	20
Skittles bite-size: 1.7 oz	45
Slo-Poke: 1 oz	24
Snickers, bar: 2 oz	33
Special Dark Bar: 1.45 oz / **Hershey's**	26
Starburst Fruit Chews: 2.1 oz	50
Sugar Babies: 1⅝ oz	40
Sugar Daddy: 1⅜ oz	33
Sugar Mama: 1 piece	17
Summit: .7 oz	12
3 Musketeers: 2.3-oz bar	49
Thin mints: 6 pieces (1⅞ oz) / **Nabisco**	44
Toffees: 1 oz / **Brach**	20
Tootsie Pop, caramel, chocolate, flavored: .49-oz pop	12
Tootsie Roll: 1 oz	23
Tootsie Roll: 1¼ oz roll	29
Tootsie Roll, .23-oz midgee	5.3
Twix Caramel: 1 oz	17
Twix Peanut Butter: .9 oz	13
Twizzler, cherry, chocolate, strawberry: 1 oz	22
Whatchamacallit, bar: 1.4 oz	22
York Mint: 1.5 oz	33
Zagnut, bar: 1 oz	20

DIETETIC CANDY

	GRAMS
Chocolates, boxed or pieces	
Peanut butter cups: 1 piece / **Estee**	3
Raisins, chocolate-covered: 6 pieces / **Estee**	4
T.V. mix: 4 pieces / **Estee**	3
Estee-ets: 5 pieces	4
Chocolate bar: 2 squares / **Estee**	4
Crunch: 2 squares / **Estee**	4
Gum drops: 4 pieces / **Estee**	3
Hard Candies: 2 pieces / **Estee**	6
Lollipops: 1 / **Estee**	3
Mints: 1 piece / **Estee**	1

Cereals

COLD, READY TO SERVE

Measurements vary according to what companies consider appropriate one-serving sizes. The servings generally are one ounce in weight.

	GRAMS
All-Bran: ⅓ cup	22
Alpha-Bits: 1 cup	24
Amaranth w bananas: 1 oz / **Health Valley**	20
Arrowhead Crunch: 1 oz / **Arrowhead Mills**	18
Bran: 1 oz / **Loma Linda**	19
Bran w apples and cinnamon: 1 oz / **Health Valley**	21
Bran w raisins: 1 oz / **Health Valley**	21
Bran flakes, 40%: ⅔ cup / **Kellogg's**	23
Bran flakes, 40%: ⅔ cup / **Post**	23
Bucwheats: ¾ cup	24
C-3PO's: ¾ cup	24
Cap'n Crunch: ¾ cup	23
Cap'n Crunch's Crunchberries: ¾ cup	23
Cap'n Crunch's Peanut Butter Cereal: ¾ cup	21

	GRAMS
Cheerio's: 1¼ cup	20
Cheerio's, Honey Nut ¾ cup	23
Cinnamon **Life:** ⅔ cup	19
Cinnamon Toast Crunch: ⅔ cup	23
Cocoa Krispies: ¾ cup	25
Cocoa Puffs: 1 cup	25
Cookie Crisp, chocolate chip or vanilla wafer: 1 cup	25
Corn bran: ⅔ cup / **Quaker**	23
Corn Chex: 1 cup	25
Corn flakes	
General Mills Country: 1 cup	25
Kellogg's: 1 cup	25
Post Toasties: 1 cup	24
Ralston: 1 cup	25
Safeway: 1 cup	24
Corn germ cereal: 1 cup / **Nutri-Dyne** Ener-G	42
Corn, puffed: ½ oz / **Arrowhead Mills**	11
Corn **Total:** 1 cup	24
Count Chocula: 1 cup	24
Cracklin' Oat Bran: ½ cup	20
Crispix: ¾ cup	24
Crispy Oatmeal & Raisin Chex: ¾ cup	31
Crispy rice	
Malt-O-Meal: 1 cup	25
Ralston: 1 cup	25
Safeway: 1 cup	25
Crispy Wheats 'n Raisins: ¾ cup	23
C. W. Post: ¼ cup	20
C. W. Post w raisins: ¼ cup	21
Donkey Kong: 1 cup	25
Donkey Kong Junior: 1 cup	25
E.T.: ¾ cup	19
FrankenBerry: 1 cup	24
Froot Loops: 1 cup	25
Frosted Flakes: ¾ cup / **Kellogg's**	26
Frosted Flakes, banana: ⅔ cup / **Kellogg's**	25
Frosted Krispies: ¾ cup	25
Frosted Mini-Wheats, sugar or apple flavored: 4 biscuits (1 oz)	24
Fruit & Fibre, apples and cinnamon: 1.2 cup	22

GRAMS

Fruit & Fibre, dates, raisins and walnuts: ½ cup	21
Fruitful Bran: ¾ cup	27
Fruit Rings: 1 cup / **Ralston**	26
Golden Grahams: ¾ cup	24
Granola	
Apple amaranth: 1 oz / **Arrowhead Mills**	19
Cinnamon and raisin: ⅓ cup / **Nature Valley**	19
Coconut and honey: ⅓ cup / **Nature Valley**	18
Fruit and nut: ⅓ cup / **Nature Valley**	19
Maple nut: 2 oz / **Arrowhead Mills**	34
Toasted oat mixture: ⅓ cup / **Nature Valley**	19
Grape-Nuts: ¼ cup	23
Grape-Nuts, raisin: 1 oz	22
Grape-Nuts Flakes: 1 oz	23
Heartland, all varieties: ¼ cup	18
Hearts O'Bran: 1 oz / **Health Valley**	19
Hearts O'Bran w apples and cinnamon: 1 oz / **Health Valley**	19
Hearts O'Bran w raisins and spice: 1 oz **Health Valley**	19
Honeycomb: 1⅓ cup	25
Honeycomb, Strawberry: 1⅓ cup	25
Honey and nut corn flakes: ¾ cup / **Kellogg's**	24
Honey nut crunch, raisin bran: 1 oz / **Post**	23
Honey Smacks: ¾ cup	25
Kaboom: 1 cup	23
King Vitamin: 1¼ cup	23
Kix: 1½ cup	24
Life: ⅔ cup	19
Lites, brown rice: ½ cup / **Health Valley**	12
Lites, golden corn: ½ cup / **Health Valley**	11
Lites, golden wheat: ½ cup / **Health Valley**	11
Lucky Charms: 1 cup	24
Marshmallow Krispies: 1¼ cup	33
Millet, whole grain, puffed: ½ oz / **Arrowhead Mills**	11
Most: ½ cup	22
Nature O's: 1 oz / **Arrowhead Mills**	20
Nutri-Grain, corn: ½ cup	24
Nutri-Grain, wheat: ⅔ cup	24

GRAMS

Nutri-Grain, wheat and raisins: ⅔ cup	33
Oat bran: 1 oz / **Arrowhead Mills**	17
Oat flakes, fortified: 1 oz / **Post**	20
Orangeola w almonds and dates: 1 oz / **Health Valley**	19
Orangeola w bananas and coconut: 1 oz / **Health Valley**	20
Pac-Man: 1 cup	25
Pebbles, cocoa: 1 oz	25
Pebbles, fruity: 1 oz	25
Product 19: ¾ cup	24
Quaker 100% Natural: ¼ cup	17
Quaker 100% Natural w apples and cinnamon: ¼ cup	18
Quaker 100% Natural w raisins and dates: ¼ cup	18
Quisp: 1⅙ cup	23
Raisin bran	
Health Valley: 1 oz	24
Kellogg's: ¾ cup	30
Post: ½ cup	22
Ralston: ¾ cup	30
Safeway: 1 oz	22
Raisins, Rice & Rye: ¾ cup	31
REAL Almond Crunch: 1 oz / **Health Valley**	20
REAL Apple Cinnamon: 1 oz / **Health Valley**	20
REAL Hawaiian Fruit: 1 oz / **Health Valley**	20
REAL Maple Nut: 1 oz / **Health Valley**	20
REAL Raisin Nut: 1 oz / **Health Valley**	20
Rice Chex: 1¼ cup	25
Rice Krispies: 1 cup	25
Rice, puffed: ½ oz / **Arrowhead Mills**	12
Rice, puffed: 1 cup / **Malt-O-Meal**	12
Rice, puffed: 1 cup / **Quaker**	13
Rice and Shine: ¼ cup / **Arrowhead Mills**	35
7-Grain Crunchy: 1 oz / **Loma Linda**	21
7-Grain, no sugar: 1 oz / **Loma Linda**	20
Seven Grain Cereal: 1 oz / **Arrowhead Mills**	17
Smurf-Berry Crunch: 1 oz	25
Special K: 1 cup	20
Sprouts 7 w banana: 1 oz / **Health Valley**	29

GRAMS

Sprouts 7 w raisins: 1 oz / **Health Valley**	20
Strawberry Krispies: ¾ cup	25
Strawberry Shortcake: 1 cup	25
Sugar Corn Pops: 1 cup	26
Sugar Frosted Flakes: ¾ cup / **Ralston**	26
Sugar Frosted Rice: 1 cup / **Ralston**	26
Sugar Puffs: ⅞ cup / **Malt-O-Meal**	26
Super Sugar Crisp: ⅞ cup	26
Tasteeos: 1¼ cup	22
Toasty O's: 1¼ cup	20
Total: 1 cup	23
Trix: 1 cup	25
Wheat Chex: ⅔ cup	23
Wheat flakes: 1 oz / **Health Valley**	24
Wheat, puffed: ½ oz / **Arrowhead Mills**	11
Wheat, puffed: 1 cup / **Malt-O-Meal**	11
Wheat, puffed: 1 cup / **Quaker**	11
Wheat & Raisin Chex: ¾ cup	31
Wheat, shredded: 1 biscuit / **Sunshine**	19
Wheat, shredded: 2 biscuits / **Quaker**	22
Wheaties: 1 cup	23

TO BE COOKED

Dry, uncooked, unless noted

Barley, pearled: ¼ cup uncooked (¾ cup cooked) / **Quaker** Scotch Brand Quick	36
Barley, pearled: ¼ cup uncooked (1 cup cooked) / **Quaker** Scotch Brand Regular	36
Bear Mush: 1 oz / **Arrowhead Mills**	21
Complete Cereal: ¼ cup / **Elam's**	17
Cracked wheat: 2 oz / **Arrowhead Mills**	40
Cracked wheat: ¼ cup / **Elam's**	26
Farina: ⅔ cup cooked / **Pillsbury**	17
4-Grain Cereal + Flax: 2 oz / **Arrowhead Mills**	18
Grits	
Bulgur-soy: 2 oz / **Arrowhead Mills**	40
Corn: 2 oz / **Arrowhead Mills**	43
Hominy: 3 tbsp / **Aunt Jemima** Quick	22
Hominy: 3 tbsp / **Aunt Jemima** Regular	22

GRAMS

Hominy: 3 tbsp / **Quaker** Quick	22
Hominy: 3 tbsp / **Quaker** Regular	22
Hominy Quick: ¼ cup dry / **Albers**	33
Instant: 1 pkt / **Quaker** Instant Grits Product	18
Instant w artificial cheese flavor: 1 pkt / **Quaker** Instant Grits Product	22
Instant w imitation bacon bits: 1 pkt / **Quaker** Instant Grits Product	22
Instant w imitation ham bits: 1 pkt / **Quaker** Instant Grits Product	21
Malt-O-Meal, chocolate flavored: 1 oz dry	22
Malt-O-Meal, quick: 1 oz	22
Oats and oatmeal	
Quaker Old Fashioned: ⅔ cup cooked	18
Quaker Quick: ⅔ cup cooked	18
Regular and Quick / **Ralston** ⅓ cup uncooked	18
3-Minute Brand Old-Fashioned: 1 oz	18
3-Minute Brand Quick: 1 oz	18
Scotch style: ¼ cup / **Elam's**	19
Steel-cut: ¼ cup / **Elam's**	30
Stone-ground: ¼ cup / **Elam's**	19
Oatmeal, instant: 1 pkt **Harvest Brand**	18
Quaker Regular	18
w apples and cinnamon / **Harvest Brand**	26
w apples and cinnamon / **Quaker**	26
w bran and raisins / **Quaker**	29
w cinnamon and spice / **Harvest Brand**	35
w cinnamon and spice / **Quaker**	35
w honey and graham / **Quaker**	27
w maple and brown sugar / **Harvest Brand**	32
w maple and brown sugar / **Quaker**	32
w peaches and cream / **Harvest Brand**	27
w raisins, dates and walnuts / **Quaker**	24
w raisins and spice / **Quaker**	31
w strawberries and cream / **Quaker**	26
Ralston, instant and regular: ¼ cup dry	20
Wheat and oatmeal: ¼ cup / **Elam's**	19
Wheat and soya: ¼ cup dry / **Fearn Soy-O**	26
¼ cup prepared w milk	32
Whole wheat: ⅔ cup cooked / **Quaker** Pettijohns	22

Cheese

	GRAMS
1 oz unless noted	
American	
Borden	1
Kraft	1
Land O Lakes	1
Slices / **Kraft**	1
Sharp / **Kraft** Old English	1
Sharp slices / **Kraft** Old English	1
Sharp / **Land O Lakes**	1
Blue / **Kraft**	1
Blue / **Land O Lakes**	1
Brick / **Kraft**	1
Brick / **Land O Lakes**	1
Brie / **Kolb-Lena Delico**	1
Camembert / **Kolb-Lena Delico**	1
Caraway / **Kraft**	1
Caraway Jack / **Health Valley**	1
Cheddar / **Land O Lakes**	1
Cheddar, mild / **Kraft**	1
Cheddar, sharp / **Kraft**	1
Cheddar, imitation, mild / **Kraft** Golden Image	1
Colby / **Health Valley**	1
Colby / **Kraft**	1
Colby / **Land O Lakes**	1
Colby, imitation / **Kraft** Golden Image	1
Edam / **Kraft**	1
Feta / **Kolb-Lena Delico**	1
Farmer: ½ cup / **Friendship**	4
Fondue / **Swiss Knight**	1
Gouda / **Kraft**	1
Gouda / **Land O Lakes**	1
Hoop: ½ cup / **Friendship**	2
Jalapeno Jack / **Health Valley**	1
Limburger / **Mohawk Valley** Little Gem Size	1
Longhorn / **Health Valley**	1
Monterey Jack / **Health Valley**	1

	GRAMS
Monterey Jack / **Land O Lakes**	1
Mozzarella / **Kraft Casino**	1
Mozzarella / **Land O Lakes**	1
Muenster / **Health Valley**	1
Muenster / **Kraft**	1
Muenster / **Land O Lakes**	1
Part-skim milk, natural / **Weight Watchers**	1
Pimento, process / **Kraft**	1
Parmesan / **Kraft**	1
Provolone / **Kraft**	1
Provolone / **Land O Lakes**	1
Romano / **Kraft** Casino	1
Scamorze, low-moisture, part-skim / **Kraft**	1

Swiss

Kolb-Lena Delico Swiss-Lo	1
Kraft, aged	1
Kraft, chunk	1
Land O Lakes	1
Processed / **Borden**	1
Slices / **Kraft**	1
Processed slices / **Kraft** Deluxe	1

COTTAGE CHEESE

½ cup unless noted

Creamed

Borden	4
Friendship California Style	4
Land O Lakes	3
Lucerne	4
Meadow Gold	4
w chives / **Lucerne**	4
w fruit salad / **Lucerne**	15
w pineapple / **Friendship**	15
w pineapple / **Lucerne**	15
Dry: **Lucerne**	3

Low-fat

Friendship	4
Friendship Pot Style	4
Liteline	4

GRAMS

Lucerne	4
Meadow Gold Viva Lowfat	4
Weight Watchers	3

CREAM AND NEUFCHATEL CHEESE

1 oz

Cream cheese	
Kraft Philadelphia Brand	1
Land O Lakes	1
Friendship	1
w chives / **Kraft Philadelphia** Brand	1
w pimentos / **Kraft Philadelphia** Brand	1
Cream cheese, whipped	
Kraft Philadelphia Brand	1
w bacon and horseradish / **Kraft Philadelphia** Brand	1
w blue cheese / **Kraft Philadelphia** Brand	2
w chives / **Kraft Philadelphia** Brand	1
w onions / **Kraft Philadelphia** Brand	2
w pimentos / **Kraft Philadelphia** Brand	2
w smoked salmon / **Kraft Philadelphia** Brand	1
Neufchatel / **Kraft**	1

GRATED AND SHREDDED CHEESE

1 oz (= about ⅓ cup)

Parmesan, grated / **Kraft**	1
Parmesan, grated / **Land O Lakes**	1
Romano, grated / **Kraft**	1
Romano, grated / **Land O Lakes**	1

CHEESE FOODS

1 oz (about 2 tbsp)

American	
Borden	3
Slices, cheese product / **Lite-Line**	1
Cheddar	
Wispride Cold Pack	2

GRAMS

Sharp / **Land O Lakes** Cold Pack	2
Sharp w wine / **Land O Lakes** Cold Pack	2
Sharp, cheese product / **Lite-Line**	1
Sharp flavor / **Weight Watchers** Cold Pack	6
Colby, cheese product / **Lite-Line**	1
Hot pepper / **Land O Lakes**	2
Monterey Jack, cheese product / **Lite-Line**	1
Muenster, cheese product / **Lite-Line**	1
Onion-flavor / **Weight Watchers**	6
Port wine / **Wispride** Cold Pack	1
Process / **Land O Lakes**	2
Smoked / **Wispride** Cold Pack	3
Smoked flavor / **Weight Watchers** Cold Pack	6
Substitute, processed / **Lite-Line**	2
Swiss: 1 slice (1 oz) / **Weight Watchers**	1
Swiss flavor, cheese product / **Lite-Line**	1

CHEESE SPREADS

1 oz

American / **Nabisco** Snack Mate	2
Cheddar / **Nabisco** Snack Mate	2
Cheese and bacon / **Nabisco** Snack Mate	2
Creamed / **Weight Watchers**	3
Jalapeno / **Kraft**	2
Pimento / **Price's**	2
Snack Mate, all flavors / **Nabisco**	2
Velveeta / **Kraft**	2
Velveeta, pimento / **Kraft**	2
Velveeta slices / **Kraft**	2

SOUFFLÉ

Cheese soufflé: 6 oz / **Stouffer's**	14

WELSH RAREBIT

Canned: ½ cup / **Snow's**	10
Frozen: 5 oz / **Stouffer's**	17

Chewing Gum

GRAMS

1 stick or piece

Adams Sour	2.3
Beech-Nut	2.3
Beechies	1.6
Big Red	2.3
Bubble Yum	7
Bubble Yum, sugarless	5
Bubblicious	2
Care Free, all flavors	2
Chiclets	1.1
Clorets	1.5
Dentyne	1.2
Doublemint / **Wrigley's**	2.3
Estee, all flavors	1
Freedent / **Wrigley's**	2.3
Fruit Stripe	2
Juicy Fruit / **Wrigley's**	2.3
Hubba Bubba, all flavors	6
Orbit, sugar free	1
Replay	4.2
Spearmint / **Wrigley's**	2.3
Trident	1.2
Wrigley's, all flavors	2

Chinese Foods

GRAMS

See also Dinners

Almond chicken, frozen: 11 oz / **Van de Kamp's**	41
Bamboo shoots, canned: 4¼ oz / **Chun King**	3
Bamboo shoots, canned: ¼ cup / **La Choy**	1

GRAMS

Bean sprouts, canned: ½ cup / **Chun King**   2
Bean sprouts, canned: ⅔ cup / **La Choy**   1
Beef Oriental, frozen: 8⅝ oz / **Stouffer's**
  Lean Cuisine   32
Beef Oriental, frozen: 10 oz / **Weight Watchers**   32
Beef pepper, frozen: 6 oz / **Chun King Pouch**   10
Beef Teryaki, frozen: 10 oz / **Stouffer's**   41
Beef and vegetables Szechwan: 11 oz /
  Van de Kamp's   37
Chicken, Oriental, frozen: 9½ oz /
  Weight Watchers   26
Chicken, sweet and sour, frozen: 9 oz /
  Weight Watchers   26
Chop suey beef, frozen: 12 oz / **Stouffer's**   48
Chop suey vegetables,:½ cup canned / **La Choy**   2
Chow mein, canned
  Beef: 10½ oz / **Chun King** Divider Pak   9
  Beef: 12 oz / **Chun King** 24-oz size   8
  Beef: ¾ cup / **La Choy**   5
  Beef: ¾ cup prepared / **La Choy** Bi-Pack   6
  Beef pepper: ¾ cup / **La Choy**   10
  Beef pepper: ¾ cup prepared /
    La Choy Bi-Pack   7
  Chicken: 10½ oz / **Chun King** Divider Pak   9
  Chicken: 12 oz / **Chun King** 24-oz size   10
  Chicken: ¾ cup / **La Choy**   6
  Chicken: ¾ cup prepared / **La Choy** Bi-Pack   5
  Meatless: ¾ cup / **La Choy** Vegetable   5
  Meatless: ¾ cup prepared / **La Choy** Bi-Pack   7
  Pork: 10½ oz / **Chun King** Divider Pak   7
  Pork: ¾ cup prepared / **La Choy** Bi-Pack   7
  Shrimp: 10½ oz / **Chun King**   8
  Shrimp: ¾ cup / **La Choy**   4
  Shrimp: ¾ cup prepared / **La Choy** Bi-Pack   7
  Vegetables: ½ cup / **Chun King**   2
Chow mein, frozen
  Beef mandarin: 11 oz / **Van de Kamp's**   29
  Beef pepper: 12 oz / **La Choy**   45
  Beef: 10 oz / **Green Giant** Entrée   33
  Chicken: 6 oz / **Chun King** Pouch   12
  Chicken: 12 oz / **La Choy**   44

GRAMS

Chicken: 9 oz / **Green Giant** Entrée	29
Chicken wo noodles: 8 oz / **Stouffer's**	10
Chicken: 11¼ oz / **Stouffer's** Lean Cuisine	36
Chicken Mandarin: 11 oz / **Van de Kamp's**	31
Shrimp: 6 oz / **Chun King** Pouch	10
Shrimp: 12 oz / **La Choy**	47
Egg rolls, frozen	
Health Valley: 1 roll	20
Van de Kamp's: 5¼ oz	41
Chicken: 1 roll / **Chun King**	4
Chicken: 1 roll / **La Choy**	4
Lobster: 1 roll / **Health Valley**	23
Lobster: 1 roll / **La Choy**	4.3
Meat and shrimp: 1 roll / **Chun King** 2-roll pkg	20
Meat and shrimp: 1 roll / **Chun King** 12-roll pkg	4.6
Meat and shrimp: 7½ oz pkg: 1 roll / **La Choy**	2.5
Meat and shrimp: 6½ oz pkg: 1 roll / **La Choy**	2
Nut: 1 roll / **Health Valley**	24
Shrimp: 1 roll / **Chun King**	5
Shrimp: 1 roll / **Health Valley**	21
Shrimp: 6½ oz pkg: 1 roll / **La Choy**	4.3
Shrimp: 6 oz pkg: 1 roll / **La Choy**	12
Teriyaki: 1 roll / **Health Valley**	24
Fried rice, canned: ¾ cup / **La Choy**	40
Fried rice w pork, frozen: ¾ cup / **La Choy**	26
Noodles, canned, Chinatown style: ¾ oz / **Chun King**	13
Noodles, canned, chow mein: ⅚ oz / **Chun King**	13
Noodles, canned, chow mein: ½ cup / **La Choy**	17
Noodles, canned, rice: ½ cup / **La Choy**	21
Pea pods, frozen: ½ pkg (3 oz) / **La Choy**	6
Pepper Oriental, canned: 10½ oz / **Chun King** Divider Pak	8
Stir fry dishes	
Chicken and vegetables, frozen: 10 oz / **Green Giant**	29
Chicken, cashew, frozen: 10 oz / **Green Giant**	37
Chicken, sweet and sour, frozen: 10 oz / **Green Giant**	47

	GRAMS
Sesame ginger, frozen: 11½ oz / **Legume**	34
Shrimp and fried rice: 10 oz / **Green Giant** Entrée	49
Szechwan beef, frozen: 10 oz / **Green Giant** Entrée	26
Teriyaki, beef, frozen: 10 oz / **Green Giant** Entrée	36
Sukiyaki, canned: ¾ cup prepared / **La Choy** Bi-Pack	8
Sweet and sour	
Chicken, canned: ¾ cup / **La Choy** Oriental	50
Chicken, frozen: ⅔ cup / **La Choy**	33
Pork, canned: ¾ cup / **La Choy** Oriental	48
Pork, frozen: 6 oz / **Chun King** Pouch	22
Pork, frozen: ⅔ cup / **La Choy**	32
Pork, frozen: 11 oz / **Van de Kamp's**	61
Vegetables, Chinese, canned: ½ cup / **La Choy**	2
Water chestnuts, canned: 4¼ oz / **Chun King**	11
Water chestnuts, canned: ¼ cup / **La Choy**	4
Won ton soup: ½ pkg / **La Choy**	6

Chips, Crisps Bars and Similar Snacks

	GRAMS
Bars: 1 bar	
All flavors / **Figurines**	10.5
Chocolate / **Milk Break**	22
Chocolate chip / **Carnation** Breakfast Bar	20
Chocolate chip / **Carnation** Slender	26
Chocolate crunch / **Carnation** Breakfast Bar	20
Chocolate mint / **Milk Break**	21
Chocolate peanut / **Carnation** Slender	24
Honey nut / **Carnation** Breakfast Bar	18

GRAMS

Natural flavor / **Milk Break**	21
Peanut butter / **Milk Break**	21
Peanut butter w chocolate chips / **Carnation** Breakfast Bar	20
Peanut butter crunch / **Carnation** Breakfast Bar	20
Vanilla / **Carnation** Slender	24

Granola bars: 1 bar

Almond / **Nature Valley**	16
Apple / **Nature Valley** Chewy	20
Chocolate chip / **Hershey's** New Trail	25
Chocolate chip / **Nature Valley** Chewy	19
Chocolate chip / **Quaker** Chewy	19
Cinnamon / **Nature Valley**	17
Coconut / **Nature Valley**	15
Honey and oats / **Quaker** Chewy	19
Honey graham / **Hershey's** New Trail	25
Oats and honey / **Nature Valley**	17
Peanut / **Nature Valley**	16
Peanut butter / **Hershey's** New Trail	23
Peanut butter / **Nature Valley**	15
Peanut butter / **Nature Valley** Chewy	18
Peanut butter / **Quaker** Chewy	18
Peanut butter, chocolate chip / **Hershey's** New Trail	23
Raisin / **Nature Valley** Chewy	20
Raisin and cinnamon / **Quaker** Chewy	19

1 ounce unless noted

Bugles	18
Bugles, nacho cheese	16
Cheddar sticks / **Flavor Tree**	12
Cheese balls, baked / **Guy's**	14
Cheese 'n Crunch	14
Cheese puffs: 1⅛ oz / **Laura Scudder's**	19
Cheese snacks / **Lite-Line** Puffed Cheese Curls	19
Chee.tos, crunch / **Frito-Lay**	15
Chee.tos, puffs / **Frito-Lay**	15
Chee.tos, puffed balls / **Frito-Lay**	15
Chee.tos, cheddar flavored / **Frito-Lay**	15

GRAMS

Cheez Balls / **Planters**	15
Cheez Curls / **Planters**	15
Cheez Doodles, crunchy	16
Cheez Doodles, puffed	16
Cheez Waffies / **Wise**	14
Cheez Waffies / **Old London**	14
Chipsters / **Nabisco**	19
Corn chips	
Flavor Tree	17
Fritos	16
Fritos, king size	16
Granny Goose	15
Laura Scudder's: 1½ oz	23
Planters	15
Bar-B-Q	16
Corn Diggers / **Nabisco**	17
Corn Crunchies / **Wise**	16
Corn & Sesame Chips / **Nabisco**	15
Corn sticks / **Flavor Tree**	15
Crispy Chinese TV Snacks / **Mother's**	17
Crunch 'N Munch: 1¼ oz / **Franklin**	33
Doo Dads / **Nabisco**	17
Fiesta Chips / **Granny Goose**	17
Flings / **Nabisco**	14
Granola nuts / **Flavor Tree**	9
Jalapeno Corn Toots / **Granny Goose**	15
Korkers / **Nabisco**	16
Mini-Tacos: 7 oz / **Laura Scudder's**	133
Party Mix / **Flavor Tree**	11
Potato chips	
Charles	14
Granny Goose	13
Laura Scudder's	15
Lay's	14
O'Grady's	16
Planter's Stackable	17
Pringle's	12
Pringle's Cheez-ums	13
Pringle's Light	17
Pringle's Rippled	13
Ruffles	15

GRAMS

Wise	14
Au Gratin flavored / **O'Grady's**	15
Bacon & cheddar flavored, waffle / **Charles**	18
Bacon and sour cream / **Ruffles**	15
Barbecue / **Granny Goose**	13
Barbecue / **Laura Scudder's**	16
Barbecue / **Lay's**	14
Barbecue / **Morton's Ridgies**	14
Barbecue / **Ruffles**	15
Green onion / **Granny Goose**	13
Ketchup and french fry flavor / **Buckeye**	14
Salt 'N Vinegar / **Lay's**	15
Sour cream and onion / **Lay's**	15
Sour cream and onion / **Ruffles**	15
Unsalted / **Lay's**	14
Unsalted / **Wise**	14
Potato sticks: 1½ oz / **O&C**	22
Pork rinds, fried / **Granny Goose**	0
Sesame chips / **Flavor Tree**	13
Sesame nuts / **Flavor Tree**	8
Sesame sticks / **Flavor Tree**	13
Sesame sticks w bran / **Flavor Tree**	11
Sesame sticks, unsalted / **Flavor Tree**	12
Sour cream and onion sticks / **Flavor Tree**	13
Tortilla chips	
Doritos	19
Doritos, nacho cheese	18
Doritos, taco flavor	18
Granny Goose	19
Laura Scudder's	19
Nabisco	19
Old El Paso Nachips: 10 chips	17
Tostitos	18
Tostitos, nacho cheese flavor	17
Nacho / **Planters**	14
Nacho cheese flavor / **Lite-Line**	19
Nacho cheese flavor / **Nabisco** Buenos	17
Nacho cheese flavor / **Wise** Bravos	17
Sour cream and onion / **Nabisco** Buenos	18
Taco / **Planters**	14

	GRAMS
Wheat nuts / **Flavor Tree**	8
Wheat Snax / **Estee**	22

Chocolate and Chips

GRAMS

For baking: 1 oz unless noted

Chips

	GRAMS
Butterscotch / **Nestlé's** Morsels	19
Chocolate, milk: ¼ cup / **Hershey's**	27
Chocolate, milk / **Nestlé's** Morsels	17
Chocolate, semi-sweet / **Borden**	20
Chocolate, semi-sweet / **Ghirardelli**	18
Chocolate, semi-sweet: ¼ cup / **Hershey's**	26
Chocolate, semi-sweet: ¼ cup / **Hershey's** Mini	26
Chocolate, semi-sweet / **Nestlé's** Morsels	18
Choco-Bake / **Nestlé's**	12
Chocolate, ground: **Ghirardelli**	23

Chocolate, solid

	GRAMS
Hershey's	7
German sweet / **Baker's**	17
Semi-sweet / **Baker's**	17
Unswt / **Baker's**	9

Cocktails

GRAMS

WITH ALCOHOL, READY-TO-SERVE

Canned: 2 fl oz

Apricot Sour / **Party Tyme**	6
Banana Daiquiri / **Party Tyme**	6
Daiquiri / **Party Tyme**	5
Gimlet / **Party Tyme**	5
Gin and Tonic / **Party Tyme**	5
Mai Tai / **Party Tyme**	6
Manhattan / **Party Tyme**	2
Margarita / **Party Tyme**	6
Martini / **Party Tyme**	0
Pina Colada / **Party Tyme**	5
Rum and Cola / **Party Tyme**	5
Scotch Sour / **Party Tyme**	6
Screwdriver / **Party Tyme**	6
Tom Collins / **Party Tyme**	6
Vodka Martini / **Party Tyme**	0
Vodka Tonic / **Party Tyme**	5

MIXES

Dry: 1 packet

Alexander / **Holland House**	16
Banana Daiquiri / **Holland House**	16
Bloody Mary / **Holland House**	14
Collins: 1 env prepared / **Bar-Tender's**	18
Daiquiri: 1 env prepared / **Bar-Tender's**	18
Daiquiri / **Holland House**	17
Gimlet / **Holland House**	17
Grasshopper / **Holland House**	17
Lite: 1 env prepared / **Bar-Tender's**	1
Mai Tai / **Holland House**	17
Margarita / **Holland House**	17

GRAMS

Mint Julep / **Holland House**	17
Pina Colada / **Holland House**	16
Pink Squirrel / **Holland House**	17
Pussycat: 1 env prepared / **Bar-Tender's**	18
Screwdriver / **Holland House**	17
Slightly Sour: 1 env prepared / **Bar-Tender's**	18
Strawberry Margarita / **Holland House**	15
Strawberry Sting / **Holland House**	18
Tequilla Sunrise / **Holland House**	15
Tom Collins / **Holland House**	17
Vodka Sour / **Holland House**	16
Wallbanger / **Holland House**	16
Whiskey Sour: 1 env prepared / **Bar-Tender's**	18
Whiskey Sour / **Holland House**	17

Liquid: 1 fl oz unless noted

Amaretto / **Holland House**	16
Apricot Sour / **Holland House**	12
Black Russian / **Holland House**	23
Blackberry Sour / **Holland House**	12
Bloody Mary / **Holland House**	2
Cocktail Host / **Holland House**	12
Cream of Coconut / **Holland House** Coco Casa	22
Daiquiri / **Holland House**	13
Dry Martini / **Holland House**	2
Gimlet / **Holland House**	10
Mai Tai / **Holland House**	8
Manhattan / **Holland House**	7
Margarita / **Holland House**	9
Old Fashioned / **Holland House**	9
Pina Colada / **Holland House**	15
Strawberry Sting / **Holland House**	8
Tom Collins / **Holland House**	16
Whiskey Sour / **Holland House** Low	22

Cocoa

GRAMS

Cocoa: ⅓ cup / Hershey's	13
Mix:	
Estee: 6 oz	9
Hershey's: 1 oz	21
Nestlé's: 1 oz	23
Instant: 1 env / **Alba**	9
Instant: 1 oz / **Carnation**	23
Instant: 3 tbsp prepared w 8 oz milk / **Hershey's**	29
Instant: 1 pkt / **Ovaltine**	8
Instant: 1 pkt / **Ovaltine** Hot 'n Rich	22
Instant: 1 env / **Superman** instant	12
Instant, chocolate marshmallow: 1 env / **Alba**	10
Instant, chocolate and mini-marshmallows: 1 oz / **Carnation**	23
Instant, mocha: 1 env / **Alba**	10
Instant, rich chocolate: 1 oz / **Carnation**	23
Instant, rich chocolate: 1 pkt / **Carnation** 70-calorie	15
Instant, sugar free: 1 pkt / **Carnation**	8
Instant, sugar free: 1 pkt / **Ovaltine**	7
Instant, sugar-free mint: 1 pkt / **Ovaltine**	7
Instant, w marshmallows: 1 oz / **Nestlé's**	23

Coconut

FRESH

GRAMS

In shell: 1 coconut	37.5
Meat: 1 piece (2 x 2 x ½ in)	4.2
Meat, shredded or grated: 1 cup	7.5
Cream (liquid from grated meat): 1 cup	20.2
Milk (liquid from mixture of grated meat and water): 1 cup	12.5
Water (liquid from coconuts): 1 cup	11.3

CANNED OR PACKAGED

GRAMS

¼ cup unless noted

Plain / **Baker's** Angel Flake	1
Plain / **Baker's** Premium Shred	9
Plain / **Baker's** Southern Style	8
Plain, shredded / **Durkee**	2
Plain, shredded or flaked: 1 oz / **Town House**	15
Cookie-coconut / **Baker's**	12

Coffee

GRAMS

Flavored coffee instant mixes, prepared: 6 fl oz	
Cafe Amaretto / **General Foods** International	7
Cafe Francais / **General Foods** International	7
Cafe Vienna / **General Foods** International	10
Irish Mocha Mint / **General Foods** International	7
Orange Cappuccino / **General Foods** International	10
Suisse Mocha / **General Foods** International	7
Postum (cereal beverage), instant: 6 fl oz	12

Condiments

GRAMS

See also Sauces *and* Seasonings.

Catsup	
Del Monte: ¼ cup	16
Del Monte No Salt: ¼ cup	16
Dia-Mel: 1 tbsp	1

GRAMS

Heinz: 1 tbsp	4
Heinz Hot: 1 tbsp	4
Heinz Lite: 1 tbsp	2
Heinz Low Sodium Lite: 1 tbsp	2
Hunt's: 1 tbsp	4
Hunt's No Salt: 1 tbsp	5
Durkee Famous Sauce: 1 tbsp	2
Horseradish, cream style: 1 tbsp / **Vita**	2
Horseradish, prepared: 1 tbsp / **Vita**	2
Hot sauce: ½ tsp / **Frank's**	0
Mint sauce: 1 tbsp / **Crosse & Blackwell**	4
Mustard	
Diablo: ¼ oz / **Gulden's**	0
French's Bold 'n Spicy: 1 tbsp	1
French's Medford: 1 tbsp	1
French's Yellow: 1 tbsp	1
Gulden's Spicy: ¼ oz	0
Gulden's Creamy Mild: ¼ oz	0
Heinz Brown: 1 tsp	.5
Mr. Mustard: 1 tsp	0
Dijon: 1 tbsp / **Grey Poupon**	1
Dijon: ¼ oz / **Gulden's**	2
w horseradish: 1 tbsp / **French's**	1
w onion: 1 tbsp / **French's**	5
Sauce Diable: 1 tbsp / **Escoffier**	4
Sauce Robert: 1 tbsp	5
Seafood cocktail: 1 tbsp / **Crosse & Blackwell**	5
Seafood cocktail: ½ oz / **Nutri-Dyne Elwood**	1
Seafood cocktail: 1 tbsp / **Vita**	3
Soy sauce: 1 oz / **Health Valley** Tamari-Ya	1.5
Steak sauce	
A.1. Sauce: 1 tbsp	3
Crosse & Blackwell: 1 tbsp	5
Lea & Perrins: 1 fl oz	10
Mrs. Dash: 1 tbsp	4
Steak Supreme: 1 tbsp	5
Taco sauce: 1 tbsp / **Ortega**	5
Tartar sauce: 1 tbsp / **Hellmann's**	0
Tartar sauce: 1 tbsp / **Vita**	2
Vinegar	
Apple cider: 1 fl oz / **Lucky Leaf**	2

	GRAMS
Apple cider: 1 fl oz / **Musselman's**	2
Red wine: 1 fl oz / **Lucky Leaf**	0
Red wine: 1 fl oz / **Musselman's**	0
Red wine: 1 fl oz / **Regina**	1
Red wine and garlic: 1 fl oz / **Regina**	1
White distilled: 1 fl oz / **Lucky Leaf**	2
White distilled: 1 fl oz / **Musselman's**	2
White wine: 1 fl oz / **Regina**	1
Wine, cooking	
Burgundy: ¼ cup / **Regina**	1
Sauterne: ¼ cup / **Regina**	1
Sherry: ¼ cup / **Regina**	5
Worcestershire	
Crosse & Blackwell: 1 tbsp	4
French's Regular: 1 tbsp	2
French's Smoky: 1 tbsp	2
Lea & Perrins: 1 tsp	1
Nutri-Dyne Elwood: ½ oz	3

Cookies

	GRAMS
1 piece unless noted	
Almond fudge, chocolate chip / **Duncan Hines**	7
Almond supreme / **Pepperidge Farm**	6.5
Almond toast / **Stella D'Oro**	10
Amond windmills / **Nabisco**	7
Angel bars / **Stella D'Oro**	7
Angelica Goodies / **Stella D'Oro**	16
Angel wings / **Stella D'Oro**	7
Anginetti / **Stella D'Oro**	5
Animal crackers	
Barnum's Animals: 11 pieces	21
Ralston Purina: 15 pieces (1 oz)	22
Sunshine: 1 piece	2

GRAMS

Animal snaps, cinnamon / **Health Valley**	3
Animal snaps, vanilla / **Health Valley**	3
Anisette sponge / **Stella D'Oro**	10
Anisette toast / **Stella D'Oro**	10
Anisette toast, large / **Stella D'Oro**	29
Apple / **Pepperidge Farm**	7.6
Apple crisp / **Nabisco**	7
Apple spice / **Pepperidge Farm**	23
Applesauce raisin, iced / **Nabisco** Almost Home	8.5
Apricot-raspberry / **Pepperidge Farm**	7.5
Apricot raspberry snack bar / **Pepperidge Farm**	36
Arrowroot biscuit / **National**	3.5
Biscos / **Nabisco**	6
Blueberry / **Pepperidge Farm**	9
Blueberry snack bar / **Pepperidge Farm**	36
Bordeaux / **Pepperidge Farm**	16
Breakfast Treat / **Stella D'Oro**	16
Brown Edge sandwich / **Nabisco**	10
Brown Edge wafers / **Nabisco**	4
Brownie chocolate nut / **Pepperidge Farm**	6.3
Brownie nut snack bar / **Pepperidge Farm**	30
Brussels / **Pepperidge Farm**	7
Brussels mint / **Pepperidge Farm**	8.3
Butter / **Pepperidge Farm**	5
Butter-flavored / **Nabisco**	3.5
Butter-flavored / **Sunshine**	4
Butterscotch / **Nutri-Dyne** Aproten	10
Butterscotch chocolate chip / **Duncan Hines**	7
Cappucino / **Pepperidge Farm**	3
Capri / **Pepperidge Farm**	10
Carob snaps / **Health Valley**	2
Champagne / **Pepperidge Farm**	4
Chessman / **Pepperidge Farm**	6
Chinese Dessert / **Stella D'Oro**	20
Chip-A-Roos / **Sunshine**	9
Chips Ahoy!	7
Chocolate chip	
Duncan Hines	7
Keebler Chips Deluxe	10
Keebler Rich 'n Chips	10

GRAMS

Nabisco Almost Home	10
Nabisco Cookie Little: 20 pieces	20
Nutri-Dyne Aproten	10
Pepperidge Farm	7
Snaps	3
Sunshine Chocolate Nuggets	3
Tastykake	7
Chocolate chip macaroon snack bar / **Pepperidge Farm**	28
Chocolate chocolate chip / **Nabisco**	7.3
Chocolate chocolate chip / **Pepperidge Farm**	6.3
Chocolate chunk pecan / **Pepperidge Farm**	7.5
Chocolate peanut bars / **Nabisco**	10
Chocolate snaps / **Nabisco**	2.7
Chocolate wafers / **Nabisco**	4.6
Cinnamon chip / **Pepperidge Farm**	7
Cinnamon honey jumbo / **Health Valley**	14
Cinnamon raisin / **Nabisco** Almost Home	9
Cinnamon sugar / **Pepperidge Farm**	7
Cinnamon treats: 9 oz / **Nabisco**	20
Cocoa chocolate chip / **Archway**	10
Coconut, dietetic / **Stella D'Oro**	6
Cocoanut bars / **Nabisco**	5.3
Cocoanut chocolate chip / **Nabisco**	9
Cocoanut macaroon, soft / **Nabisco**	11.5
Coconut chocolate chip / **Archway**	10
Coconut granola / **Pepperidge Farm**	6.3
Coconut macaroon snack bar / **Pepperidge Farm**	28
Coconut snaps / **Health Valley**	2
Coconut squares / **Archway**	16
Como delights / **Stella D'Oro**	17
Cookie Break, mixed / **Nabisco**	7
Cookie Break, vanilla / **Nabisco**	7.5
Creme wafer sticks / **Nabisco**	6.3
Date nut granola / **Pepperidge Farm**	6.6
Date nut snack bar / **Pepperidge Farm**	30
Date pecan / **Health Valley**	4
Date pecan / **Pepperidge Farm**	7.3
Dietetic / **Estee**	3
Dixie Vanilla / **Sunshine**	10

	GRAMS
Duplex / **Estee**	5
Egg biscuits	
Stella D'Oro	7
Stella D'Oro dietetic	7
Anise-rum / **Stella D'Oro**	18
Brandy-vanilla / **Stella D'Oro**	18
Sugared / **Stella D'Oro**	14
Egg jumbo / **Stella D'Oro**	9
Fig bars / **Sunshine**	9
Fig bars, whole wheat / **Nabisco** Fig Wheats	12
Fig Newtons / **Nabisco**	11
Frosty lemon / **Archway**	22
Fruit crescent / **Stella D'Oro**	11
Fruit sticks, all flavors / **Nabisco** Almost Home	14
Fudge bar / **Tastykake**	38
Fudge chocolate chip / **Nabisco** Almost Home	10
Fudge stripes / **Keebler**	7
Geneva / **Pepperidge Farm**	6.3
Gingerman / **Pepperidge Farm**	5
Ginger snaps / **Health Valley**	2
Ginger snaps / **Nabisco**	5.5
Ginger snaps / **Sunshine**	3
Golden bars / **Stella D'Oro**	16
Golden fruit / **Sunshine**	14
Graham crackers	
Honey Maid	6
Nabisco	5
Nabisco Fancy Dip	8
Nabisco Party	9
I. Rokeach	2.5
Chocolate / **Nabisco**	7
Cinnamon / **Keebler**	3
Cinnamon / **Sunshine**	3
Fudge-covered / **Keebler**	5.5
Honey / **Keebler**	3
Sugar honey / **Ralston**	3
Sugar honey / **Sunshine**	3
Hazelnut / **Pepperidge Farm**	7
HeyDay / **Nabisco**	13
Hostess assortment / **Stella D'Oro**	5
Hydrox, chocolate	7

GRAMS

Hydrox, vanilla | 7
Irish oatmeal / **Pepperidge Farm** | 7
Kettle cookies / **Nabisco** | 5
Kichel, dietetic / **Stella D'Oro** | 1
Lady Stella assortment / **Stella D'Oro** | 5
Lemon coconut / **Archway** | 9
Lemon coolers / **Sunshine** | 5
Lemon nut crunch / **Pepperidge Farm** | 6
Lemon snaps / **Health Valley** | 2
Lido / **Pepperidge Farm** | 11
Lorna Doones | 5
Love cookies, dietetic / **Stella D'Oro** | 14
Mallomars | 8.5
MalloPuffs / **Sunshine** | 12
Margherite chocolate / **Stella D'Oro** | 10
Margherite vanilla / **Stella D'Oro** | 11
Marseilles assortment / **Pepperidge Farm** | 6
Marshmallow puffs / **Nabisco** | 14
Marshmallow twirls / **Nabisco** | 20
Milano / **Pepperidge Farm** | 7
Mint chocolate chip / **Duncan Hines** | 7
Mint Milano / **Pepperidge Farm** | 8.3
Mollases / **Nabisco** Pantry | 9.5
Molasses crisps / **Pepperidge Farm** | 4
Mystic Mints / **Nabisco** | 11
Nassau / **Pepperidge Farm** | 9
Nilla Wafers / **Nabisco** | 3
Nutter Butter | 9
Nutter Butter, chocolate | 7.3
Oatmeal

Archway	19
Drake's	10
Health Valley	5
Keebler	12
Nabisco Bakers Bonus	12
Nabisco Cookie Little	1
Sunshine	9
Date filled / Archway	18
Creme / Nabisco Almost Home	21
Honey / Health Valley Jumbo	14
Iced / Nabisco Almost Home	9.5

GRAMS

Raisin / **Nabisco** Almost Home	10
Raisin / **Pepperidge Farm**	8
Raisin bar / **Tastykake**	37
Oatmeal and nut / **Archway**	10
Old fashion molasses / **Archway**	21
Orange / **Pepperidge Farm**	9
Orange Milano / **Pepperidge Farm**	8
Oreo	7.3
Oreo, Double Stuff	9
Orleans / **Pepperidge Farm**	4
Orleans sandwich / **Pepperidge Farm**	7
Peanut brittle cookies / **Nabisco**	6.3
Peanut butter	
Health Valley	5
Nabisco Almost Home	8
Chip / **Archway**	9
Chip / **Pepperidge Farm**	6.3
Fudge / **Nabisco**	7
Fudge / **Nabisco** Almost Home	8
Fudge and chocolate chip / **Duncan Hines**	7
Honey / **Health Valley** Jumbo	15
Peanut creme patties / **Nabisco**	4
Pecan crunch / **Archway**	9
Pecan sandies / **Keebler**	9
Pecan shortbread / **Nabisco**	8.5
Pfeffernusse / **Stella D'Oro**	7
Piccolo crepe / **Nabisco**	3
Pirouettes, original / **Pepperidge Farm**	4
Pirouettes, chocolate-laced / **Pepperidge Farm**	4
Pitter Patter / **Keebler**	11
Pretzel, coated / **Tastykake**	14
Pretzel, coated, mini / **Tastykake**	3
Raisin bran / **Health Valley**	5
Raisin bran / **Pepperidge Farm**	7
Raisin fruit biscuit / **Nabisco**	12
Raisin spice snack bar / **Pepperidge Farm**	31
Royal Nuggets, dietetic / **Stella D'Oro**	1
Sandwich, creme	
Nabisco Baronet	8
Nabisco Cameo	10

	GRAMS
Nabisco Mayfair	9
Nabisco Mayfair Crown	8
Nabisco Mayfair Tea Rose	8
Nabisco Swiss	7.5
Chocolate fudge / **Sunshine**	9
Coconut / **Sunshine** Coconut Cremers	7
Fudge / **Keebler** Fudge Cremers	8
Fudge / **Nabisco**	8
Fudge / **Nabisco** Gaiety	7
Fudge and chocolate / **Nabisco** Almost Home	20
Oatmeal / **Keebler**	11
Oatmeal peanut / **Sunshine**	11
Peanut butter / **Nabisco** Almost Home	20
Vanilla / **Sunshine** Cup Custard	9
Sandwich, malted milk peanut butter / **Nabisco**	4.5
Sesame / **Stella D'Oro**	6
Sesame, dietetic / **Stella D'Oro**	6
Seville / **Pepperidge Farm**	7
Shortbread / **Pepperidge Farm**	8.5
Shortcake / **Nabisco** Cookie Little	1
Shortcake / **Nabisco** Melt-a-Way	8
Social Tea Biscuit / **Nabisco**	3.3
Southport assortment / **Pepperidge Farm**	6
Spiced wafers / **Nabisco**	6
Sprinkles / **Sunshine**	12
Strawberry / **Pepperidge Farm**	8
Striped shortbread / **Nabisco**	6
Sugar / **Pepperidge Farm**	7
Sugar rings / **Nabisco**	10
Sugar wafers / **Nabisco** Biscos	2.5
Swiss fudge / **Stella D'Oro**	8
Tahiti / **Pepperidge Farm**	8.5
Tea Time Biscuit / **Nabisco** Mayfair	4
Toy cookies / **Sunshine**	2
Twiddle Sticks / **Nabisco**	7
Vanilla shortbread cookie tub / **Tastykake**	6
Vienna fingers / **Sunshine**	10
Wafers	
Creme-filled, assorted / **Estee**	4
Creme-filled, chocolate / **Estee**	3

	GRAMS
Creme-filled, vanilla / **Estee**	3
Peanut butter / **Sunshine**	5
Snack, chocolate, strawberry, vanilla / **Estee**	11
Snack, chocolate-coated / **Estee**	14
Sugar / **Sunshine**	6
Vanilla / **Keebler**	8
Vanilla / **Sunshine**	2
Waffle cremes / **Nabisco** Biscos	6
Yum Yums / **Sunshine**	10

COOKIE MIXES

Brownies	
Estee: 2-in square	8
Duncan Hines Double Fudge: 1 square	20
Betty Crocker Family Size: 1/24 pkg	21
Betty Crocker Supreme Fudge: 1/24 pkg	25
Betty Crocker Supreme Golden: 1/24 pkg	19
Pillsbury: 2-in square	23
Pillsbury Family Size: 2-in square	22
Walnut / **Betty Crocker** Family Size: 1/24 pkg	19
Walnut / **Betty Crocker** Regular: 1/16 pkg	22
Walnut / **Pillsbury** Family Size: 2-in square	23
Chocolate chip	
Betty Crocker Big Batch: 1/18 pkg (2 cookies)	16
Duncan Hines: 2 cookies	19
Pillsbury: 3 cookies	23
Duncan Hines Double: 2 cookies	19
Quaker: 8/10 oz dry	18
Coconut macaroon / **Betty Crocker:** 1/14 pkg	10
Date bar / **Betty Crocker:** 1/32 pkg	9
Double chocolate / **Pillsbury:** 3 cookies	23
Fudge: 1 bar	
Brown sugar and oatmeal / **Pillsbury** Fudge Jumbles	15
Chocolate chip and oatmeal / **Pillsbury** Fudge Jumbles	14
Coconut and oatmeal / **Pillsbury** Fudge Jumbles	14
Peanut butter and oatmeal / **Pillsbury** Fudge Jumbles	14

	GRAMS
Oatmeal / **Betty Crocker** Big Batch: 1/18 (2 cookies)	17
Oatmeal raisin: 2 cookies / **Duncan Hines**	18
Peanut butter: 2 cookies / **Duncan Hines**	15
Peanut butter: 3 cookies / **Pillsbury**	20
Sugar: 1/18 (2 cookies) / **Betty Crocker** Big Batch	18
Sugar: 2 cookies / **Duncan Hines** Golden	17
Sugar: 3 cookies / **Pillsbury**	23
Vienna Dream Bar: 1/14 pkg / **Betty Crocker**	10

REFRIGERATED DOUGH

1 cookie

Chocolate chip / **Merico**	8
Chocolate chip w pecan / **Merico**	7.5
Chocolate chip: 1/36 pkg / **Pillsbury**	7
Fudge brownie: 1/16 pkg / **Pillsbury**	17
Peanut butter / **Merico**	7.5
Peanut butter: 1/36 pkg / **Pillsbury**	6
Sugar / **Merico**	7.5
Sugar: 1/36 pkg / **Pillsbury**	8

Crackers

	GRAMS
1 cracker unless noted	
Amaranth / **Health Valley**	4
Bacon 'n Dip / **Nabisco**	1
Banquet Wafers / **Sunshine**	2
Buttery Flavored Sesame / **Nabisco**	2
Cheddar: 1 oz / **Charles**	14
Cheddar Snacks / **Ralston**	1
Cheddar Triangles / **Nabisco**	1
Cheddar 'n Sesame / **Nabisco** Country	1
Cheese Nips / **Nabisco**	1

GRAMS

Cheese Peanut Butter Sandwich / **Nabisco**	4
Cheese Sandwich / **Nabisco**	3
Cheese Snacks / **Ralston**	1
Cheese Tid-Bit / **Nabisco**	1
Cheese Wheels: 1 oz / **Health Valley**	14
Cheez-It / **Sunshine**	1
Chicken in a Biskit / **Nabisco**	1
Chippers / **Nabisco**	2
Club: smallest piece when broken on score line / **Keebler**	2
Cracked Wheat / **Pepperidge Farm**	4
Crown Pilot / **Nabisco**	13
Dip in a Chip / **Nabisco**	1
Dixies / **Nabisco**	1
English Water Biscuit / **Pepperidge Farm**	3
Escort / **Nabisco**	3
French Onion / **Nabisco**	2
Goldfish: 1 piece has about 3 calories	
Cheddar Cheese: 45 / **Pepperidge Farm**	18
Parmesan Cheese: 45 / **Pepperidge Farm**	18
Pizza Flavored: 45 / **Pepperidge Farm**	18
Pretzel: 40 / **Pepperidge Farm**	18
Salted: 45 / **Pepperidge Farm**	18
Harvest Wheats / **Keebler**	3
Hearty Wheat / **Pepperidge Farm**	3
Herb: 1 oz / **Health Valley**	18
Herb: 1 oz / **Health Valley** No Salt	18
Hi Ho / **Sunshine**	2
Holland Rusk / **Nabisco**	8
Matzos: 1 sheet or 1 cracker	
American / **Manischewitz**	23
Egg 'n Onion / **Manischewitz**	24
Egg Passover / **Manischewitz**	26
Thin Tea / **Manischewitz**	24
Thin Tea Passover / **Manischewitz**	24
Whole Wheat w bran / **Manischewitz**	24
Meal Mates / **Nabisco**	3
Melba Toast: 1 piece	
Old London	3
Bacon / **Old London** Bacon Rounds	2

GRAMS

Cheese / **Old London** Cheese Rounds	2
Garlic / **Old London** Garlic Rounds	2
Onion / **Old London** Onion Rounds	2
Pumpernickel / **Old London**	3
Rye / **Old London**	3
Salty Rye / **Old London** Salty-Rye Rounds	2
Sesame / **Old London** Sesame Rounds	2
Unsalted / **Old London**	3
Whole Grain / **Old London**	3
Milk Crackers / **Nabisco** Royal Lunch	8
Oyster / **Ralston**	1
Oyster / **Sunshine**	1
Rich & Crisp / **Ralston**	2
Ritz / **Nabisco**	2
Rye	
Wasa Golden	8
Wasa Hearty	11
Wasa Lite	6
Wasa Sport	9
Wasa Fiber Plus	5
Rye Snacks / **Ralston**	1
Ry Krisp, Natural	5
Ry Krisp, Seasoned	5
Ry Krisp, Sesame	5
Saltines and soda crackers	
Krispy / **Sunshine**	2
Krispy, unsalted / **Sunshine**	2
Premium / **Nabisco**	2
Premium, unsalted tops / **Nabisco**	2
Ralston	2
Rokeach Kosher	2
Zesta / **Keebler**	2
Sea Rounds / **Nabisco**	8
Sesame: 1 oz / **Health Valley**	18
Sesame: 1 oz / **Health Valley** No Salt	17
Sesame / **Pepperidge Farm**	3
Sesame Wheats! / **Nabisco**	2
7-Grain: 1 oz / **Health Valley**	17
7-Grain: 1 oz / **Health Valley** No Salt	17
Snack / **Rokeach**	2

GRAMS

Snackers / **Ralston**	2
Snacks Ahoy / **Nabisco**	1
Snack sticks	
Cheese / **Pepperidge Farm**	2
Original / **Pepperidge Farm**	3
Pumpernickel / **Pepperidge Farm**	3
Rye / **Pepperidge Farm**	3
Sesame / **Pepperidge Farm**	2
Sociables / **Nabisco**	1
Soup and Oyster: 40 / **Nabisco** Dandy	20
Soup and Oyster: 36 / **Nabisco** Oysterettes	20
Swiss Cheese Flavor / **Nabisco**	1
Tams, garlic / **Manischewitz**	2
Tams, onion / **Manischewitz**	2
Tams, wheat / **Manischewitz**	2
Tam Tams / **Manischewitz**	2
Tam Tams, no salt / **Manischewitz**	2
Thins	
Bacon Flavored / **Nabisco**	1
Butter Flavored / **Pepperidge Farm**	3
Cheese / **Pepperidge Farm**	2
Salted / **Pepperidge Farm**	2
Vegetable / **Nabisco**	1
Wheat / **Nabisco**	1
Wheat / **Pepperidge Farm**	2
Toasted Rye / **Keebler**	2
Toasted Sesame / **Keebler**	2
Toasted Wheat / **Keebler**	2
Town House / **Keebler**	2
Triscuit / **Nabisco**	3
Tuc / **Keebler**	3
Twigs / **Nabisco**	2
Uneeda Biscuit / **Nabisco**	4
Unsalted crackers / **Estee**	3
Unsalted top / **Ralston**	2
Waverly Wafers / **Nabisco**	3
Wheat	
Estee 6 Calorie Wheat Wafers	1
Wasa Poppyseed	9
Wasa Sesame	11

GRAMS

Wheat Snacks / **Ralston**	1
Wheat, stoned: 1 oz / **Health Valley**	18
Wheat, stoned: 1 oz / **Health Valley** No Salt	18
Wheat, stoneground	
Hain Rich	2
Cheese / **Hain** Rich	2
Cheese & Garlic / **Hain** Rich	1
Onion / **Hain**	2
Sesame / **Hain**	1
Sour Cream & Chive / **Hain**	1
Sourdough / **Hain**	2
Vegetable / **Hain**	2
Wheat & Rye / **Hain**	2
Wheat & Sweet Rye: 1 oz / **Health Valley**	17
Wheat & Sweet Rye: 1 oz / **Health Valley** No Salt	17
Wheat Wafers / **Sunshine**	2
Wheatsworth / **Nabisco**	2
Yogurt & Green Onion: 1 oz / **Health Valley**	17
Yogurt & Green Onion: 1 oz / **Health Valley** No Salt	17
Zwieback / **Nabisco**	5

Cream

	GRAMS
Half and half (cream and milk, 11.7% fat)	
1 cup	0
1 tbsp	0
Light, coffee or table (20.6% fat)	
1 cup	0
1 tbsp	0
Light whipping (31.3% fat)	
1 cup (about 2 cups whipped)	0
1 tbsp	0
Heavy whipping (37.6% fat)	
1 cup (about 2 cups whipped)	0
1 tbsp	0

NONDAIRY CREAMERS

Dry	
Coffee-mate	
1 pkt	2
1 tsp	1
1 fl oz	2.6
Coffee Tone: 1 tsp / **Lucerne**	1
Cremora: 1 tsp	1
Liquid	
Coffee Tone, freezer pack: ½ fl oz (1 tbsp) /	
Lucerne	2
Lucerne Cereal Blend: 1 fl oz	1

SOUR CREAM

Sour cream	
1 tbsp	0
1 cup	0

GRAMS

Sour cream, half and half
    1 tbsp   0
    1 cup   0
Imitation sour cream: 1 tbsp / **Pet**   1

Dinners

FROZEN

1 dinner	GRAMS
Beans and franks: 10¼ oz / **Banquet**	64
Beans and franks: 10¾ oz / **Morton**	79
Beans and franks: 12½ oz / **Swanson**	75
Beef	
Banquet: 10 oz	19
Banquet Extra Helping: 16 oz	72
Morton: 10 oz	20
Swanson: 11½ oz	34
Burgundy: 10¼ oz / **Dinner Classics**	23
Chopped: 11 oz / **Banquet**	23
Chopped: 18 oz / **Banquet** Extra Helping	70
Chopped sirloin: 11½ oz / **Swanson**	32
Chopped sirloin: 12¼ oz / **Le Menu**	30
Chopped sirloin: 9½ oz / **Morton** Steak House	43
Chopped steak: 17¼ oz / **Swanson** Hungry Man	42
Pepper oriental / **Chun King**	43
Pepper steak: 10 oz / **Classic Lite**	28
Short ribs: 10¼ oz / **Dinner Classics**	32
Sirloin tips: 11 oz / **Dinner Classics**	28
Sirloin tips: 11½ oz / **Le Menu**	24
Sliced: 14 oz / **Morton** Country Table	57
Sliced: 16 oz / **Swanson** Hungry Man	60
Sliced: 10¼ oz / **Classic Lite**	30
Steak, sirloin strip: 9½ oz / **Morton** Steak House	43
Steak, rib eye: 9 oz / **Morton** Steak House	38
Stroganoff: 11¼ oz / **Dinner Classics**	28

Tenderloin: 9½ oz / **Morton** Steak House	43
Burrito, Grande: 14¾ oz / **Van de Kamp's**	69
Burrito, bean and beef: 15¾ oz / **Swanson**	88

Chicken

À la king: 10¼ oz / **Le Menu**	29
Boneless: 10 oz / **Morton**	24
Boneless: 17 oz / **Morton** King Size	55
Boneless: 17½ oz / **Swanson** Hungry Man	77
Burgundy: 11¼ oz **Classic Lite**	24
Fricassee: 11¾ oz / **Dinner Classics**	32
Fried: 11 oz / **Banquet**	46
Fried: 17 oz / **Banquet** Extra Helping	92
Fried: 11 oz / **Morton**	49
Fried: 15 oz / **Morton** Country Table	96
Fried: 17 oz / **Morton** King Size	91
Fried, barbecue: 9½ oz / **Swanson**	51
Fried, breast portion: 10¾ oz / **Swanson**	62
Fried, breast portion: 14 oz / **Swanson** Hungry Man	77
Fried, dark meat: 10¼ oz / **Swanson**	55
Fried, dark portions: 14 oz / **Swanson** Hungry Man	79
Oriental: 10 oz / **Classic Lite**	24
Parmigiana: 20 oz / **Swanson** Hungry Man	55
Parmigiana, breast of chicken / **Le Menu**	26
Sweet and sour: 11 oz / **Dinner Classics**	43
Sweet and sour: 11¼ oz / **Le Menu**	45
w dressing: 19 oz / **Banquet** Extra Helping	89
w dumplings: 19 oz / **Banquet** Extra Helping	91
Chicken Suiza: 14¾ oz / **Van de Kamp's**	64

Chow mein

Chicken / **Chun King**	43
Chicken and sweet and sour pork / **Chun King**	52
Shrimp / **Chun King**	43
Shrimp and beef pepper / **Chun King**	51

Enchilada

El Charrito	56
Beef: 12 oz / **Banquet**	72
Beef: 11 oz / **Morton**	44
Beef / **Patio**	70
Beef: 15 oz / **Swanson**	57

GRAMS

Beef: 16 oz / **Swanson** Hungry Man	65
Beef: 12 oz / **Van de Kamp's** Holiday	45
Beef w rice and corn: 14¾ oz / **Van de Kamp's**	60
Beef w chili and beans / **Patio**	76
Beef and cheese / **Patio**	83
Beef and cheese: 14¾ oz / **Van de Kamp's**	59
Cheese: 12 oz / **Banquet**	71
Cheese: 21¼ oz / **Banquet** Extra Helping	105
Cheese / **El Charrito**	64
Cheese / **Patio**	68
Cheese: 12 oz / **Van de Kamp's** Holiday	44
Cheese w rice and beans: 14¾ oz / **Van de Kamp's**	60

Fish

Banquet: 8¾ oz	45
Morton: 9 oz	22
Van de Kamp's: 12 oz	27
and chips: 14 oz / **Banquet** Extra Helping	97
and chips: 10½ oz / **Swanson**	59
and chips: 14¾ oz / **Swanson** Hungry Man	78
Cod almondine: 12 oz / **Dinner Classics**	33
Cod divan: 13¼ oz / **Classic Lite**	32
9 oz	6
Seafood newburg: 10½ oz / **Dinner Classics**	33
Seafood natural herbs: 12 oz / **Classic Lite**	40

Green peppers, stuffed: 12 oz / **Dinner Classics**	37
Ham: 10 oz / **Banquet**	61
Ham: 10 oz / **Morton**	57
Italian style: 12 oz / **Banquet**	71
Lasagna: 10 oz / **Dinner Classics**	38
Lasagna: 13 oz / **Swanson**	54
Lasagna w meat: 18¾ oz / **Swanson** Hungry Man	90
Macaroni and beef: 10 oz / **Morton**	46
Macaroni and beef: 12 oz	46
Macaroni and cheese: 11 oz / **Morton**	54
Macaroni and cheese: 12¾ oz / **Swanson**	47

Meat loaf

Banquet: 11 oz	30
Banquet Extra Helping: 19 oz	80
Morton: 11 oz	28

	GRAMS
Swanson: 11 oz	49
Meatballs, Swedish: 11½ oz / **Dinner Classics**	32
Mexican style	
Banquet: 12 oz	62
Banquet Combination: 12 oz	72
El Charrito	78
Morton: 11 oz	45
Patio	60
Patio Combination	66
Patio Fiesta	68
Swanson: 16 oz	66
Swanson Hungry Man: 22 oz	103
Van de Kamp's Holiday: 11½ oz	43
Noodles and chicken: 10½ oz / **Swanson**	37
Pepper steak: 11½ oz / **Le Menu**	34
Polynesian style: 12 oz / **Swanson**	65
Pork, loin: 11¼ oz / **Swanson**	26
Pork, sweet and sour: 11½ oz / **Dinner Classics**	41
Queso / **El Charrito**	74
Rice, fried w pork / **Chun King**	24
Salisbury steak	
Banquet: 11 oz	24
Banquet Extra Helping: 19 oz	72
Dinner Classics: 11 oz	39
Morton: 11 oz	25
Morton Country Table: 15 oz	62
Morton King Size: 19 oz	65
Swanson: 11 oz	46
Swanson Hungry Man: 16½ oz	45
Saltillo / **El Charrito**	73
Spaghetti and meatballs: 11 oz / **Morton**	61
Spaghetti and meatballs: 12½ oz / **Swanson**	57
Spaghetti in tomato sauce w veal: 8¼ oz / **Swanson**	29
Swiss steak: 10 oz / **Swanson**	38
Tacos, beef / **Patio**	64
Teriyaki, chicken: 10¼ oz / **Dinner Classics**	52
Teriyaki steak: 10 oz / **Dinner Classics**	31
Turkey	
Banquet: 11 oz	41
Banquet Extra Helping: 19 oz	98
Le Menu: 11¼ oz	36

GRAMS

Morton: 11 oz	35
Morton Country Table: 15 oz	80
Morton King Size: 19 oz	65
Swanson: 11½ oz	42
Swanson Hungry Man: 18½ oz	80
Turkey parmesan: 11 oz / **Classic Lite**	24
Turf and Surf: 10 oz / **Classic Lite**	15
Veal parmigiana	
Banquet: 11 oz	43
Banquet Extra Helping: 20 oz	116
Dinner Classics: 10¾ oz	36
Morton: 11 oz	27
Morton King Size: 20 oz	83
Swanson: 12¾ oz	42
Swanson Hungry Man: 20 oz	64
Veal pepper steak: 11 oz / **Classic Lite**	27
Western style	
Banquet: 11 oz	43
Morton: 11⅘ oz	32
Swanson: 12¼ oz	44
Swanson Hungry Man: 17½ oz	61
Yankee pot roast: 11 oz / **Le Menu**	29

DINNER MIXES

GRAMS

⅕ prepared dinner unless noted

Beef Noodle / **Hamburger Helper**	25
Beef Romanoff / **Hamburger Helper**	28
Burger 'N Cheese Dinner / **Creamette** Hamburger Mate	32
Cheeseburger Macaroni / **Hamburger Helper**	28
Chili Tomato / **Hamburger Helper**	32
Country Dumplings, Noodles and Tuna / **Tuna Helper**	31
Creamy Noodles and Tuna / **Tuna Helper**	31
Hamburger Hash / **Hamburger Helper**	24
Hamburger Pizza Dish / **Hamburger Helper**	33
Hamburger Stew / **Hamburger Helper**	23
Lasagne / **Hamburger Helper**	29

GRAMS

Noodles, Cheese Sauce and Tuna / **Tuna Helper**	28
Potatoes Au Gratin / **Hamburger Helper**	27
Potato Stroganoff / **Hamburger Helper**	27
Rice Oriental / **Hamburger Helper**	35
Stroganoff: 1 cup prepared dinner / **Durkee**	7
Tamale Pie / **Hamburger Helper**	27
Tuna Tetrazzini / **Tuna Helper**	26

Doughnuts

GRAMS

1 doughnut

Chocolate / **Dolly Madison**	18
Chocolate-coated / **Hostess**	14
Chocolate-coated / **Hostess** Donette	6
Cinnamon / **Hostess**	15
Cinnamon-apple / **Earth Grains**	36
Devil's food / **Earth Grains**	36
Krunch / **Hostess**	16
Old fashioned / **Hostess**	22
Old fashioned, glazed / **Earth Grains**	34
Old fashioned, glazed / **Hostess**	30
Old fashioned, powdered / **Earth Grains**	29
Plain / **Hostess**	12
Powdered / **Hostess** Donette	5
Powdered, sugar / **Dolly Madison**	19
Powdered, sugar / **Hostess**	15

FROZEN

1 doughnut

Bavarian creme / **Morton**	22
Boston creme / **Morton**	28
Chocolate iced / **Morton**	20

	GRAMS
Chocolate iced / **Morton** Morning Light	26
Fudge iced / **Tastykake** Morning Fresh	40
Glazed / **Morton**	19
Glazed / **Morton** Morning Light	26
Honey wheat old fashioned / **Tastykake** Morning Fresh	40
Honey wheat, mini / **Tastykake** Morning Fresh	9
Jelly / **Morton**	23
Jelly / **Morton** Morning Light	33
Mini / **Morton**	16
Mini, powdered sugar / **Tastykake** Morning Fresh	8
Powdered old fashioned / **Tastykake** Morning Fresh	31

DOUGHNUT HOLES

Doughnut Holes: 1½ oz

Devil's food: / **Morton**	22
Honey wheat / **Morton**	21
Vanilla / **Morton**	22

Eggs and Egg Dishes

EGGS

Chicken
    Raw, hard cooked or poached
Extra large	.5
Large	.5
Medium	.4

    Raw, white only
Extra large	.3
Large	.3
Medium	.2
1 cup	1.9

    Raw, yolk only
Extra large	.1
Large	.1
Medium	.1

    Fried
Extra large	.2
Large	.1
Medium	.1

    Scrambled in fat
Extra large	1.8
Large	1.5
Medium	1.3

Duck, raw: 1 egg	.5
Goose, raw: 1 egg	1.9
Turkey, raw: 1 egg	1.3

EGG DISHES, FROZEN

Omelet w cheese sauce and ham: 7 oz / **Swanson**	11
Omelet, Spanish style: 8 oz / **Swanson**	16

GRAMS

Scrambled eggs, Canadian bacon and cheese in pastry: 1 piece / **Pepperidge Farm** Deli's	24

EGG MIXES AND SEASONINGS

Egg, imitation	
Country Morning: 1 fl oz	1
Morningstar Farms Scramblers: ¼ cup	2
Scramblend: 1 fl oz	3
Omelet mix, Western: 1 pkg dry / **Durkee**	9
Quiche filling: 4⅓ oz / **Land O Lakes** Pour-A-Quiche	4
Scrambled, mix: 1 pkg dry / **Durkee**	4
Scrambled, mix w bacon: 1 pkg dry / **Durkee**	6

$\mathbf{F}$ish and Seafood

FRESH

All fish, all varieties, fresh: any quantity	0
Abalone, raw: 3½ oz	3.4
Abalone, canned: 3½ oz	2.3
Bass, black sea, baked, stuffed: 1 lb	51.7
Bass, striped, oven fried: 1 fillet	
(8¾ x 4½ x ⅝ in thick)	13.4
Bass, striped, oven fried: 1 oz	1.9
Bass, striped, oven fried: 1 lb	30.4
Bluefish, fried: 1 fillet	9.2
Bluefish, fried: 1 oz	1.3
Caviar, sturgeon, granular: 1 tbsp	.5
Caviar, sturgeon, pressed: 1 tbsp	.8
Clams, 4 cherrystone or 5 little neck clams	4.1
Clams, hard or round, raw, meat only: 1 pint (1 lb)	26.8
Clams, soft, raw, meat only: 1 pint (1 lb)	9.1
Crab, cooked, flaked: 1 cup	.6
Crab, cooked, pieces: 1 cup	.8
Crayfish, freshwater, raw, meat only: 3½ oz	1.2
Eel, raw: 4 oz	0
Frog legs, raw, meat only: 3½ oz	0
Haddock, fried: 1 fillet	6.4
Haddock, fried: 1 oz	1.6
Lobster, northern, cooked pieces: 1 cup	.4
Lobster, whole, steamed, meat only: 3½ oz	.3
Oysters, raw: 3 oz.	2.9
Cooked, fried: 4 Select (medium)	9.5
Smoked: 3 oz.	4.7
Roe, carp, cod, haddock, shad: 3½ oz	1.5

	GRAMS
Scallops, bay and sea, raw: 4 oz	3.7
Shrimp, french fried: 1 oz	2.8
Shrimp, raw, peeled: 4 oz	1.7
Snails, raw: 1 oz	.6
Squid, raw, edible portion only: 3½ oz	1.5
Turtle, green, raw, meat only: 3½ oz	0
Whitefish, cooked, stuffed: 1 oz	1.6
Whitefish, smoked:	0

CANNED AND FROZEN

Catfish fillets, frozen: 1 fillet / **Mrs. Paul's**	14
Catfish fingers, frozen: 4 oz / **Mrs. Paul's**	17
Clams	
Minced, canned: 6½ oz / **Snow's**	4
Fried, frozen: 5 oz / **Howard Johnson's**	46
Fried, frozen: 2½ oz / **Mrs. Paul's**	20
Juice: 8 fl oz / **Doxsee**	4
Juice: 3 fl oz / **Snow's**	2
Cod, frozen: 4 oz / **Van de Kamp's** Today's Catch	0
Cod, frozen, breaded: 5 oz / **Van de Kamp's**	11
Crab	
Deviled, frozen: 1 pc (3 oz) / **Mrs. Paul's**	20
Deviled, frozen: 3½ oz / **Mrs. Paul's**	
Miniatures	18
King, frozen: 3 oz / **Wakefield**	1
Snow, frozen: 3 oz / **Wakefield**	1
and shrimp, frozen: 3 oz / **Wakefield**	1
Fancy Gems, frozen: 3 oz / **Wakefield**	11
Fish, frozen	
Cakes: 2 cakes (4 oz) / **Mrs. Paul's**	24
Cakes: 2 cakes (5 oz) / **Mrs. Paul's** Thins	25
Filet: 8 oz / **Wakefield**	12
Filets: 2 oz / **Van de Kamp's** Light & Krispy	9
Fillets: 4 oz / **Van de Kamp's** Today's Catch	0
Fillets, batter-fried: 2 fillets (6 oz) /	
Mrs. Paul's	27
Fillets, batter-fried: 2 fillets (4½ oz) /	
Mrs. Paul's Crunchy Light	27

GRAMS

Fillets, batter-fried: 1 fillet (3⅝ oz) / **Mrs. Paul's**
  Supreme Light 19
Fillets, batter-fried: 3 oz / **Van de Kamp's** 14
Fillets, breaded, fried: 2 fillets (4¼ oz) /
  Mrs. Paul's Crispy Crunchy 22
Fillets, breaded, fried: 1 fillet (6 oz) /
  Mrs. Paul's Light and Natural 21
Fillets, buttered: 2 fillets (5 oz) / **Mrs. Paul's** 0
Fillets, country seasoned: 2 oz /
  Van de Kamp's 12
Nuggets: 2 oz / **Van de Kamp's** Light & Crispy 9
Portions, batter-fried: 3 oz / **Van de Kamp's** 14
Sticks, Alaskan 3½ oz / **Health Valley** 5
Sticks, batter-fried: 4 sticks (3½ oz) /
  Mrs. Paul's Crunchy Light 21
Sticks, batter-fried: 4 oz / **Van de Kamp's** 15
Sticks, breaded, fried: 4 sticks (3 oz) /
  Mrs. Paul's Crispy Crunchy 17
Sticks: 3¾ oz / **Van de Kamp's**
  Light & Crispy 16
Flounder, frozen
  Mrs. Paul's Light & Natural: 1 fillet (6 oz) 24
  Van de Kamp's Today's Catch: 4 oz 2
  Batter-fried: 2 fillets (4½ oz) / **Mrs. Paul's**
    Crunchy Light 26
  Breaded: 5 oz / **Van de Kamp's** 17
  Breaded, fried: 2 fillets (4 oz) / **Mrs. Paul's**
    Crispy Crunchy 25
Gefilte fish, canned or in jars: 1 piece unless noted
  Mother's in jellied broth 2
  Mother's Old Fashioned in liquid broth 7
  Mother's Old World, jellied 7
  Rokeach, jelled 4
  Rokeach, in jellied broth, low sodium 3
  Rokeach in natural liquid broth 4
  Rokeach Old Vienna in jellied broth 8
  Whitefish and pike, jellied / **Mother's** 4
  Whitefish and pike, in jellied broth / **Rokeach** ... 4
Haddock, frozen
  Van de Kamp's Today's Catch: 4 oz 0

GRAMS

Fillets, fried: 2 oz / **Van de Kamp's** Light & Crispy	10
Fried: 2 fillets (4 oz) / **Mrs. Paul's** Crispy Crunchy	25
Fried: 1 fillet (6 oz) / **Mrs. Paul's** Light and Natural	25
Fried in batter: 2 fillets (4½ oz) / **Mrs. Paul's** Crunchy Light	28
Halibut, frozen: 3½ oz / **Health Valley**	0
Halibut, frozen: 8 oz / **Wakefield**	1
Halibut, frozen, fried: 4 oz / **Van de Kamp's**	17
Herring, pickled in jars: 1 oz	
Lunch herring / **Vita**	4
Party snacks / **Vita**	4
Salad / **Vita**	3
in sour cream / **Vita**	3
Oysters wo shell, canned: ½ cup / **Bumble Bee**	8
Perch, frozen	
Van de Kamp's Today's Catch: 4 oz	0
Fried: 2 fillets (4 oz) / **Mrs. Paul's** Crispy Crunchy	21
Fried: 4 oz / **Van de Kamp's**	21
Fried: 2 oz / **Van de Kamp's** Light & Crispy	10
Salad Gems, frozen: 3 oz / **Wakefield**	8
Salmon, canned	
Keta: ½ cup / **Bumble Bee**	0
Pink: ½ cup / **Bumble Bee**	0
Pink: ½ cup / **Del Monte**	0
Pink: 7¾ oz / **Libby's**	0
Red: ½ cup / **Del Monte**	0
Red sockeye: ½ cup / **Bumble Bee**	0
Red sockeye: 7¾ oz / **Libby's**	0
Salmon, smoked, Nova: 1 oz / **Vita**	0
Salmon steak, frozen: 3½ oz / **Health Valley**	0
Sardines, canned	
in olive oil: 3 oz / **King Oscar**	1
in tomato sauce: ½ cup / **Del Monte**	45
in tomato sauce: 1 can (3¾ oz) / **Underwood**	1
Scallops, frozen: 4 oz / **Wakefield** Scallop Gems	14
Scallops, fried, frozen: 3½ oz / **Mrs. Paul's**	23

GRAMS

Seafood combination, fried, frozen: 9 oz / **Mrs. Paul's**	49
Shrimp, frozen: 3 oz / **Mrs. Paul's**	15
Sole, frozen	
Van de Kamp's Today's Catch: 4 oz	0
Fried: 1 fillet (6 oz) / **Mrs. Paul's**	
Light and Natural	19
Fried in batter: 4 oz / **Van de Kamp's**	24
Fried, breaded: 5 oz / **Van de Kamp's**	17
Trout, boned, frozen: 3½ oz / **Health Valley**	0
Tuna, canned	
Health Valley No Salt Dietetic: 7 oz	0
Light, chunk in oil: 2 oz / **A & P**	0
Light, chunk in oil: ½ cup undrained / **Bumble Bee**	0
Light, chunk in oil: 1 cup / **Chicken of the Sea**	0
Light, chunk in water: 2 oz / **A & P**	0
Light, chunk in water: ½ cup undrained / **Bumble Bee**	0
Light, chunk in water: 1 cup / **Chicken of the Sea**	0
Light, solid in oil: 1 cup / **Chicken of the Sea**	0
Light, solid in water: 1 cup / **Chicken of the Sea**	0
White, chunk in oil: 1 cup / **Chicken of the Sea**	0
White, chunk in water: 2 oz / **A & P**	0
White, chunk in water: 1 cup / **Chicken of the Sea** Dietetic Pack, Low Sodium	0
White, solid in oil: 2 oz / **A & P**	0
White, solid in oil: ½ cup undrained / **Bumble Bee**	0
White, solid in oil: 1 cup / **Chicken of the Sea**	0
White, solid in water: 2 oz / **A & P**	0
White, solid in water: ½ cup undrained / **Bumble Bee**	0

FISH AND SEAFOOD ENTRÉES, FROZEN

Fish and chips: 7 oz / **Van de Kamp's**	36
Fish Dijon: 8½ oz / **Mrs. Paul's**	11

GRAMS

Fish Divan: 12⅜ oz / **Stouffer's Lean Cuisine**	16
Fish Florentine: 9 oz / **Mrs. Paul's**	16
Fish Florentine: 9 oz / **Stouffer's Lean Cuisine**	13
Fish Kabobs: 4 oz / **Van de Kamp's**	15
Fish Mornay: 10 oz / **Mrs. Paul's**	11
Fish Parmesan: 5 oz / **Mrs. Paul's**	16
Haddock, au gratin: 10 oz / **Howard Johnson's**	12
Lobster Newburg: 6½ oz / **Stouffer's**	9
Scallops: 10 oz / **Light and Elegant**	30
Scallops Mediterranean: 11 oz / **Mrs. Paul's**	36
Scallops Oriental: 11 oz / **Stouffer's Lean Cuisine**	32
Scallops and Shrimp Mariner: 10¼ oz / **Stouffer's**	40
Seafood Newburg: 8½ oz / **Mrs. Paul's**	34
Seafood Potato: 3 oz / **Wakefield**	12
Shrimp Creole: 10 oz / **Light and Elegant**	31
Shrimp Croquettes: 6 oz / **Howard Johnson's**	14
Shrimp Marinara: 11 oz / **Buitoni**	24
Shrimp Oriental: 11 oz / **Mrs. Paul's**	42
Shrimp Primavera: 11 oz / **Mrs. Paul's**	42
Sole Florentine: 8 oz / **Wakefield**	6
Sole w stuffing: 8 oz / **Wakefield**	12
Tuna noodle casserole: 5¾ oz / **Stouffer's**	18

Flour and Meal

FLOUR

GRAMS

1 cup unless noted

Biscuit mix / **Bisquick**	76
Buckwheat, dark, sifted	71
Buckwheat, light, sifted	78
Carob	113
Lima bean, sifted	79
Peanut, defatted	19

GRAMS

Rye
Light	69
Medium / **Pillsbury**'s Best	83
Dark	87
and wheat / **Pillsbury**'s Best Bohemian Style	86

Tortilla, corn / **Quaker** Masa Harina	100
Tortilla, wheat / **Quaker** Masa Trigo	108

White
Aunt Jemima Self-Rising: ¼ cup	24
Ballard All-Purpose	87
Drifted Snow: 4 oz	87
Gold Medal All-Purpose	87
Gold Medal Self-Rising: 4 oz	83
Gold Medal Unbleached	87
Pillsbury's Best All-Purpose	87
Pillsbury's Best Bread	83
Pillsbury's Self-Rising	84
Pillsbury's Best Unbleached	86
Red Band Plain	87
Red Band Self-Rising	83
Red Band Unbleached	87
Softasilk: 4 oz	23
Wondra	87
High protein / **Gold Medal** Better for Bread	83
Thickening: 2 tbsp **Pillsbury**'s Best	
Sauce 'n Gravy	11

Wheat
All-purpose	104
Bread	102
Cake or pastry	94
Gluten	66
Self-rising	93
Whole wheat	85
Whole wheat: 4 oz / **Gold Medal**	78
Pillsbury's Best	80

MEAL

Note: 1 ounce equals about 4 tablespoons

Almond, partially defatted: 1 oz	8

GRAMS

Corn
White: 1 oz / **Albers**	22
White: 1 oz / **Aunt Jemima** Enriched	22
White: 1 oz / **Quaker** Enriched	22
White: ⅙ cup / **Aunt Jemima**	21
White: ⅙ cup / **Aunt Jemima** Self-Rising	20
Yellow: 1 oz / **Albers**	22
Yellow: 1 oz / **Aunt Jemima** Enriched	22
Yellow: 1 oz / **Quaker** Enriched	22

Matzo meal: 1 oz / **Manischewitz**   23
Passover cake meal: 1 cup / **Manischewitz**   120

Frostings

READY TO SPREAD

GRAMS

¹⁄₁₂ can unless noted

Butter pecan / **Betty Crocker**	25
Cake and cookie decorator, all colors: 1 tbsp / **Pillsbury**	12
Caramel pecan / **Pillsbury**	21
Cherry / **Betty Crocker**	26
Chocolate / **Betty Crocker**	23
Chocolate chocolate chip / **Betty Crocker**	24
Chocolate chip / **Betty Crocker**	26
Chocolate fudge / **Pillsbury**	24
Chocolate mint / **Pillsbury**	24
Chocolate nut / **Betty Crocker**	22
Coconut almond / **Pillsbury**	17
Coconut pecan / **Betty Crocker**	24
Coconut pecan / **Pillsbury**	17
Cream cheese / **Betty Crocker**	26
Cream cheese / **Pillsbury**	26
Dark Dutch fudge / **Betty Crocker**	23

GRAMS

Double Dutch / **Pillsbury**	22
Lemon / **Betty Crocker**	26
Lemon / **Pillsbury**	26
Milk chocolate / **Betty Crocker**	24
Milk chocolate / **Pillsbury**	23
Orange / **Betty Crocker**	26
Sour cream chocolate / **Betty Crocker**	22
Sour cream vanilla / **Pillsbury**	27
Sour cream white / **Betty Crocker**	26
Strawberry / **Pillsbury**	26
Vanilla / **Betty Crocker**	27
Vanilla / **Pillsbury**	26

MIXES

¹⁄₁₂ pkg, prepared

Banana / **Betty Crocker**	30
Butter brickle / **Betty Crocker**	30
Butter pecan / **Betty Crocker**	30
Caramel / **Pillsbury** Rich 'n Easy	24
Cherry, creamy / **Betty Crocker**	30
Chocolate / **Duncan Hines**	24
Chocolate almond fudge / **Betty Crocker**	27
Chocolate fudge / **Betty Crocker**	30
Chocolate fudge / **Pillsbury** Rich 'n Easy	27
Coconut almond / **Betty Crocker**	18
Coconut almond / **Pillsbury**	16
Coconut pecan / **Betty Crocker**	18
Coconut pecan / **Pillsbury**	20
Cream cheese and nuts / **Betty Crocker**	24
Dark chocolate fudge / **Betty Crocker**	30
Dark Dutch fudge / **Duncan Hines**	24
Double Dutch / **Pillsbury** Rich 'n Easy	26
Lemon / **Betty Crocker**	30
Lemon / **Pillsbury** Rich 'n Easy	25
Milk chocolate / **Betty Crocker**	30
Milk chocolate / **Duncan Hines**	24
Milk chocolate / **Pillsbury**	26
Sour cream chocolate fudge / **Betty Crocker**	30
Sour cream white / **Betty Crocker**	31

	GRAMS
Strawberry / **Pillsbury** Rich 'n Easy	25
Vanilla / **Duncan Hines**	24
Vanilla / **Pillsbury** Rich 'n Easy	25
White / **Betty Crocker** Creamy	31
White / **Betty Crocker** Fluffy	16
White / **Pillsbury** Fluffy	15

Fruit

FRESH

	GRAMS
Acerola cherries: 10 fruits	5.6
Apples	
w skin: 1 small (about 4 per lb)	15.3
w skin: 1 medium (about 3 per lb)	20
w skin: 1 large (about 2 per lb)	30.7
Peeled: 1 small (about 4 per lb)	13.9
Peeled: 1 medium (about 3 per lb)	18.2
Peeled: 1 large (about 2 per lb)	27.9
Apricots	
Raw, halves: 1 cup	19.8
Raw, halves: 1 lb	58.1
Raw, whole: 3 apricots	13.7
Raw, whole (12 per lb): 1 lb	54.6
Avocados	
California: ½ average	6.5
California, cubed: 1 cup	9
California, puree: 1 cup	13.8
Florida: ½ average	13.5
Florida, cubed: 1 cup	13.2
Florida, puree: 1 cup	20.2
Bananas	
1 small (7¾ in)	21.1
1 medium (8¾ in)	26.2
1 large (9¾ in)	30.2

	GRAMS
Mashed: 1 cup	50
Red: 7¼ in, 1 banana	30.7
Red, sliced: 1 cup	35.1
Sliced: 1 cup	33.3
Dehydrated or flakes: 1 tbsp	5.5
Dehydrated or flakes: 1 cup	88.6
Blackberries (including dewberries, boysenberries, youngberries), raw: 1 cup	18.6
Blueberries, raw: 1 cup	22.2
Blueberries, raw: 1 lb	69.4
Cherries	
Raw, sour, red: 1 cup	14.7
Raw, sour, red: 1 lb	58.4
Raw, sweet: 1 cup	20.4
Raw, sweet: 1 lb	71
Cranberries, raw, chopped: 1 cup	11.9
Cranberries, raw, whole: 1 cup	10.3
Figs, raw, whole: 1 small	8.1
Figs, raw, whole: 1 medium	10.2
Figs, raw, whole: 1 large	13.2
Grapefruit, 3½-in diam: half	10.3
Grapefruit, sections: 1 cup	24.4
Grapes	
Concord, Delaware, Niagara, Catawba, Scuppernong: 10 grapes	4.1
Flame Tokay, Emperor: 10 grapes	9.9
Ribier: 10 grapes	11.5
Thompson Seedless, Malaga, Muscat: 10 grapes	8.7
Groundcherries (poha or cape-gooseberries): 1 cup	15.7
Lemons, wedge: 1 from large lemon	2.2
Lemons, whole fruit: 1 large	8.7
Limes, raw: 1 lime	6.4
Loganberries, raw: 1 cup	21.5
Loquats, raw: 10 fruits	15.3
Lychees, raw: 10 fruits	14.8
Mangoes, raw, whole: 1 fruit	38.8
Muskmelons	
Cantaloupes, cubed, diced or balls: 1 cup	12
Cantaloupes, 5-in diam half:	20.4
Casaba, cubed, diced or balls: 1 cup	11.1
Casaba, whole (about 6 lbs): 1 melon	88.5

GRAMS

Honeydew, cubed, diced or balls: 1 cup	13.1
Honeydew, whole (about 5¼ lbs): 1 melon	115.5
Nectarines, raw, 2½-in diam: 1 nectarine	23.6
Oranges	
California navels (winter): 1 small	11.3
California navels (winter): 1 medium	17.8
California navels (winter): 1 large	21.8
California navels, sections: 1 cup	19.1
Valencias (summer): 1 small	12.2
Valencias (summer): 1 medium	15
Valencias (summer): 1 large	23.4
Valencias, sections: 1 cup	22.3
Florida: 1 small	14.5
Florida: 1 medium	18.1
Florida: 1 large	22.6
Florida, sections: 1 cup	22.2
Papaws, raw, whole: 1 pawpaw	16.4
Papayas, raw, cubed, ½-in pieces: 1 cup	14
Papayas, raw, whole (about 1 lb): 1 papaya	30.4
Peaches	
Raw, pared, sliced: 1 cup	16.5
Raw, whole, peeled: 1 small (about 4 per lb)	9.7
Raw, whole, peeled: 1 large	
(about 2½ per lb)	14.8
Raw, whole, peeled: 1 lb	38.3
Pears	
Raw, sliced or cubed: 1 cup	25.2
Raw, whole, Bartlett: 1 pear (about 2½ per lb)	25.1
Raw, whole, Bosc: 1 pear (about 3 per lb)	21.6
Raw, whole, D'Anjou: 1 pear (about 2 per lb)	30.6
Persimmons, raw, Japanese or kaki: 1 persimmon	33.1
Persimmons, raw, native: 1 persimmon	8.2
Pineapple, raw, diced pieces: 1 cup	21.2
Pineapple, raw, sliced, ¾-in thick: 1 slice	11.5
Plums	
Raw, whole, Damson, 1-in diam: 10 plums	17.8
Raw, whole, Damson: 1 lb	73.5
Raw, Japanese and hybrid, 2⅛-in diam: 1 plum	8.1
Raw, Japanese and hybrid: 1 lb	80.7
Prune type, raw, 1½-in diam: 1 plum	5.6
Prune type, raw: 1 lb	84

	GRAMS
Pomegranate, 3⅜-in diam: 1 pomegranate	25.3
Raspberries, raw, black: 1 cup	21
Raspberries, raw, red: 1 cup	16.7
Rhubarb, raw, diced: 1 cup	4.5
Rhubarb, cooked w sugar: 1 cup	97.2
Strawberries, raw, whole: 1 cup	12.5
Tangerines, raw, whole: 1 large (2½-in diam)	11.7
Watermelon	
Raw: 1 lb	29
Raw, diced pieces: 1 cup	10.2
Raw, slice: 10-in diam x 1-in thick	27.3
Raw, wedge: 4-in x 8-in radius	27.3

CANNED AND FROZEN

	GRAMS
Apples, canned	
Sliced	
Lucky Leaf Chipped: 4 oz	12
Lucky Leaf Diced: 4 oz	12
Lucky Leaf Syrup Pack: 4 oz	13
Lucky Leaf Water Pack: 4 oz	12
Musselman's Chipped: 4 oz	12
Musselman's Diced: 4 oz	12
Musselman's Syrup Pack: 4 oz	13
Musselman's Water Pack: 4 oz	12
Dessert: 4 oz / **Lucky Leaf**	16
Dessert: 4 oz / **Musselman's**	16
Fried: 8 oz / **Luck's**	47
Unpeeled: 4 oz / **Lucky Leaf**	22
Unpeeled: 4 oz / **Musselman's**	22
Whole	
Lucky Leaf: 1 apple	21
Musselman's: 1 apple	21
Baked: 1 apple / **Lucky Leaf**	28
Baked: 1 apple / **Musselman's**	28
Apples, frozen, escalloped: 4 oz / **Stouffer's**	28
Apples, frozen, sliced: 4 oz / **Lucky Leaf**	28
Apples, frozen, sliced: 4 oz / **Musselman's**	28
Apple rings, spiced, canned: 4 oz / **Lucky Leaf**	24

GRAMS

Apple rings, spiced, canned: 4 oz / **Musselman's**	24
Applesauce in cans or jars	
A & P: ½ cup	25
A & P Natural Style: ½ cup	13
Del Monte: ½ cup	24
Del Monte Lite: ½ cup	13
Lucky Leaf Chunky: 4 oz	20
Lucky Leaf Juice Pack: 4 oz	12
Lucky Leaf Sweetened: 4 oz	20
Lucky Leaf Unsweetened: 4 oz	12
Lucky Leaf w Cranberry: 4 oz	19
Mott's: 8 oz	55
Mott's Natural Style: 8 oz	22
Musselman's Chunky: 4 oz	20
Musselman's Juice Pack: 4 oz	12
Musselman's Sweetened: 4 oz	20
Musselman's Unsweetened: 4 oz	12
Seneca: ½ cup	22
Seneca Cinnamon: ½ cup	22
Seneca Golden Delicious: ½ cup	22
Seneca Mcintosh: ½ cup	22
Seneca Natural: ½ cup	12
Apricots, canned: ½ cup	
Halves / **Del Monte**	26
Halves / **Del Monte** Lite	16
Halves, unpeeled / **Scotch Buy**	20
Halves, unpeeled / **Town House**	28
Unpeeled, in heavy syrup / **A & P**	28
Whole / **Del Monte**	27
Whole peeled / **Town House**	26
Blueberries, canned: 4 oz / **Lucky Leaf** Water Pack	9
Blueberries, canned: 4 oz / **Musselman's** Water Pack	9
Blueberries, canned, in heavy syrup: ½ cup / **A & P**	28
Cherries, canned	
Dark, sweet w pits: ½ cup **Del Monte**	23
Dark, sweet, pitted: ½ cup / **Del Monte**	24
Light, sweet w pits: ½ cup / **Del Monte**	26
Red tart: ½ cup / **A & P**	12
Red tart, pitted: 4 oz / **Lucky Leaf**	11

GRAMS

Red tart, pitted: 4 oz / **Musselman's**	11
Cherries, frozen: 4 oz / **Lucky Leaf**	31
Cherries, frozen: 4 oz / **Musselman's**	31
Crabapples, spiced, canned: 4 oz / **Lucky Leaf**	28
Crabapples, spiced, canned: 4 oz / **Musselman's**	28
Cranberry orange, crushed: 2 oz / **Ocean Spray**	26
Cranberry orange relish: 2 oz / **Ocean Spray**	26
Cranberry sauce, canned: ¼ cup / **A & P**	25
Cranberry sauce, canned: ½ oz / **Nutri-Dyne** Elwood	1
Cranberry sauce, jellied: 2 oz / **Ocean Spray**	22
Cranberry sauce, whole: 2 oz / **Ocean Spray**	21
Figs, canned: ½ cup / **Del Monte**	28
Figs, canned, in heavy syrup: 1 cup / **Town House**	54
Fruit cocktail, canned: ½ cup	
A & P, in heavy syrup	24
A & P, in pear juice	14
Del Monte	23
Del Monte Lite	15
Town House	24
Weight Watchers	15
Fruit compote, canned: 4 oz / **Rockeach**	31
Fruits for salad, canned: ½ cup / **Del Monte**	22
Fruit salad, canned: ½ cup / **Del Monte** Tropical	26
Mixed, canned	
A & P Fruit Mix: ½ cup	20
Del Monte Chunky: ½ cup	23
Del Monte Chunky Lite: ½ cup	14
Del Monte Fruit Cup: 5 oz	27
Mother's: 4 oz	31
Scotch Buy Fruit Mix: ½ cup	20
Mixed, frozen: 5 oz / **Birds Eye** Quick Thaw	27
Oranges, Mandarin, canned: ½ cup / **A & P**	20
Oranges, Mandarin, canned: 5½ cup / **Del Monte**	25
Peaches, canned: ½ cup unless noted	
Weight Watchers	15
Cling / **Del Monte**	22
Cling: 5 oz / **Del Monte** Fruit Cup	28
Cling, halves, in heavy syrup / **A & P**	25
Cling, halves or slices / **Del Monte** Lite	13
Cling, halves, in light syrup / **Scotch Buy**	18

GRAMS

Cling, halves, in light syrup / **Town House**	25
Cling, halves, in pear juice / **A & P**	12
Cling, slices, in heavy syrup / **A & P**	25
Cling, slices, in light syrup / **Scotch Buy**	18
Cling, sliced, in light syrup / **Town House**	25
Cling, sliced, in pear juice / **A & P**	12
Freestone / **Del Monte** Lite	13
Freestone, halves or slices / **Del Monte**	23
Freestone, halves / **Town House**	26
Freestone, pieces, in light syrup / **Scotch Buy**	18
Freestone, slices, in light syrup / **Town House**	26
Spiced, w pits: 3½ oz / **Del Monte**	20
Pears, canned: ½ cup unless noted	
Weight Watchers: 2 halves + 2 tbsp juice	15
Bartlett, halves or slices / **Del Monte**	22
Bartlett, halves or slices / **Del Monte** Lite	14
Halves, in heavy syrup / **A & P**	25
Halves, in light syrup / **A & P**	20
Halves, in pear juice / **A & P**	15
Slices, in heavy syrup / **A & P**	25
Slices, in light syrup / **A & P**	20
Slices, in pear juice / **A & P**	15
Pineapple, canned	
All cuts, in juice: ½ cup	
Del Monte	18
Dole	18
Libby's	18
All cuts, in syrup: ½ cup	
Del Monte	23
Dole	25
Libby's	25
Chunks, in heavy syrup: ½ cup w syrup / **A & P**	23
Chunks, in heavy syrup: ½ cup / **Town House**	23
Chunks, in juice, unsweetened: ½ cup / **A & P**	18
Chunks, in juice, unsweetened: ½ cup / **Town House**	18
Crushed, in heavy syrup: ½ cup w syrup / **A & P**	23

Crushed, in heavy syrup: ½ cup / **Town House**	23
Crushed, in juice, unsweetened: ½ cup / **A & P**	18
Crushed, in juice, unsweetened: ½ cup / **Town House**	18
Slices, in heavy syrup: 2 slices w syrup / **A & P**	23
Slices, in heavy syrup: ½ cup / **Town House**	23
Slices, in juice, unsweetened: 2 slices w juice / **A & P**	18
Slices, in juice, unsweetened: ½ cup / **Town House**	18
Spears, in juice: 2 spears / **Del Monte**	14
Prunes, canned, stewed: ½ cup / **Rokeach**	25
Raspberries, red, frozen: 5 oz / **Birds Eye** Quick Thaw	26
Strawberries, frozen, halves in lite syrup: 5 oz / **Birds Eye** Quick Thaw	16
Strawberries, frozen, halves in syrup: 5 oz / **Birds Eye** Quick Thaw	30
Strawberries, frozen, whole, in lite syrup: 4 oz / **Birds Eye**	14

DRIED, UNCOOKED

Apples: 2 oz / **Del Monte**	37
Apples: 2 oz / **Sun-Maid**	42
Apples: 1 pkg / **Weight Watchers** Fruit Snacks	13
Apricots: 2 oz / **Del Monte**	35
Apricots: 2 oz / **Sun-Maid**	35
Apricots: 2 oz / **Sunsweet**	35
Currants, Zante: ½ cup / **Del Monte**	53
Dates, chopped: ¼ cup / **Dromedary**	31
Dates, pitted: 5 dates / **Dromedary**	23
Figs, California Mission: ½ cup / **Blue Ribbon**	50
Figs, California Mission: ½ cup / **Sun-Maid**	50
Figs, Calimyrna: ½ cup / **Blue Ribbon**	58
Figs, Calimyrna: ½ cup / **Sun-Maid**	58

GRAMS

Mixed
Carnation All Fruit Mix: 1 pouch	18
Del Monte: 2 oz	34
Sun-Maid: 2 oz	39
Sun-Maid Fruit Bits: 2 oz	40
Sunsweet: 2 oz	39
Weight Watchers Fruit Snacks: 1 pkg	13
Weight Watchers Tropical Snacks: 1 pkg	13
Peaches: 2 oz / **Del Monte**	35
Peaches: 2 oz / **Sun-Maid**	38
Peaches: 2 oz / **Sunsweet**	38

Prunes: 2 oz
Del Monte Moist-Pak	30
Sunsweet	32
Town House	36
w pits / **Del Monte**	31
pitted / **Del Monte**	35
pitted / **Sunsweet**	36

Raisins
Town House: 1½ oz	33
Golden: 3 oz / **Del Monte**	68
Natural: 3 oz / **Del Monte**	68
Seedless: ½ cup / **Sun-Maid**	69

Fruit rolls: 1 roll
All flavors / **Sunkist**	11
Apple / **Betty Crocker** Fruit Roll-Ups	12
Apple / **Flavor Tree**	23
Apricot / **Betty Crocker** Fruit Roll-Ups	12
Apricot / **Flavor Tree**	23
Cherry / **Betty Crocker** Fruit Roll-Ups	12
Cherry / **Flavor Tree**	23
Fruit Punch / **Flavor Tree**	23
Grape / **Betty Crocker** Fruit Roll-Ups	12
Grape / **Flavor Tree**	23
Orange / **Flavor Tree**	23
Peach / **Flavor Tree**	23
Plum / **Flavor Tree**	23
Raspberry / **Flavor Tree**	23
Strawberry / **Betty Crocker** Fruit Roll-Ups	12
Strawberry / **Flavor Tree**	23

GRAMS

CANDIED

Cherry: 1 cherry	3
Citron: 1 oz	23
Lemon peel: 1 oz	23
Orange peel: 1 oz	23
Pineapple slice: 1 slice	45

Fruit Drinks and Fruit-Flavored Beverages

In bottles, cans, cartons, pouches, frozen or as a packaged mix: 6 fl ounces unless noted

GRAMS

Apple Drinks	
Apple + Plus / **Juicy Juice**	22
CapriSun: 6¾ fl oz	23
Hawaiian Punch*	22
Hi-C	22
Sunkist: 250 ml	22
Mix: 8 fl oz / **Kool-Aid**	24
Mix: 8 fl oz / **Wyler's Crystals**	22
Hot spiced cider, mix / **Boyd's Today**	18
Apple-cherry / **Musselman's BC**	26
Apple-cranberry / **Lucky Leaf**	32
Apple-grape / **Musselman's BC**	28
Banana Frost, mix: 7 fl oz prepared / **Libby**	25
Berry / **Hawaiian Punch** Very Berry*	90
Black cherry, mix, unswt: 8 fl oz / **Wyler's** Cherry	1

---

*For both frozen concentrate and shelf.

GRAMS

Hawaiian Punch*	23
Hi-C	23
Mix, prepared: 8 fl oz / **Kool-Aid**	23
Mix, prepared: 8 fl oz / **Kool-Aid** Sugar Free	0
Mix, prepared: 8 fl oz / **Safeway**	23
Cranberry juice cocktail	
A & P	26
Ocean Spray	26
Ocean Spray Low Calorie	9
Ocean Spray, frozen, reconstituted	28
P & Q	24
Town House	26
Welch's, frozen, reconstituted	26
Cranberry-apple	
A & P	32
Ocean Spray Cranapple	32
Ocean Spray Low Calorie	7
P & Q	32
Town House	32
Frozen, reconstituted / **Ocean Spray** Cranapple	29
Frozen, reconstituted / **Welch's**	3
Cranberry-apricot / **Ocean Spray** Cranicot	26
Cranberry-grape / **Ocean Spray** Cran-Grape	26
Cranberry-grape, frozen, reconstituted / **Welch's**	27
Cranberry-orange / **Ocean Spray** Cranorange	25
Fruit / **Hawaiian Punch** Island, Juicy Red and Tropical	22
Funny Face, mix, swt: 8 fl oz	22
Funny Face, swt w aspartame: 8 fl oz	1
Golden Good / **Juicy Juice**	24
Grape / **Welchade**	23
Grape	
CapriSun: 6¾ fl oz	26
Hawaiian Punch*	23
Hi-C	23

---

*For both frozen concentrate and shelf.

GRAMS

Texsun in "brik-pak"	24
Welch's, frozen, reconstituted	23
Welch's Concord Juice Cocktail	27
Welch's Grape Juice Drink	27
Frozen / **A & P**	25
Mix: 8 fl oz / **Kool-Aid**	23
Mix, prepared / **Kool-Aid** Sugar Free: 8 fl oz	0
Mix, prepared / **Tang**	23
Mix, prepared / **Safeway**	23
Grape and apple / **Welch's** Concord 'N Apple Juice Cocktail	27
Grapefruit, mix, prepared / **Tang**	22
Lemonade	
CapriSun: 6¾ fl oz	23
Sunkist	
Frozen, reconstituted: 8 fl oz / **A & P**	28
Frozen, reconstituted / **Minute Maid**	20
Mix, prepared: 8 fl oz / **Country Time**	22
Mix, prepared: 8 fl oz / **Country Time** Sugar Free	0
Mix, prepared: 8 fl oz / **Crystal Light** Sugar Free	0
Mix, prepared / **Elam's** Sweetened	33
Mix, prepared / **Elam's** Unsweetened	3
Mix, prepared: 8 fl oz / **Kool-Aid**	22
Mix, prepared: 8 fl oz / **Kool-Aid** Sugar Free	0
Mix, prepared: 8 fl oz / **Safeway**	23
Mix, prepared: 8 fl oz / **Wyler's** Crystals	22
Mix, prepared: 8 fl oz / **Wyler's** Sugar Free	2
Lemon-lime	
Gatorade: 8 fl oz	14
Mix, prepared: 8 fl oz / **Country Time**	22
Mix, prepared: 8 fl oz / **Gatorade**	15
Mix, prepared: 8 fl oz / **Crystal Light** Sugar Free	0
Orange	
Awake, frozen, reconstituted / **Birds Eye**	21
Bama	22
CapriSun: 6¾ fl oz	26
Gatorade: 8 fl oz	14

GRAMS

Hawaiian Punch*	24
Hi-C	24
Orange Plus, frozen, reconstituted	24
Sunkist, in carton: 250 ml	
Texsun, in "brik-pak"	23
Mix, prepared: 4 fl oz / **Borden** Instant Breakfast Drink	16
Mix, prepared: 8 fl oz / **Crystal Light** Sugar Free	0
Mix, prepared: 8 fl oz / **Gatorade**	15
Mix, prepared: 8 fl oz / **Kool-Aid**	22
Mix, prepared: 8 fl oz / **Libby** Orange Frost	29
Mix, prepared: 8 fl oz / **Safeway**	23
Mix, prepared / **Tang**	22
Mix, prepared, unswt: 8 fl oz / **Wyler's**	1
Orange-apricot / **Musselman's** BC	21
Orange-pineapple / **Musselman's** BC	23
Pineapple, mix, prepared / **Libby** Pineapple Frost	22
Pineapple-grapefruit / **Del Monte**	24
Pineapple-orange / **Del Monte**	24
Pineapple–pink grapefruit / **Del Monte**	24
Pineapple–pink grapefruit / **Dole**	25
Punch	
Bama	22
CapriSun: 6¾ fl oz	26
Hawaiian Punch Low Sugar*	8
Hi-C Florida	26
Sunkist	na
Sunkist, in portion cup: 4 fl oz	na
Texsun, in "brik-pak"	22
Mix, prepared / **Crystal Light** Sugar Free	0
Mix, prepared: 8 fl oz / **Kool-Aid** Rainbow	25
Mix, prepared: 8 fl oz / **Kool Aid** Sunshine	24
Mix, prepared: 8 fl oz / **Kool-Aid** Tropical	25
Mix, prepared: 8 fl oz / **Kool-Aid** Sugar Free	0
Mix, prepared: 8 fl oz / **Safeway**	23
Mix, prepared: 8 fl oz / **Wyler's** Crystal Tropical	22

---

*For both frozen concentrate and shelf.

GRAMS

Mix, prepared: 8 fl oz / **Wyler's Tropical** Sugar Free	1
Pure Purple / **Juicy Juice**	25
Raspberry, mix: 8 fl oz / **Kool-Aid**	22
Raspberry-cranberry / **A & P**	27
Real Red / **Juicy Juice**	26
Strawberry, mix, prepared: 8 fl oz / **Kool-Aid**	22
Strawberry, mix, prepared: 8 fl oz / **Safeway**	23
Strawberry, mix, prepared: 8 fl oz / **Libby** Strawberry Frost	21
Wild berry / **Hi-C**	23
Wild cherry, mix: 8 fl oz / **Wyler's Crystals**	22
Wild cherry, mix: 8 fl oz / **Wyler's Sugar Free**	1
Wild fruit / **Hawaiian Punch***	23
Wild grape, mix: 8 fl oz / **Wyler's Crystals**	22
Wild grape, mix: 8 fl oz / **Wyler's Sugar Free**	1

Fruit Juices

FRESH

GRAMS

1 cup unless noted

Acerola cherry	11.6
Grapefruit	22.6
Lemon	19.5
Lemon: 1 tbsp	1.2
Lime: 1 tbsp	1.4
Orange	
California navels	28.1
Florida	24.7
Valencias	26
Tangerine	24

*For both frozen concentrate and shelf.

BOTTLED, CANNED AND FROZEN

6 fl oz unless noted | GRAMS

Apple
A & P, frozen	22
Mott's	19
Mott's Natural Style	19
Seneca	22
Seneca Natural	22
Lucky Leaf	21
Musselman's	21
Sunkist, in portion cup: 4 fl oz	
Texsun, in "brik-pak"	22
Town House	23

Apple cider / **Lucky Leaf**	21
Apple cider, sparkling / **Lucky Leaf**	18
Apple cider / **Musselman's**	21
Apple-grape / **Welch's**	23

Apricot nectar
Del Monte	26
Libby's	27
Town House	26

Banana nectar / **Libby's**	14
Blend / **Welch's** Frozen Harvest	23
Cranberry / **Lucky Leaf**	26

Grape
A & P	50
Lucky Leaf	32
Minute Maid	25
Seneca, bottled, canned	27
Seneca, frozen, reconstituted	26
Welch's, red and white, bottled, canned	30
Welch's, frozen, reconstituted	25
Welch's Orchard, frozen, reconstituted	30
Sparkling, red or white / **Welch's**	30

Grapefruit
A & P, frozen, reconstituted	18
Del Monte	17
Libby's, unswt	18
Minute Maid, frozen, reconstituted	18
Ocean Spray	15
Ocean Spray, frozen reconstituted	16

	GRAMS
Texsun, in "brik-pak"	18
pink / **Texsun**	18
Guava nectar / **Libby's**	17
Lemon	
A & P: 2 tbsp	2
Lucky Leaf	6
Minute Maid, frozen, reconstituted	13
Realemon: 2 tbsp	2
Seneca: 2 tbsp	2
Mango nectar / **Libby's**	14
Mixed: ⅓ cup / **Weight Watchers** Fruit Juice Medley	11
Orange	
A & P, frozen, reconstituted	19
Citrus Hill	20
Del Monte, unswt	19
Libby's, swt	23
Libby's, unswt	20
Minute Maid, frozen, reconstituted	21
Minute Maid, in carton	20
Texsun	20
Texsun, in "brik-pak"	20
Orange-grapefruit, unswt / **Libby's**	19
Orange-pineapple / **Texsun**	21
Peach nectar / **Libby's**	23
Pear nectar / **Libby's**	25
Pear-passion fruit nectar / **Libby's**	14
Pineapple	
Del Monte	25
Dole	25
Texsun	24
Pineapple-grapefruit / **Texsun**	22
Prune	
Del Monte	33
Lucky Leaf	36
Mott's	30
Sunsweet	33
Strawberry / **Libby's**	14

Gelatin

	GRAMS
All flavors, mix, prepared: ½ cup / **D-Zerta**	0
All flavors, mix, prepared: ½ cup / **Dia-Mel**	0–1
All flavors, mix, prepared: ½ cup / **Estee**	0–1
All flavors, mix, prepared: ½ cup / **Jell-O**	19
All flavors, mix, prepared: ½ cup / **Nutri-Dyne** Elwood	0
All flavors, mix, prepared: 2.7 oz / **Nutri-Dyne** Prono Gelled Dessert	14
All flavors, mix, prepared: ½ cup / **Safeway**	19
Gel-a-thin: ½ cup / **Dia-Mel**	0–1
Orange flavor: 1 envelope / **Knox**	10
Unflavored: 1 envelope / **Knox**	0

Gravies

	GRAMS
¼ cup unless noted	
Au jus	
Canned / **Franco-American**	1
Mix, prepared / **Durkee**	2
Mix, prepared / **French's**	2
Mix w roasting bag: 1 pkg / **Durkee** Roastin' Bag	14
Beef, canned / **Franco-American**	3
Brown	
Mix, prepared / **Durkee**	3

113

GRAMS

Mix, prepared / **French's**	3
Mix, prepared: ¼ pkg / **McCormick**	3
Mix, prepared / **Pillsbury**	3
Mix, prepared / **Spatini** Family Style	4
Mix, prepared / **Weight Watchers**	1
w mushrooms, mix, prepared / **Durkee**	3
w mushrooms, mix, prepared / **Weight Watchers**	2
w onions, canned / **Franco-American**	4
w onions, mix, prepared / **Durkee**	3
w onions, mix, prepared / **Weight Watchers**	2
Chicken	
Canned / **Franco-American**	3
Mix, prepared / **Durkee**	4
Mix, prepared / **McCormick**	3
Mix, prepared / **Pillsbury**	4
Mix, prepared / **Weight Watchers**	2
Mix w roasting bag: 1 pkg / **Durkee** Roastin' Bag	24
Creamy, mix, prepared / **Durkee**	4
Creamy, mix, w roasting bag: 1 pkg / **Durkee** Roastin' Bag	22
Giblet, canned / **Franco-American**	3
Italian style, mix w roasting bag: 1 pkg / **Durkee** Roastin' Bag	31
for chicken, mix, prepared / **French's**	4
Homestyle, mix, prepared / **Durkee**	3
Homestyle, mix, prepared / **French's**	4
Homestyle, mix, prepared / **Pillsbury**	3
Meatloaf, mix w roasting bag: 1 pkg / **Durkee** Roastin' Bag	18
Mushroom, canned / **Franco-American**	3
Mushroom, mix, prepared / **Durkee**	3
Mushroom, mix, prepared / **French's**	3
Onion, mix, prepared / **Durkee**	4
Onion, mix, prepared / **French's**	4
Onion, mix, prepared / **McCormick**	2
Pork	
Canned / **Franco-American**	3
Mix, prepared / **Durkee**	4

Mix w roasting bag: 1 pkg / **Durkee** Roastin' Bag	26
for pork, mix, prepared / **French's**	3
Pot roast and stew, mix w roasting bag: 1 pkg / **Durkee** Roastin' Bag	25
Pot roast, onion, mix w roasting bag: 1 pkg / **Durkee** Roastin' Bag	24
Swiss steak, mix, prepared / **Durkee**	3
Swiss steak, mix w roasting bag: 1 pkg / **Durkee** Roastin' Bag	28
Turkey	
Canned / **Franco-American**	3
Mix, prepared / **Durkee**	4
For turkey, mix, prepared / **French's**	4

Health and "Natural" Foods

Flour, Grains, Meal, Rice, Yeast

	GRAMS
Amaranth, whole grain: 2 oz / **Arrowhead Mills** Baking Mix	35
Brown rice: ½ cup dry / **Fearn**	44
Brown rice: 1 cup dry / **Nutri-Dyne** Ener-G	99
Low protein: 3½ oz dry / **Nutri-Dyne** Aproten	84
White rice: ½ cup dry / **Fearn**	53
White rice: 1 cup dry / **Nutri-Dyne** Ener-G	170
Barley, pearled: 2 oz / **Arrowhead Mills**	45
Barley, hulled: 2 oz / **Arrowhead Mills**	34
Buckwheat groats, brown or white: 2 oz / **Arrowhead Mills**	41
Corn: 2 oz / **Arrowhead Mills**	43
Corn bran: 1 cup / **Nutri-Dyne** Ener-G	3
Corn germ: ¼ cup / **Fearn** Naturfresh	12
Flax seeds: 2 oz / **Arrowhead Mills**	11
Flour	
Barley: 2 oz / **Arrowhead Mills**	43
Brown rice: 2 oz / **Arrowhead Mills**	44
Brown rice: ¼ cup / **Elam's**	26
Brown rice: 1 cup / **Nutri-Dyne** Ener-G	107
Buckwheat: 2 oz / **Arrowhead Mills**	41
Buckwheat: ½ cup / **Elam's**	54
Durum: 2 oz / **Arrowhead Mills**	40
Graham: 2 oz / **Arrowhead Mills**	40
Millet: 2 oz / **Arrowhead Mills**	41
Oat: 2 oz / **Arrowhead Mills**	43
Pastry: 2 oz / **Arrowhead Mills**	41

	GRAMS
Rye: 2 oz / **Arrowhead Mills**	39
Rye: ½ cup / **Elam's**	48
Soy: 2 oz / **Arrowhead Mills**	18
Soy: ¼ cup / **Elam's**	10
Tapioca: 1 cup / **Nutri-Dyne** Ener-G	101
Triticale: 2 oz / **Arrowhead Mills**	41
White, unbleached: 2 oz / **Arrowhead Mills**	53
White w wheat germ: ½ cup / **Elam's**	43
White rice: 1 cup / **Nutri-Dyne** Ener-G	98
Whole wheat: 2 oz / **Arrowhead Mills**	40
Whole wheat: ½ cup / **Elam's**	43
Whole wheat pastry: ¼ cup / **Elam's**	25
Grain side dishes: ½ cup prepared	
Herb / **Hain**	17
Italian / **Hain**	23
Spanish / **Hain**	14
Meal, corn: 2 oz / **Arrowhead Mills**	43
Meal, corn: ¼ cup / **Elam's**	25
Millet, hulled: 2 oz / **Arrowhead Mills**	21
Oats, hulled (oat groats): 2 oz / **Arrowhead Mills**	38
Oats, steel cut: 2 oz / **Arrowhead Mills**	37
Rice bran: 1 cup / **Nutri-Dyne** Ener-G	39
Rice mix: 1 cup / **Nutri-Dyne** Ener-G	107
Rye, whole grain: 2 oz / **Arrowhead Mills**	42
Sesame seeds: 2 oz / **Arrowhead Mills**	6
Triticale, whole grain: 2 oz / **Arrowhead Mills**	42

Seasonings and Gravy

Catch-up: 1 tbsp / **Health Valley**	3
Catsup: ½ oz / **Nutri-Dyne** Elwood	1
Chef Seasoning: 1 tsp / **Nutri-Dyne** Chef Otto	2
Chicken, mix: 1 oz dry / **Nutri-Dyne** Chef Otto	20
Mustard: ½ oz / **Nutri-Dyne** Elwood	1
Savorex: 1 oz / **Loma Linda**	4

Soy Milk and Beverage Mixes

80% Protein Mix: ¼ cup / **Fearn**	1
Liquid soya lecithin: 1 tbsp / **Fearn**	0
Liquid soya lecithin, mint: 1 tbsp / **Fearn**	1

GRAMS

Nutquick-almond milk powder: 8½ oz
prepared / **Nutri-Dyne**   2

Soy milk, powder: 8 oz prepared / **Nutri-Dyne**
Soyquick   4

Soy Moo, dry: 1 cup / **Health Valley**   13

Soy Moo, dry, carob: 1 cup / **Health Valley**   16

Soya granules: ¼ cup / **Fearn**   12

Soya powder: ½ cup / **Fearn**   6

Soyamel, powder: 1 oz dry / **Worthington**   15

Soya protein isolate: 4 tbsp / **Fearn**   0

Soybeans and Legumes

Beans

Adzuki: 2 oz dry / **Arrowhead Mills**   35

Black turtle: 2 oz dry / **Arrowhead Mills**   35

Boston baked: 4 oz / **Health Valley**   24

Boston baked, no salt: 4 oz /
Health Valley   22

Great Northern: 2 oz / **Arrowhead Mills**   35

Kidney: 2 oz / **Arrowhead Mills**   35

Navy: 2 oz / **Arrowhead Mills**   35

Pinto: 2 oz / **Arrowhead Mills**   36

Soybeans: 2 oz / **Arrowhead Mills**   19

Soybeans canned: 7½ oz / **Hain**   13

Soybeans, chili, canned: ½ cup / **Hain**   15

Tri-bean casserole, mix: 1.9 oz dry /
Fearn   27

Vegetarian w miso: 4 oz / **Health Valley**   19

Chickpeas: 2 oz / **Arrowhead Mills**   35

Lentils, red: 2 oz / **Arrowhead Mills**   34

Lentils, green: 2 oz / **Arrowhead Mills**   35

Peas, split: 2 oz / **Arrowhead Mills**   35

Spreads and Sandwich Fillings: 2 tbsp unless noted

Almond butter, raw / **Hain**   3

Almond butter, toasted / **Hain**   3

Cashew butter, raw / **Hain**   8

Cashew butter, toasted / **Hain**   8

Peanut butter

Creamy old-fashioned / **Hain**   3

GRAMS

Creamy toasted / **Hain**	6
Creamy / **Health Valley**	6
Chunky / **Health Valley**	6
Crunchy / **Health Valley**	6
Crunchy old-fashioned / **Hain**	3
Unsalted, raw / **Hain**	5
Unsalted, toasted / **Hain**	6
Unsalted / **Health Valley**	6
w wheat germ / **Elam's**	3
Peanut-sesame butter / **Hain**	4
Sandwich spread: 3 tbsp / **Loma Linda**	4
Sesame butter / **Hain**	7
Sesame tahini / **Sahadi**	4
Sunflower butter / **Hain**	6

Sweets, Nuts and Snacks: 1 oz unless noted

Almonds, dry roast, smoke-flavored / **Laura Scudder's**	4.2
Apple Bakes: 1 bar / **Health Valley**	16.5
Apple date fruit and nut mix / **Harmony**	15
Apricot bars, whole wheat / **Harmony**	19
Banana chips / **Harmony**	17
Carob almonds / **Harmony**	15
Carob cashews / **Harmony**	16
Carob coconut clusters / **Harmony**	37
Carob drops / **Harmony**	22
Carob fruit and nut clusters / **Harmony**	15
Carob granola clusters / **Harmony**	19
Carob maltballs / **Harmony**	21
Carob peanuts / **Harmony**	15
Carob peanut clusters / **Harmony**	13
Carob raisins / **Harmony**	21
Carob walnuts / **Harmony**	15
Cashews, dry roasted: 1 oz / **Laura Scudder's**	8
Cashews, oil roasted: ¾ oz / **Laura Scudder's**	6
Cheddar Lites, regular or no salt / **Health Valley**	12
Corn chips / **Health Valley**	15
Corn chips w cheese, / **Health Valley**	13
Corn chips w cheese, no salt / **Health Valley**	15

GRAMS

Corn snacks party mix / **Harmony**	3
Country chips / **Health Valley**	12
Country Ripples / **Health Valley**	12
Crunchy raisins / **Harmony**	16
Date Bakes: 1 bar / **Health Valley**	16
Deluxe super trail mix / **Harmony**	13
Deluxe tamari nut mix / **Harmony**	16
Dip chips / **Health Valley**	12
Fig bars, whole wheat / **Harmony**	19
Golden Hawaiian / **Health Valley**	15
Granola Snack: 1 pouch	
Cinnamon / **Nature Valley**	19
Honey nut / **Nature Valley**	19
Oats and honey / **Nature Valley**	19
Peanut butter / **Nature Valley**	23
Raspberry glaze / **Nature Valley**	27
Vanilla glaze / **Nature Valley**	28
Halvah / **Sahadi**	13
Hot Stuff / **Harmony**	9
Mint yogurt raisins / **Harmony**	15
Mixed munchies / **Harmony**	14
Oat bran snack bar: 1 bar / **Elam's**	18
Oriental party mix / **Harmony**	11
Peanuts: 1 oz unless noted / **Arrowhead Mills**	5
Dry Roast / **Laura Scudder's** Snackin'	4
Roasted in shell: 1¾ oz / **Laura Scudder's**	
Goober	7
Spanish, oil roasted / **Laura Scudder's**	3.5
Virginia, oil roasted: 1¼ oz /	
Laura Scudder's	4
Pistachios, roasted in shell: 1¼ oz /	
Laura Scudder's	3
Potato chips: 1 oz / **Health Valley**	15
Pretzels, mini: 1 oz / **Health Valley**	23
Pretzels, mini, whole wheat: 1 oz /	
Health Valley	20
Pretzels, sesame whole wheat: 1 oz /	
Health Valley	25
Raisin Bakes: 1 bar / **Health Valley**	16.5
Raisins and nuts: 1 pouch / **Carnation**	11
Rice thins: 4 / **Nutri-Dyne** Hol-Grain	7

	GRAMS
Rice thins, unsalted: 4 / **Nutri-Dyne** Hol-Grain	10
Ruskets biscuits / **Loma Linda**	22
Rusks / **Nutri-Dyne** Aproten	2.3
Seeds, sunflower	
Arrowhead Mills	3
Laura Scudder's, dry roasted	11
Roasted in shell: 1¼ oz / **Laura Scudder's**	4
Sesame sticks / **Harmony**	13
Sesame walnut mix / **Harmony**	10
Tamari roasted almonds / **Harmony**	5
Trail mix: 1 pouch / **Carnation Deluxe**	9
Trail mix, raw / **Harmony**	12
Tortilla chips / **Health Valley**	17
Tortilla chips, nacho cheese and chili / **Health Valley**	17
Tropical Fruit & Nuts: 1 pouch / **Carnation**	16
Tropical Trail Mix / **Harmony**	15
Yogurt almonds / **Harmony**	15
Yogurt coconut clusters / **Harmony**	18
Yogurt fruit and nut clusters / **Harmony**	37
Yogurt granola clusters / **Harmony**	18
Yogurt maltballs / **Harmony**	20
Yogurt peanuts / **Harmony**	14
Yogurt raisins / **Harmony**	20
Yogurt raisin fruit and nut mix / **Harmony**	13
Yogurt raspberry clusters / **Harmony**	14

Tofu and Tofu Dishes

Tofu, hard: 4 oz / **Health Valley** Tofu-Ya	5
Tofu, soft: 4 oz / **Health Valley** Tofu-Ya	2
Cannelloni Florentine: 11 oz / **Legume**	23
Lasagna, vegetable: 12 oz / **Legume**	28
Sesame ginger, stir-fry: 11½ oz / **Legume**	34
Stuffed shells Provencale: 11 oz / **Legume**	22
Tofu Bourguignon: 11¼ oz / **Legume**	34
Tofu Lasagna: 8 oz / **Legume**	28
Tofu Maniccoti: 8 oz / **Legume**	24
Tofu Tetrazzini: 10¼ oz / **Legume**	31

GRAMS

Vegetarian Meat Substitutes

Beef style	
Hain: ½ cup prepared	18
Frozen: 1 slice / **Worthington**	2
Frozen, smoked: 1 slice / **Worthington**	1
Bologna, meatless, frozen: 2 slices /	
Loma Linda	5
Bolono, frozen: 2 slices / **Worthington**	3
Brazil nut burger mix: ¼ cup dry / **Fearn**	10
Breakfast patty mix: ¼ cup dry / **Fearn**	11
Chicken style	
Hain: ½ cup prepared	20
Loma Linda Chicken Supreme:	
¼ cup dry	4
1 slice prepared	4
fried, canned: 2 pieces / **Loma Linda**	4
fried, frozen: 1 piece / **Loma Linda**	2
frozen: 1 slice / **Worthington**	1
frozen: 1 oz / **Worthington** Chic-Ketts	2
frozen: 1 piece / **Worthington** Chik Stiks	4
Chili, canned: ½ cup / **Worthington**	20
Choplets, canned: 1 piece / **Worthington**	3
Corned beef style, frozen: 1 slice / **Worthington**	1
Corn dogs, frozen: 1 corn dog / **Loma Linda**	21
Cutlets, canned: 1½ slices / **Worthington**	5
Dinner cuts, canned: 2 cuts / **Loma Linda**	4
Dinner roast, frozen: 2 oz / **Worthington**	4
Falafel mix: .8 oz dry / **Fearn**	12
Fillets, frozen: 2 pieces / **Worthington**	11
Frankfurters, canned: 1 frank / **Loma Linda**	
Big Franks	4
Frankfurters: 2 franks / **Loma Linda**	
Sizzle Franks	3
Fri Chik, canned: 1 piece / **Worthington**	1
Fri Pats, frozen: 1 patty / **Worthington**	3
Gran Burger: 1 oz dry / **Worthington**	10
Griddle Steaks, frozen: 1 steak / **Loma Linda**	5
Linketts, canned: 2 links / **Loma Linda**	5
Little Links, canned: 2 links / **Loma Linda**	2

GRAMS

Nuteena (peanut butter base), canned: ½" slice /
  Loma Linda — 5
Non-meat balls, canned: 1 piece / **Worthington** — 2
Numete, canned: ½" slice / **Worthington** — 9
Ocean fillets, frozen: 1 fillet/ **Loma Linda** — 5
Ocean platter, canned / **Loma Linda**
  ¼ cup dry — 5
  1 slice prepared — 5
Patty mix, canned / **Loma Linda:**
  ¼ cup dry — 4
  1 patty prepared — 4
Prime Stakes, canned: 1 piece w gravy /
  Worthington — 5
Prosage links, frozen: 1 link / **Worthington** — 2
Prosage patties, frozen: 1 patty / **Worthington** — 4
Prosage roll, frozen: ⅜" slice / **Worthington** — 4
Proteena (gluten–peanut butter base), canned:
  ½" slice / **Loma Linda** — 5
Redi-Burger, canned: ½" slice / **Loma Linda** — 5
Salami, meatless, frozen: 2 slices /
  Worthington — 3
Saucettes, canned: 1 link / **Worthington** — 2
Savory dinner loaf, canned / **Loma Linda:**
  ¼ cup dry — 4
  1 slice prepared — 4
Sesame burger mix: ¼ cup dry / **Fearn** — 8
Sizzle burger, frozen: 1 burger / **Loma Linda** — 13
Skallops, vegetable, canned: ½ cup /
  Worthington — 3
Stakelets, frozen: 1 piece / **Worthington** — 7
Stripples, frozen: 1 slice / **Worthington** — 1
Sunflower burger, mix: ¼ cup dry / **Fearn** — 15
Super-Links, canned: 1 link / **Worthington** — 4
Swedish meatballs, frozen: 8 pieces /
  Loma Linda — 7
Swiss steak, canned: 1 steak / **Loma Linda** — 8
Tastee Cuts, canned: 2 cuts / **Loma Linda** — 2
Tender Bits, canned: 4 pieces / **Loma Linda** — 4
Tender Rounds, canned: 6 pieces / **Loma Linda** — 7
Tuno, frozen: 2 oz / **Worthington** — 3
Turkey style, frozen: 1 slice / **Worthington** — 1

GRAMS

Vege-Burger, canned: ½ cup / **Loma Linda**	4
Vegelona, canned: ½″ slice / **Loma Linda**	6
Vege-Scallops, canned: 6 pieces / **Loma Linda**	2
Vegetable steaks, canned: 2½ pieces / **Worthington**	7
Vegetarian burger, canned: 1/3 cup / **Worthington**	9
Veja-Bits, canned: 4.3 oz / **Worthington**	4
Veja-Links, canned: 1 link / **Worthington**	2
Vita-Burger, canned: 3 tbsp / **Loma Linda**	7
Wham, frozen: 1 slice / **Worthington**	1

Wheat and Wheat Germ

Bran, unprocessed: 1 oz	15
Bulgur, club wheat: 1 cup dry	140
Bulgur: 2 oz dry / **Arrowhead Mills**	43
Wheat, hard red winter or soft pastry: 2 oz / **Arrowhead Mills**	41
Wheat bran: 2 oz / **Arrowhead Mills**	30
Wheat bran: 2 tbsp / **Elam's** Miller's Bran	5
Wheat germ: 2 oz / **Arrowhead Mills**	26
Wheat germ: 2 tbsp / **Elam's**	6
Wheat germ: ¼ cup / **Fearn**	13
Wheat germ, toasted: ¼ cup / **Kretschmer**	13
Wheat germ, toasted w brown sugar and honey: ¼ cup / **Kretschmer**	17
Wheat germ w almonds and dates: 1 oz / **Health Valley**	20
Wheat germ w bananas: 1 oz / **Health Valley**	20
Wheat starch: 1 oz / **Nutri-Dyne** Aproten	24

Ice Cream and Similar Frozen Products

GRAMS

FROZEN DESSERT

Chocolate supreme: ½ cup / **Toffuti**	21
Frozen dessert: 5 fl oz / **Weight Watchers**	19
Frosted treat: ¾ cup / **Weight Watchers** / **Frappe**	22
Maple walnut: ½ cup / **Toffuti**	21
Mountain coffee: ½ cup (1 scoop) / **Baskin-Robbins**	17
Snack cups: 1 Snack Cup (5 fl oz) / **Weight Watchers**	19
Sundae cone: 1 cone / **Weight Watchers**	22
Sunny orange: ½ cup (1 scoop) / **Baskin-Robbins**	17
Wild strawberry: ½ cup (1 scoop) / **Baskin-Robbins**	16
Wildberry supreme: ½ cup / **Toffuti**	21

ICE CREAM

Black raspberry: ½ cup / **Breyer's**	18
Butter almond: ½ cup / **Sealtest**	16
Butter almond chocolate: ½ cup / **Breyer's**	16
Butter brickle: ½ cup / **Sealtest**	19
Butter pecan: 1 scoop / **Baskin-Robbins**	16
Butter pecan: ½ cup / **Haagen-Dazs**	28
Butter pecan: ½ cup / **Lady Borden**	16
Butter pecan: ½ cup / **Lucerne**	15
Butter pecan: ½ cup / **Sealtest**	16
Caramel pecan crunch: ½ cup / **Breyer's**	18
Carob: ½ cup / **Haagen-Dazs**	20
Cherry nugget: ½ cup / **Sealtest**	16
Cherry-vanilla: ½ cup / **Breyer's**	17

	GRAMS
Cherry-vanilla: ½ cup / **Sealtest**	17
Chocolate	
Baskin-Robbins: 1 scoop	20
Breyer's: ½ cup	19
Haagen-Dazs: ½ cup	26
Howard Johnson's: ½ cup	29
Lady Borden: ½ cup	16
Lucerne: ½ cup	16
Meadow Gold: ½ cup	18
Meadow Gold Olde Fashioned: ½ cup	16
Chocolate almond: ½ cup / **Breyer's**	18
Chocolate almond: ½ cup / **Sealtest**	18
Chocolate chip: ½ cup / **Haagen-Dazs**	26
Chocolate chip: ½ cup / **Lucerne**	17
Chocolate chip: ½ cup / **Sealtest**	17
Chocolate chip, mint: ½ cup / **Breyer's**	17
Chocolate cups: 3 fl oz / **A & P**	11
Chocolate fudge: 1 scoop / **Baskin-Robbins**	21
Chocolate marble: ½ cup / **Lucerne**	19
Chocolate marshmallow marble: ½ cup / **Lucerne**	20
Chocolate mint: 1 scoop / **Baskin-Robbins**	17
Chocolate mousse royale: 1 scoop / **Baskin-Robbins**	23
Coffee: ½ cup / **Breyer's**	15
Coffee: ½ cup / **Sealtest**	16
Coffee: ½ cup / **Haagen-Dazs**	24
Cookies & cream: ½ cup / **Haagen-Dazs**	24
Dutch chocolate: ½ cup / **Borden**	16
Dutch chocolate almond: 1.2 cups / **Borden** All Natural	18
French vanilla	
Baskin-Robbins: 1 scoop	16
Borden All Natural: ½ cup	16
Lady Borden: ½ cup	20
Lucerne: ½ cup	16
Honey: ½ cup / **Haagen-Dazs**	18
Jamoca: 1 scoop / **Baskin-Robbins**	16
Macadamia nut: ½ cup / **Haagen-Dazs**	20
Maple nut: ½ cup / **Lucerne**	16
Maple walnut: ½ cup / **Haagen-Dazs**	22
Maple walnut: ½ cup / **Sealtest**	16
Mint chocolate chip: ½ cup / **Lucerne**	17

GRAMS

Mocha chip: ½ cup / **Haagen-Dazs**	22
Neapolitan: ½ cup / **Lucerne**	16
Peach: ½ cup / **Haagen-Dazs**	28
Peach: ½ cup / **Sealtest**	18
Pralines 'n cream: 1 scoop / **Baskin-Robbins**	24
Rocky road: 1 scoop / **Baskin-Robbins**	27
Rocky road: ½ cup / **Lucerne**	18
Rum raisin: ½ cup / **Haagen-Dazs**	26
Strawberry	
Baskin-Robbins: 1 scoop	16
Borden: ½ cup	17
Breyer's: ½ cup	17
Haagen-Dazs: ½ cup	26
Howard Johnson's: ½ cup	27
Lucerne: ½ cup	16
Meadow Gold: ½ cup	19
Sealtest: ½ cup	18
Strawberry cheesecake: ½ cup / **Lucerne**	20
Swiss chocolate almond: ½ cup / **Haagen-Dazs**	26
Vanilla	
Baskin-Robbins: 1 scoop	16
Borden: ½ cup	15
Borden All Natural: ½ cup	17
Breyer's: ½ cup	15
Haagen-Dazs: ½ cup	24
Howard Johnson's: ½ cup	24
Land O Lakes: ½ cup	16
Lucerne: ½ cup	16
Meadow gold: ½ cup	16
Sealtest: ½ cup	16
Vanilla cups: 3 fl oz / **A & P**	11
Vanilla ice cream and orange sherbet: ½ cup / **Lucerne**	21
Vanilla slices: 1 slice / **Good Humor**	13
Vanilla slices: 1 slice / **Good Humor** Cal-Control	11
Vanilla swiss almond: ½ cup / **Haagen-Dazs**	28

ICE MILK

Banana-strawberry twirl: ½ cup / **Sealtest** Light N' Lively	21

GRAMS

Chocolate: ½ cup / **Borden** All Natural	17
Chocolate: ½ cup / **Sealtest** Light N' Lively	19
Coffee: ½ cup / **Sealtest** Light N' Lively	17
Fudge twirl: ½ cup / **Sealtest** Light N' Lively	18
Strawberry: ½ cup / **Borden** All Natural	18
Vanilla: ½ cup / **Borden** All Natural	16
Vanilla: ½ cup / **Land O Lakes**	14
Vanilla: ½ cup / **Sealtest** Light N' Lively	17

SHERBET AND ICES

All flavors: ½ cup / **Land O Lakes**	27
Daiquiri ice: 1 scoop / **Baskin-Robbins**	21
Lemon ice: ½ cup / **Haagen-Dazs**	34
Lemon: ½ cup / **Borden**	25
Orange	
Baskin-Robbins: 1 scoop	21
Borden: ½ cup	25
Haagen-Dazs: ½ cup	34
Howard Johnson's: ½ cup	33

ICE CREAM BARS

1 bar or piece

Almond toasted / **Good Humor**	28
Bon Bon, ice cream nugget, chocolate	3
Bon Bon, ice cream nugget, vanilla	3
Caramel toasted / **Good Humor**	21
Chip crunch / **Good Humor**	16
Chocolate dip / **Weight Watchers**	11
Chocolate eclair / **Good Humor**	24
Chocolate fudge: 2 oz bar / **Ann Page**	19
Chocolate fudge: 2½ oz bar / **Ann Page**	20
Chocolate fudge cake / **Good Humor**	25
Chocolate malt / **Good Humor**	16
Chocolate mint treat / **Weight Watchers**	19
Chocolate treat / **Weight Watchers**	19
Cookie sandwich: 2.7 oz / **Good Humor** ice milk	42
Cookie sandwich: 4 oz / **Good Humor** ice milk	59
Fat Frog / **Good Humor** ice milk	17

	GRAMS
Heart / **Good Humor** ice milk	21
Heath toffee	16
Orange vanilla treat / **Weight Watchers**	19
Pops / **Ann Page**	11
Pudding Pops, all flavors / **Jell-O**	16
Pudding sticks / **Good Humor**	15
Sandwich / **Ann Page**	23
Sandwich, mint / **Weight Watchers**	28
Sandwich, vanilla / **Good Humor**	28
Sandwich, vanilla / **Weight Watchers**	28
Shark / **Good Humor** ice milk	17
Strawberry vanilla treat / **Weight Watchers**	19
Twin pops / **Ann Page**	17
Vanilla / **Ann Page**	12
Vanilla / **Ann Page** ice milk	12
Vanilla / **Good Humor**	16
Whammy / **Good Humor** ice milk	9

CONES

1 cone (alone)

Cones / **Comet**	4
Cake cones / **Baskin-Robbins**	4
Sugar cones / **Baskin-Robbins**	11
Sugar cones / **Comet**	9

Italian Foods

	GRAMS
See also Dinners, Pizza *and* Spaghetti	
Cannelloni, canned: 7½ oz / **Chef Boy-ar-dee**	33
Cannelloni, canned: 7½ oz / **Ezo**	31
Cannelloni, beef and pork, frozen: 9⅝ oz /	
Stouffer's Lean Cuisine	24

GRAMS

Cannelloni, cheese, frozen: 9⅛ oz / **Stouffer's** Lean Cuisine	24
Cannelloni Florentine, frozen: 11 oz / **Legume**	23
Chicken cacciatore, frozen: 11¼ oz / **Stouffer's**	29
Chicken cacciatore, frozen: 10 oz / **Weight Watchers**	30
Chicken parmigiana, frozen: 9½ oz / **Weight Watchers**	26
Eggplant parmigiana, frozen: 12 oz / **Buitoni**	33
Fettucine Alfredo: 2.85 oz dry / **Pasta Suprema**	46
Fettucine Alfredo, frozen: 10 oz / **Buitoni**	36
Fettucine Alfredo, frozen: 5 oz / **Stouffer's**	19
Fettucine Alfredo, mix: ¼ pkg / **Betty Crocker**	23
Fettucine carbonara, frozen: 10 oz / **Buitoni**	36
Fettucine primavera, frozen: 10 oz / **Buitoni**	86
Lasagna	
Canned: 7½ oz / **Chef Boy-ar-dee**	28
Canned: 8 oz / **Chef Boy-ar-dee**, 40 oz can	31
Canned: 6 oz / **Chef Boy-ar-dee** Dinner	44
Canned: 7 oz / **Ezo**	30
Frozen: 9½ oz / **Green Giant**	42
Frozen: 12 oz / **Legume** (tofu)	28
Frozen: 10½ oz / **Stouffer's**	36
Frozen: 11 oz / **Van de Kamp's**	30
Frozen: 11 oz pkg / **Weight Watchers**	33
Frozen, chicken: 12 oz / **Green Giant**	47
Frozen, deep-dish: 11 oz / **Buitoni**	55
Frozen, deep-dish w meat sauce: 10½ oz / **Buitoni**	45
Frozen, Florentine: 9½ oz / **Buitoni**	36
Frozen, Florentine: 11¼ oz / **Light and Elegant**	32
Frozen w meat: 8 oz / **Banquet** Buffet Supper	42
Frozen w meat sauce: 12¾ oz / **Swanson** Hungry Man	63
Frozen w meat sauce: 13¼ oz / **Swanson** Main Course	45
Frozen w meat sauce: 14 oz / **Buitoni**	64
Frozen w meat sauce: 10½ oz / **Green Giant**	45
Frozen w meat sauce: 12 oz / **Green Giant** Single Serve	44

GRAMS

Frozen w meat sauce and cheese: 12 oz pkg /
   Weight Watchers   38
Frozen w sausage: 11 oz / **Van de Kamp's**   34
Frozen, spinach: 12 oz / **Green Giant**   41
Frozen, spinach: 9 oz / **Health Valley**   34
Frozen, spinach: 11 oz / **Van de Kamp's**   36
Frozen, zucchini: 11 oz / **Stouffer's**
   Lean Cuisine   28
Linguini w clam sauce, frozen: 10½ oz / **Stouffer's**   36
Manicotti, frozen: 5⅓ oz / **Banquet** Buffet Supper   23
Manicotti, frozen: 6 oz / **Buitoni**   31
Manicotti w sauce, frozen: 13 oz / **Buitoni**   55
Mostaccioli, frozen: 8 oz / **Banquet** Buffet Supper   34
Pizza style pastry, cheese filling in pastry w
   tomato sauce: 1 pastry / **Pepperidge Farm** Deli's   29
Ravioli
   Beef, canned: ½ can / **Chef Boy-ar-dee**
      Mini 15-oz can   33
   Beef, canned: ⅕ can (8 oz) / **Chef Boy-ar-dee**
      Mini 40-oz can   36
   Beef, canned: 8 oz / **Dia-Mel**   35
   Beef, canned: 7 oz / **Ezo**   27
   Beef, canned: 7½ oz / **Ezo** Chef's Special   32
   Beef, canned: 7½ oz / **Franco American**   36
   Beef, canned: 7½ oz / **Lido Club**   31
   Beef, canned in sauce: 8 oz / **Chef Boy-ar-dee**   33
   Beef, canned in tomato-meat sauce: ½ can
      (7½ oz) / **Chef Boy-ar-dee**   31
   Cheese, canned in beef-tomato sauce: ½ can
      (7½ oz) / **Chef Boy-ar-dee**   34
   Cheese, canned in tomato sauce: ½ can
      (7½ oz) / **Chef Boy-ar-dee**   33
   Cheese, canned in tomato sauce: 7½ oz /
      Ezo   34
   Cheese, frozen: 3¾ oz / **Buitoni**   44
   Cheese, frozen, parmesan: 12 oz / **Buitoni**   57
   Cheese, frozen, round: 5½ oz / **Buitoni**   42
   Chicken, canned: ½ can (7½ oz) /
      Chef Boy-ar-dee   29
   Chicken, canned: ½ can (7½ oz) /
      Chef-Boy-ar-dee Mini   29

GRAMS

Meat, frozen: 3¾ oz / **Buitoni**	44
Meat, frozen, parmesan: 12 oz / **Buitoni**	75
Meat, frozen, round: 5½ oz / **Buitoni**	58
Sausage, canned: ½ can (7½ oz) / **Chef-Boy-ar-dee**	29
RavioliOs, canned: 7½ oz / **Franco American**	34
Shells	
Frozen w sauce: 10½ oz / **Buitoni**	55
Stuffed, frozen w sauce: 10 oz / **Buitoni**	39
Stuffed, frozen: 11 oz / **Legume** Provencale (tofu)	22
Stuffed, frozen w sauce: 9 oz / **Stouffer's**	28
Stuffed w broccoli, frozen: 5 oz / **Buitoni**	24
Stuffed w cheese, frozen: 9 oz / **Stouffer's**	30
Stuffed w chicken, frozen: 9 oz / **Stouffer's**	24
Stuffed w spinach, frozen: 5½ oz / **Buitoni**	24
Tortellini, frozen: 10 oz / **Buitoni**	55
Veal parmigian, frozen: 6⅖ / **Banquet** Buffet Supper	25
Veal parmigian, frozen: 5 oz / **Banquet** Cookin' Bag	23
Veal parmigiana, frozen: 5 oz / **Morton** Boil-in bag	14
Veal parmigiana, frozen: 8 oz / **Morton** Family Meal	25
Ziti, frozen: 10½ oz / **Buitoni**	64
Ziti w meat, frozen: 11¼-oz pkg / **Weight Watchers**	30

Jams, Jellies, Preserves, Butters, Marmalade and Spreads

	GRAMS
1 tsp unless noted	
Butters	
Apple / **Bama**	3
Apple: 1 oz / **Lucky Leaf**	12
Apple: 1 oz / **Musselman's**	12
Apple / **Smucker's**	3
Peach / **Smucker's**	4
Jams	
All flavors / **Smucker's**	5
All flavors, imitation / **Smucker's** Low calorie Slenderella	2
All flavors / **Welch's**	5
Red plum / **Bama**	4
Jellies	
All flavors: 1 tbsp / **Crosse & Blackwell**	13
All flavors / **Dia-Mel**	0
All flavors / **Smucker's**	5
All flavors, imitation / **Smucker's** Low Calorie Slenderella	2
All flavors / **Welch's**	5
Apple: 1 oz / **Lucky Leaf**	19
Apple: 1 oz / **Musselman's**	20
Apple: ½ oz / **Nutri-Dyne** Elwood	0–1
Apple blackberry: 1 oz / **Musselman's**	19
Apple cherry: 1 oz / **Musselman's**	19
Apple grape: 1 oz / **Musselman's**	20

135

GRAMS

Apple raspberry: 1 oz / **Musselman's**	19
Apple strawberry: 1 oz / **Musselman's**	20
Black raspberry: ½ oz / **Nutri-Dyne** Elwood	0–1
Grape / **Bama**	4
Grape: 1 oz / **Musselman's**	20
Grape: ½ oz / **Nutri-Dyne** Elwood	1
Mint flavored apple / **Bama**	4
Strawberry: ½ oz / **Nutri-Dyne** Elwood	1
Marmalade	
All flavors: about 1 tbsp / **Crosse & Blackwell**	15
Orange: ½ oz / **Nutri-Dyne** Elwood	7
Preserves	
All flavors: about 1 tbsp / **Crosse & Blackwell**	15
All flavors / **Dia-Mel**	0
All flavors / **Safeway**	5
All flavors / **Smucker's**	5
Apricot / **Bama**	4
Spreads	
All flavors / **Smucker's** Low Sugar	2
All flavors / **Welch's** Lite	3

Liqueurs and Brandies

BRANDIES

1 fl oz

Leroux Deluxe	1
Apricot / **Leroux**	9
Blackberry / **Leroux**	8
Blackberry / **Leroux** Polish type	9
Cherry / **Leroux**	8
Cherry / **Leroux** Kirschwasser	0
Coffee / **Leroux**	8
Ginger / **Leroux**	4
Peach / **Leroux**	9

LIQUEURS

1 fl oz

Anesone / **Leroux**	3
Anisette / **Leroux**	10
Apricot / **Leroux**	9
Aquavit / **Leroux**	0
Banana / **Leroux**	11
Blackberry / **Leroux**	7
Cherry / **Kijafa**	5
Cherry / **Leroux**	8
Cherry / **Leroux** Cherry Karise	8
Chocolate, cherry / **Cheri-Suisse**	10
Chocolate, minted / **Vandermint**	10
Chocolate, orange / **Sabra**	10
Claristine / **Leroux**	11
Coffee / **Pasha** Turkish Coffee	13
Creme de Cacao, brown / **Leroux**	14

137

	GRAMS
Creme de Cacao, white / **Leroux**	13
Creme de Cafe / **Leroux**	14
Creme de Cassis / **Leroux**	15
Creme de Menthe, green / **Leroux**	15
Creme de Menthe, white / **Leroux**	13
Creme de Noya / **Leroux**	15
Curacao / **Leroux**	10
Gold-O-Mint / **Leroux**	15
Grenadine / **Leroux**	15
Kummel / **Leroux**	4
Maraschino / **Leroux**	10
Peach / **Leroux**	9
Peppermint Schnapps / **Leroux**	9
Raspberry / **Leroux**	8
Rock and Rye / **Leroux**	11
Rock and Rye–Irish Moss / **Leroux**	13
Sloe Gin / **Leroux**	6
Strawberry / **Leroux**	8
Triple Sec / **Leroux**	9

Macaroni

	GRAMS
Plain, all types, cooked to "al dente" firm stage: 1 cup	39
Plain, all types, cooked to tender stage: 1 cup	32
Macaroni and beef	
Canned: 7½ oz / **Franco American** BeefyOs	30
Canned: 7¼ oz / **Heinz** Mac 'n Beef	23
Frozen: 5¾ oz / **Stouffer's**	20
Macaroni and cheese	
Canned: 7 oz / **Ezo**	23
Canned: 7⅜ oz / **Franco American**	24
Canned: 7½ oz / **Heinz**	26
Frozen: 8 oz / **Banquet** Buffet Supper	37
Frozen: 8 oz / **Banquet** Casserole	36
Frozen: 5 oz / **Banquet** Cookin' Bag	25
Frozen: 9 oz / **Green Giant**	36
Frozen: 10 oz / **Howard Johnson's**	50
Frozen: ⅓ pkg / **Howard Johnson's** 19-oz size	32
Frozen: 8 oz / **Morton** Casserole	36
Frozen: 8 oz / **Morton** Family Meal	34
Frozen: 6 oz / **Stouffer's**	24
Frozen: 12 oz / **Swanson**	43
Mix: 2 oz dry / **Creamette**	47
Mix: ¼ pkg dry / **Golden Grain**	38
Mix: ¾ cup prepared / **Kraft** Dinner	34
Mix: ¾ cup prepared / **Kraft** Dinner Family Size	36
Mix: ¾ cup prepared / **Kraft** Deluxe Dinner	36
Mix: ¾ cup prepared / **Kraft** Dinner Spiral	32
Mix: ½ cup prepared / **Lipton**	25

GRAMS

Macaroni in pizza sauce, canned: 7½ oz /
    Franco American PizzOs   35
Macaroni in tomato sauce, canned: 7½ oz /
    Chef Boy-ar-dee   31

Mayonnaise

GRAMS

1 tbsp

Bama	0
Hellman's	0
Mrs. Filbert's Real	0
NuMade	0
Nutri-Dyne Elwood: ½ oz	0
Scotch Buy	0
Weight Watchers reduced calorie	less than 1
Imitation	
Dia-Mel	0
Mrs. Filbert's	1
Scotch Buy	1
Hain Naturals (eggless)	0

Meat

FRESH

GRAMS

Beaver, roasted: 3 oz	0
Beef, ground, lean (10% fat), raw: 4 oz	0
Beef, ground, regular (21% fat), raw: 4 oz	0

GRAMS

Beef, roast, oven-cooked, no liquid added	
Relatively fat, such as rib:	
3 oz lean and fat	0
1.8 oz lean only	0
Relatively lean, such as heel of round:	
3 oz lean and fat	0
2.7 oz lean only	0
Brains, all varieties, raw: 4 oz	.9
Hamburger (ground beef), broiled	
3 oz lean	0
3 oz regular	0
Heart: 4 oz	
Beef, lean, cooked	.8
Beef, lean, raw	.8
Calf, cooked	2
Calf, raw	2
Lamb, cooked	1.1
Lamb, raw	1.1
Kidney: 4 oz	
Beef, cooked	.9
Beef, raw	1
Lamb, raw	1
Lamb cooked	
Chop, 4.8 oz thick w bone, broiled	0
4.0 oz lean and fat, broiled	0
2.6 oz lean only, broiled	0
Leg, roasted	
3 oz lean and fat	0
2.5 oz lean only	0
Shoulder, roasted:	
3 oz lean and fat	0
2.3 oz lean only	0
Liver: 4 oz	
Beef, fried	6
Calf, fried	4.6
Lamb, broiled	3.3
Pork, fresh, cooked:	
Chop, 3.5 oz thick w bone	0
2.3 oz lean and fat	0
1.7 lean only	0

	GRAMS
Roast, oven-cooked, no liquid added:	
3 oz lean and fat	0
2.4 oz lean only	0
Cuts, simmered:	
3 oz lean and fat	0
2.2 oz lean only	0
Quail: 8 oz dressed, ready to cook	0
Rabbit, domesticated: 1 lb dressed, ready to cook	0
Rabbit, wild: 1 lb dressed, ready to cook	0
Steak, broiled	
Relatively fat such as sirloin:	
3 oz lean and fat	0
2 oz lean only	0
Relatively lean such as round:	
3 oz lean and fat	0
2.4 oz lean only	0
Sweetbreads, cooked: 4 oz	
Beef	0
Calf	0
Lamb	0
Tongue, cooked: 4 oz	
Beef	.5
Calf	1.1
Lamb	.6
Veal, med fat, cooked, bone removed:	
Cutlet, 3 oz	0
Roast, 3 oz	0

CANNED, CURED, PROCESSED

Bacon, cooked	
Hormel Black Label: 1 slice	0
Hormel Range Brand: 1 slice	0
Hormel Red Label: 1 slice	0
Oscar Mayer: 1 slice	0
Swift: 1 slice	0
Bits / **Oscar Mayer:** ¼ cup	0
Canadian: 1 oz / **Eckrich** Calorie Watcher	1
Canadian: 1 slice / **Oscar Meyer**	0
Banquet loaf: 1 slice / **Eckrich** Beef Smorgas Pack	1
Bar-B loaf: 1 slice / **Eckrich** Calorie Watcher	1

GRAMS

Bar-B-Q loaf: 1 slice / **Oscar Mayer**	2
Beef breakfast strips: 1 strip / **Oscar Mayer** Lean 'n Tasty	.2
Beef, corned, canned: 3 oz / **Dinty Moore**	
Beef, corned, canned: 2.3 oz / **Libby's** 7-oz can	2
Beef, corned, canned: 2.4 oz / **Libby's** 12-oz can	2
Beef, corned, chopped: 1 oz / **Safeway**	0
Beef, corn, jellied loaf: 1 slice / **Oscar Mayer**	0
Beef, corned, sliced: 1 oz / **Eckrich** Calorie Watcher	1
Beef, dried, chunked and formed: ¾ oz / **Swift** Premium	0
Beef pastry w bacon sauce: 1 piece / **Pepperidge Farm** Deli's	26
Beef pastry w barbecue sauce: 1 piece / **Pepperidge Farm** Deli's	28
Beef, sliced: 1 oz / **Eckrich** Calorie Watcher	1
Beef, smoked, sliced: 1 oz / **Safeway**	0
Beef steaks, breaded, frozen: 4 oz / **Hormel**	
Bologna	
Eckrich: 1 slice	2
Eckrich German Brand: 1 slice	1
Eckrich Smorgas Pac (12-oz pkg): 1 slice	1
Eckrich Smorgas Pac (1-lb pkg): 1 slice	2
Oscar Mayer: 1 slice	.4
Beef: 1 slice / **Eckrich**	2
Beef: 1 slice / **Eckrich** Beef Smorgas Pac	1
Beef: 1 oz / **Health Valley**	.5
Beef: 1 slice / **Oscar Mayer**	.6
Beef, thick sliced: 1 slice / **Eckrich**	2
Beef, thin sliced: 2 slices / **Eckrich**	2
Chicken: 1 oz / **Health Valley**	.5
Chub: 1 oz / **Eckrich** German Brand	1
Garlic: 1 slice / **Eckrich**	2
Lunch, chub: 1 oz / **Eckrich**	2
Ring: 1 oz / **Eckrich**	2
Ring, pickled: 1 oz / **Eckrich**	2
Sandwich: 1 slice / **Eckrich**	2
Sliced: 1 slice / **Eckrich** (12- oz pkg)	2
Sliced: 1 slice / **Eckrich** (1-lb pkg)	2
Thick sliced: 1 slice / **Eckrich**	3
Thin sliced: 2 slices / **Eckrich**	2

GRAMS

w cheese: 1 slice / **Eckrich**	2
w cheese: 1 slice / **Oscar Mayer**	.6
Braunschweiger: 1 oz / **Oscar Mayer**	.8
Braunschweiger, chub: 1 oz / **Eckrich**	1
Breakfast strips, pork: 1 strip / **Oscar Mayer**	
Lean 'N Tasty	.2
Corn Dogs: 1 piece / **Oscar Mayer**	27
Frankfurters: 1 frankfurter unless noted	
Eckrich	2
Oscar Mayer	.8
Beef / **Eckrich**	2
Beef / **Oscar Mayer**	.9
Beef, jumbo / **Eckrich**	3
Cheese / **Oscar Mayer**	.7
Chicken: 1 oz / **Health Valley**	.6
Turkey: 1 oz / **Health Valley**	.5
Gourmet loaf: 1 slice / **Eckrich** Beef Smorgas Pac	2
Gourmet loaf: 1 slice / **Eckrich** Calorie Watcher	2
Ham	
Canned: 1 oz / **Oscar Mayer** Jubilee	.1
Chopped: 1 slice / **Eckrich** Calorie Watcher	1
Chopped: 1 slice / **Eckrich** Smorgas Pac	1
Chopped: 1 slice / **Oscar Mayer**	.8
Cooked, sliced: 1 slice / **Eckrich**	1
Cooked, sliced: 1 slice / **Eckrich** Calorie Watcher	1
Cooked, smoked: 1 slice / **Oscar Mayer**	0
Danish: 1 oz / **Eckrich**	1
Loaf: 1 slice / **Eckrich**	1
Slice: 1 oz / **Oscar Mayer** Jubilee	0
Smoked, boneless: 1 oz / **Oscar Mayer** Jubilee	.2
Smoked, sliced: 1 oz / **Eckrich** Calorie Watcher	1
Smoked, sliced: 1 oz / **Safeway**	0
Smoked, sweet: 1 slice / **Eckrich**	
Calorie Watcher	1
Steaks: 1 slice / **Oscar Mayer** Jubilee	0
And cheese loaf: 1 slice / **Eckrich**	1
And cheese loaf: 1 slice / **Oscar Mayer**	.6
Head cheese: 1 slice / **Oscar Mayer**	0
Honey loaf: 1 slice / **Oscar Mayer**	1
Honey style loaf: 1 slice / **Eckrich** Calorie Watcher	3

GRAMS

Honey style loaf: 1 slice / **Eckrich** Smorgas Pac (12-oz pkg)	2
Honey style loaf: 1 slice / **Eckrich** Smorgas Pac (1-lb pkg)	3
Kielbasa: 1 oz / **Eckrich** Polska	1
Kielbasa, links, skinless: 2 links / **Eckrich** Polska	2
Kielbasa, skinless: 1 link / **Eckrich** Polska	2
Knockwurst: 1 oz / **Health Valley**	.5
Liver cheese: 1 slice / **Oscar Mayer**	.6
Luncheon meat: 1 slice / **Oscar Mayer**	.4
Luxury loaf: 1 slice / **Oscar Mayer**	1.5
Macaroni-cheese loaf: 1 slice / **Eckrich**	3
Old-fashioned loaf: 1 slice / **Eckrich**	3
Old-fashioned loaf: 1 slice / **Eckrich** Smorgas Pac (12-oz pkg)	2
Old-fashioned loaf: 1 slice / **Eckrich** Smorgas Pac (1-lb pkg)	2
Old-fashioned loaf: 1 slice / **Oscar Mayer**	2
Olive loaf: 1 slice / **Eckrich**	2
Olive loaf: 1 slice / **Oscar Mayer**	3
Pastrami, sliced: 1 oz / **Eckrich** Calorie Watcher	1
Pastrami, sliced, smoked: 1 oz / **Safeway**	0
Peppered loaf: 1 slice / **Eckrich** Calorie Watcher	1
Peppered loaf: 1 slice / **Oscar Mayer**	1.3
Pepperoni, sliced: 1 oz / **Eckrich**	1
Pickle loaf: 1 slice / **Eckrich**	2
Pickle loaf: 1 slice / **Eckrich** Smorgas Pac	2
Pickle loaf, beef: 1 slice / **Eckrich** Beef Smorgas Pac	1
Pickle and pimento loaf: 1 slice / **Oscar Mayer**	3
Picnic loaf: 1 slice / **Oscar Mayer**	1.5
Pork, slender sliced, smoked: 1 oz / **Eckrich** Calorie Watcher	1
Salami	
Beer, sliced: 1 slice / **Eckrich**	1
Beer: 1 slice / **Oscar Mayer**	.4
Beer, beef: 1 slice / **Oscar Mayer**	.2
Chub, cooked: 1 oz / **Eckrich**	1
Cotto: 1 slice / **Eckrich**	1
Cotto: 1 slice / **Oscar Mayer**	.4
Cotto, beef: 1 slice / **Eckrich**	1

GRAMS

Cotto, beef: 1 slice / **Oscar Mayer**	.6
Hard: 1 slice / **Oscar Mayer**	.2
Hard, sliced: 1 oz / **Eckrich**	1

Sausage

Cheese-smoked: 2 oz / **Eckrich**	2
Ham roll: 1 slice / **Oscar Mayer**	.5
Honey roll, beef 1 slice / **Oscar Mayer**	.7
Luncheon, pressed: 1 slice / **Oscar Mayer**	.7
Luncheon roll: 1 slice / **Oscar Mayer**	.2
Minced roll: 1 slice / **Eckrich**	1
New England Brand: 1 slice / **Eckrich** Calorie Watcher	1
New England Brand: 1 slice / **Oscar Mayer**	.6
Patty, fresh: 1 patty / **Eckrich**	1
Patty, pork: 1 patty / **Oscar Mayer** Southern Brand	0
Pork: 2 oz / **Eckrich**	1
Pork roll, hot, fresh: 2 oz / **Eckrich**	1
Smoked: 2 oz / **Eckrich**	1
Smoked, beef: 2 oz / **Eckrich**	1

Sausage Links

Eckrich: 1 link	.5
Oscar Mayer Little Friers: 1 link	.2

Sausage links, smoked

Eckrich Cheese: 1 link	2
Eckrich Hot: 1 link	3
Eckrich Skinless: 1 link	2
Eckrich Smok-y-Links, beef: 1 link	1
Eckrich Smok-y-Links, ham: 1 link	1
Eckrich Smok-y-Links, maple-flavored: 1 link	1
Eckrich Smok-y-Links, skinless: 1 link	1
Oscar Mayer Beef Smokies: 1 link	.9
Oscar Mayer Cheese Smokies: 1 link	.4
Oscar Mayer Smoky Links: 1 link	.6

Summer Sausage

Eckrich Smoky Tang: 1 oz	1
Eckrich Sliced: 1 slice	1
Oscar Mayer: 1 slice	.2
Beef: 1 slice / **Oscar Mayer**	.7
Vienna sausage, canned in barbeque sauce: 2½ oz / **Libby's**	2

Vienna sausage, canned in beef broth: 1 link /
    Libby's 5-oz can   .4
Vienna sausage, canned in beef broth: 1 link /
    Libby's 9-oz can   .4

MEAT ENTRÉES, FROZEN

Beef burgundy: 9 oz / **Green Giant**	33
Beef, chipped, creamed: 4 oz / **Banquet** Cookin'Bag	8
Beef, chipped, creamed: 5 oz / **Morton** Boil-in-Bag	9
Beef, chipped, creamed: 5½ oz / **Stouffer's**	10
Beef julienne: 8½ oz / **Light and Elegant**	27
Beef patty: 5 oz / **Morton** Boil-in-bag	8
Beef patties: 8 oz / **Morton** Family Meal	12
Beef patties w onion gravy: 8 oz / **Morton** Family Meal	14
Beef shortribs: 5¾ oz / **Stouffer's**	2
Beef shortribs / **Green Giant**	40
Beef, sliced	
Morton Boil-in-bag: 5 oz	5
Morton Family Meal: 8 oz	7
w barbeque sauce: 4 oz / **Banquet** Cookin'Bag	13
w gravy: 8 oz / **Banquet** Buffet Supper	6
w gravy: 4 oz / **Banquet** Cookin'Bag	4
w gravy: 8 oz / **Swanson**	18
Sirloin: 13 oz / **Weight Watchers**	16
Beef steak in green pepper sauce: 9¾ oz / **Weight Watchers**	14
Beef stroganoff: 9 oz / **Green Giant**	35
Beef stroganoff: 9¾ oz / **Stouffer's**	31
Beef teriyaki: 8 oz / **Light and Elegant**	37
Cabbage rolls stuffed w beef: ½ pkg / **Green Giant**	19
Crepes, ham and asparagus: 6¼ oz / **Stouffer's**	21
Crepes, ham and swiss cheese: 7½ oz / **Stouffer's**	23
Green pepper steak: 10½ oz / **Stouffer's**	35
Green peppers stuffed w beef: 7¾ oz / **Stouffer's**	18
Green peppers stuffed w veal: 11¾ oz / **Weight Watchers**	22
Hash, roast beef: 5¾ oz / **Stouffer's**	11
Meatballs w brown gravy: 8½ oz / **Swanson**	20
Meatballs, Swedish: 11 oz / **Stouffer's**	33

GRAMS

Meatballs, sweet and sour: 9.4 oz / **Green Giant**	57
Meat Loaf	
Banquet Buffet Supper: 6 oz	12
Banquet Cookin'Bag: 5 oz	10
w tomato sauce: 8 oz / **Morton** Family Meal	17
w tomato sauce: 9 oz / **Swanson**	30
Salisbury steak	
Banquet Buffet Supper: 5⅓ oz	5
Banquet Cookin'Bag: 5 oz	5
Morton: 10.3 oz	36
Morton Boil-in-bag: 5 oz	7
Morton Family Meal: 8 oz	13
Swanson: 5½ oz	20
Swanson Main Course: 10 oz	16
Swanson Hungry Man: 11¾ oz	30
w creole sauce: 9 oz / **Green Giant**	11
w gravy: ½ pkg / **Green Giant**	11
w Italian sauce: 9½ oz / **Stouffer's** Lean Cuisine	14
w mashed potatoes: 11 oz / **Green Giant**	27
w onion gravy: 6 oz / **Stouffer's**	5
Sausage and peppers: 10½ oz / **Buitoni**	49
Sloppy Joe: 5 oz / **Morton** Boil-in-bag	12
Steak w green peppers: 9 oz / **Green Giant**	32
Steak w green peppers: 8½ oz / **Swanson** Main Course	11
Stew, beef	
Banquet Buffet Supper: 8 oz	21
Green Giant: 9 oz	20
Morton Family Meal: 8 oz	14
Stouffer's: 10 oz	16
Stew, meatball: 10 oz / **Stouffer's** Lean Cuisine	21
Swiss steak w stuffed potato: 1 pkg / **Green Giant**	37
Veal patty Pomodoro: 10½ oz / **Buitoni**	53

MEAT ENTRÉES, CANNED

Beef goulash: 7½ oz / **Heinz**	22
Hash, corned beef: 7 oz / **Ezo**	20
Hash, corned beef: 7½ oz / **Libby's** 15 oz	20
Hash, corned beef: 8 oz / **Libby's** 24 oz	21

GRAMS

Meatballs in gravy: ½ can / **Chef Boy-ar-dee**	18
Sloppy Joe, beef: ⅓ cup / **Libby's**	7
Sloppy Joe, pork: ⅓ cup / **Libby's**	6
Stew, beef	
Dia-Mel: 8 oz	19
Ezo: 7 oz	16
Heinz: 7½ oz	19
Libby's 15 oz: 7½ oz	18
Libby's 24 oz: 8 oz	19
Stew, meatball: ⅓ can (8 oz) / **Chef Boy-ar-dee**	24

MEAT SUBSTITUTES

Bacon: 1 tbsp / **Bac*Os**	2
Bacon: 1 tsp / **French's** Crumbles	.5
Bacon: 3 strips / **Morningstar Farms** Breakfast Strips	4
Hamburger: 1 patty / **Morningstar Farms** Grillers	5
Sausage: 3 links / **Morningstar Farms** Breakfast	5
Sausage: 2 patties / **Morningstar Farms** Breakfast Patties	7

Mexican Foods

GRAMS

See also Dinners

Beans	
Chili, canned: 7½ oz / **Dennison's**	32
Chili, canned: 4 oz / **Hunt Wesson**	18
Chili, hot, canned: ½ cup / **A & P**	24
Chili, hot, canned: 7½ oz / **Luck's**	34
Chili, Mexican, canned: 8 oz / **Van Camp**	39
Chili in meat sauce, canned: 7 oz / **Ezo** Chef's Special	29

GRAMS

Garbanzo, canned: ½ cup / **Old El Paso**	12
Refried, canned: ½ cup / **Del Monte**	20
Refried, canned: ¼ cup / **Old El Paso**	10
Refried w green chiles, canned: ¼ cup / **Old El Paso**	10
Refried w sausage, canned: ¼ cup / **Old El Paso**	8
Refried, spicy, canned: ½ cup / **Del Monte**	20
Refried, frozen: ½ cup / **Patio** Boil-in-bag	23
Burritos, frozen: 1 burrito unless noted	
El Charrito Red Hot	46
El Charrito Red Hot, preferred	37
Beef / **El Charrito** Classic Chunky	83
Beef / **El Charrito** Red Hot	40
Beef and bean: 6 oz / **Van de Camp's**	44
Beef and bean / **El Charrito** Red Hot	41
Beef and bean / **El Charrito,** prefried	37
Beef and bean / **Patio**	21
Beef and bean w green chili / **El Charrito**	43
Beef and bean w red chili / **El Charrito**	45
Beef and bean w red chili / **Patio**	22
Beef and bean w green chili / **Patio**	23
Beef and bean, large / **Patio**	13
Beef and bean, large w green chili / **Patio**	15
Beef and bean, large w red chili / **Patio**	13
Crispy fried w guacamole: 6 oz / **Van de Kamp's**	40
Sirloin: 11 oz / **Van de Kamp's** burrito grande	51
Burrito entrée, frozen: 1 entrée / **El Charrito**	65
Burrito rolls, beef entrée, frozen: 1 entrée / **El Charrito**	119
Burrito filling mix: ½ oz / **Del Monte**	20
Chilies	
canned: ½ cup / **Del Monte**	5
canned / **Old El Paso:** 1 chili	1
canned / **Ortega:** 1 oz	1
Chili con carne, canned	
Chef Boy-ar-dee: ½ can (7½ oz)	14
Dennison's: 7½ oz	15
Health Valley: 4 oz	12
Heinz: 7¾ oz	27

GRAMS

Libby's: 7½ oz	11
Old El Paso: 1 cup	12
Van Camp: 8 oz	13
Chili con carne w beans, canned	
Chef Boy-ar-dee: ½ can (7½ oz)	30
Dennison's: 7½ oz	27
Dennison's hot: 7½ oz	26
Dia-Mel: 8 oz	31
Ezo: 7 oz	26
Ezo, hot: 7 oz	28
Health Valley, mild: 4 oz	14
Health Valley, spicy: 4 oz	14
Heinz, hot: 7¾ oz	30
Libby's: ½ 15-oz can (7½ oz)	25
Libby's: ⅓ 24-oz can (8 oz)	27
Luck's: 7½ oz	30
Old El Paso: 1 cup	27
Van Camp: 8 oz	21
Chili con carne w beans, frozen: 8¾ oz / **Stouffer's**	25
Dips, Mexican-style	
Bean: 4 tbsp / **Hain** Natural	6
Bean w onion: 4 tbsp / **Hain** Natural	5
Bean Jalapeno: 4 tbsp / **Hain** Natural	6
Enchilada: 3⅛ oz / **Fritos**	13
Taco: ¼ cup / **Hain** Natural	4
Enchiladas, frozen	
Beef: 8 oz / **Banquet** International Buffet	37
Beef: 6 oz / **Banquet** International Cookin' Bag	34
Beef: 2 enchiladas / **Patio**	30
Beef: 1 w gravy / **Patio** Boil-in-bag	29
Beef: 7½ oz / **Van de Kamp's** Holiday	21
Beef: 8½ oz **Van de Kamp's** Holiday	33
Cheese: 2 enchiladas / **Patio**	26
Cheese: 7½ oz / **Van de Kamp's** Holiday	23
Cheese: 5½ oz / **Van de Kamp's** Holiday	22
Cheese: 8½ oz / **Van de Kamp's** Holiday	29
Chicken: 7½ oz / **Van de Kamp's**	24
Chicken: 5½ oz / **Van de Kamp's**	24
Enchilada entrées, frozen: 1 entrée unless noted	
Green Giant Sonora style: 12 oz	48

GRAMS

Beef: 2 enchiladas / **El Charrito**	41
Beef: 6 enchiladas / **El Charrito**	89
Beef, shredded / **El Charrito** Classic	72
Beef / **Swanson:** 11¼ oz	49
Beef / **Swanson:** Hungry Man: 16 oz	65
Beef / **Van de Kamp's:** 5½ oz	16
Beef and Bean / **El Charrito** Grande	94
Beef and Cheese / **El Charrito**	95
Cheese: 2 enchiladas / **El Charrito**	44
Cheese / **El Charrito** Classic	75
Cheese: 10 oz / **Health Valley**	48
Cheese: 5½ oz / **Van de Kamp's** Ranchero	22
Chicken / **El Charrito** Classic	58
Chicken: 5½ oz / **Van de Kamp's** Suiza	21
Hot peppers: 1 oz / **Ortega**	2
Jalapeno peppers, canned: ½ cup / **Del Monte**	6
Jalapeno peppers, canned: 2 peppers / **Old El Paso**	1
Mexican-style pastry w chili sauce and cheese filling: 1 pastry / **Pepperidge Farm** Deli's	31
Quesorito entrée, frozen: 1 entrée / **El Charrito**	97
Ranchorito entrée, frozen: 1 entrée / **El Charrito**	90
Salsa, green chile: 1 oz / **Ortega**	1
Taco entrée, beef, frozen: 6 tacos / **El Charrito**	104
Taco and bean entrée, frozen / **El Charrito** Grande	97
Tacos: 1 taco / **Ortega**	15
Tacos: beef, frozen: 2 tacos / **Patio**	29
Tacos, beef, snack, frozen: 4 tacos/ **Patio**	17
Taco shell: 1 shell / **Ortega**	8
Taco Starter: 8 oz / **Del Monte**	28
Tamales, canned: 2 tamales / **Old El Paso**	17
Tamales w gravy, frozen: 1 tamale / **Patio** Boil-in-bag	27
Tamalitos w gravy, canned: 7½ oz / **Dennison's**	37
Taquitos, beef, frozen: 1 pkg (6 taquitos) / **El Charrito**	76
Taquitos, beef, frozen w guacamole: 8 oz / **Van de Kamp's**	47
Tomatoes and green chilies, canned: ¼ cup / **Old El Paso**	3
Tomatoes and jalapenos, canned: 1 oz / **Ortega**	1
Tortillas, corn frozen: 2 tortillas / **El Charrito**	9

	GRAMS
Tortillas, flour, frozen: 2 tortillas / **El Charrito**	29
Tortillas, frozen: 2 tortillas / **Patio**	21
Tostada shell: 1 shell / **Ortega**	8
Tostada, beef, frozen: 8½ oz / **Van de Kamp's**	35

Milk

	GRAMS
Non-brand name: 8 fl oz (1 cup)	
Whole, 3.3% fat	11
Lowfat, 2% fat	12
Lowfat, 1% fat	12
Nonfat, skim	12
Buttermilk: 8 fl oz (1 cup)	
.5% fat / **A & P**	12
.5% fat / **Borden**	9.5
.5% fat / **Meadow Gold**	12
1% fat / **Borden**	12
1.5% fat / **Borden**	9.5
1.5% fat / **Friendship**	12
3.5% fat / **Borden**	12
Condensed, sweetened	
Borden Dime Brand: ¼ cup	42
Borden Eagle Brand: ¼ cup	20
Carnation: ½ cup	83
Eagle: ⅓ cup	52
Magnolia: ⅓ cup	54
Dry, nonfat	
Fearn: 3 tbsp dry	13
Reconstituted / **Carnation:** 1 cup	12
Reconstituted / **Land O Lakes:** 1 cup	12
Reconstituted / **Lucerne:** 1 cup	12
Evaporated, canned	
Carnation: ½ cup	12
Lucerne: ½ cup	12
Pet: ½ cup	12

	GRAMS
Low-fat / **Carnation:** ½ cup	12
Skim / **Carnation:** ½ cup	14
Skim / **Pet:** ½ cup	14
Imitation milk: 8 fl oz / **Lucerne**	11
Lowfat: 8 fl oz	
1% fat / **A & P**	12
2% fat / **A & P**	12
2% fat / **Land O Lakes**	12
2% fat / **Lucerne** Two-Ten	13
2% fat / **Meadow** Gold Viva	11
Fortified, 2% fat / **Borden**	13
Skim (.5% fat): 8 fl oz	
A & P	12
Borden	12
Lucerne	12
Meadow Gold	12
Weight Watchers	13
Fortified, skim / **Borden**	13
Whole (3.5% fat): 8 fl oz	
A & P	11
Blossom Time	11
Borden	11
Dairy Land	11
Land O Lakes	12
Lucerne	11
Meadow Gold	11

FLAVORED MILK BEVERAGES

All flavors: 10-fl-oz can / **Carnation** Slender	34
Chocolate: 8 fl oz / **Borden** Frosted	36
Chocolate: dairy pack: 8 fl oz / **Land O Lakes**	26
Chocolate, dairy pack, low-fat (1.5% fat) / **Lucerne**	25
Chocolate, dairy pack: 8 fl oz / **Meadow Gold**	26
Chocolate, dairy pack, low-fat: 8 fl oz / **Meadow Gold**	25
Chocolate, Dutch, dairy pack: 8 fl oz / **Borden**	26
Chocolate, skim, dairy pack: 8 fl oz / **Land O Lakes**	26
Chocolate mixes	
Alba '77 Fit 'n Frosty: 1 env	11

Carnation Instant Breakfast: 1 env dry	23
Carnation Slender: 1 env dry	21
Lucerne Instant Breakfast: 1 env	26
Ovaltine: ¾ oz (4–5 heaping tsp)	16
Pillsbury Instant Breakfast: 1 pouch dry	26
Quik: 2 tsp	19
Quik prepared w whole milk: 8 fl oz	30
Quik prepared w low-fat milk: 8 fl oz	31
Quik prepared w skim milk: 8 fl oz	31
Chocolate fudge: 1 env dry / **Lucerne** Instant Breakfast	26
Dutch chocolate: 1 env dry / **Carnation** Slender	21
Malt: 1 env dry / **Carnation** Instant Breakfast	22
Malt: 1 env dry / **Lucerne** Instant Breakfast	26
Malt: 1 pouch dry / **Pillsbury** Instant Breakfast	26
Malt: 3 heaping tsp / **Carnation** Instant	18
Coffee, mix: 1 env dry / **Carnation** Instant Breakfast	24

Eggnog

Mix: 6 fl oz (1 pkt prepared) **Boyd's** Today Instant Hot Nog	21
Mix: 1 env dry / **Carnation** Instant Breakfast	23
Mix: 1 env dry / **Lucerne** Instant Breakfast	28
Malt, mix: ¾ oz (4–5 heaping tsp) / **Ovaltine**	17
Malt, mix: 3 heaping tsp / **Carnation** Instant Natural	16

Strawberry

Canned: 8 fl oz / **Borden** Frosted	36
Mix: 1 env dry / **Alba** '77 Fit 'n Frosty	11
Mix: 1 env dry / **Carnation** Instant Breakfast	24
Mix: 1 env dry / **Lucerne** Instant Breakfast	28
Mix: 1 pouch / **Pillsbury** Instant Breakfast	27
Mix: 2 tsp / **Quik**	2
Mix: 8 fl oz prepared / **Quik**	33

Vanilla

Mix: 1 env dry / **Alba** '77 Fit 'n Frosty	11
Mix: 1 env dry / **Carnation** Instant Breakfast	24
Mix: 1 env dry / **Lucerne** Instant Breakfast	28
Mix: 1 pouch / **Pillsbury** Instant Breakfast	27

GRAMS

French vanilla, mix: 1 env dry **Carnation**
Slender   22

Muffins: English and Sweet

GRAMS

1 muffin unless noted

Apple cinnamon, mix / **Betty Crocker**	18
Apple, spicy, mix / **Duncan Hines**	20
Banana nut, mix / **Duncan Hines**	20
Blueberry	
Thomas' Toast-R-Cakes	17
Frozen / **Howard Johnson's** Toastees	17
Frozen / **Morton**	23
Frozen / **Morton Rounds**	21
Frozen / **Pepperidge Farm**	27
Mix, prepared / **Duncan Hines**	17
Mix, / **Betty Crocker**	18
Bran	
Thomas' Toast-R-Cakes	17
Mix, prepared / **Arrowhead Mills**	22
Mix, prepared / **Duncan Hines**	16
Mix: 3 tbsp dry / **Elam's**	16
w raisins / **Pepperidge Farm**	28
Carrot walnut / **Pepperidge Farm**	27
Cherry, mix / **Betty Crocker**	18
Cinnamon swirl / **Pepperidge Farm**	30
Corn	
Thomas' Toast-R-Cakes	19
Frozen / **Howard Johnson's** Toastees	20
Frozen / **Morton**	20
Frozen / **Pepperidge Farm**	27
Mix, prepared / **Dromedary**	20
English	
Arnold Extra Crisp	30

GRAMS

Earth Grains	31
Merico	24
Pepperidge Farm	26
Thomas'	26
Wonder	26
Bacon and cheese / **Pepperidge Farm**	25
Bran / **Arnold** Bran'nola	30
Cinnamon apple / **Pepperidge Farm**	27
Cinnamon chip / **Pepperidge Farm**	28
Cinnamon raisin / **Merico**	30
Cinnamon raisin / **Pepperidge Farm**	28
Multi-grain / **Merico**	26
Raisin / **Arnold**	35
Raisin / **Earth Grains**	30
Raisin / **Thomas'**	30
Sourdough / **Pepperidge Farm**	27
Wheat / **Pepperidge Farm**	26
Wheat, honey / **Thomas**	27
Wheatberry / **Earth Grains**	29
Whole wheat / **Earth Grains**	29
Orange, frozen / **Howard Johnson's** Toastees	16
Orange-cranberry / **Pepperidge Farm**	30
Raisin Rounds / **Wonder**	28
Sour dough / **Wonder**	27

Nuts

UNSALTED AND UNFLAVORED

GRAMS

Almonds	
Dried, in shell: 10 nuts	2
Dried, in shell: 1 cup	6.1
Dried, shelled, chopped: 1 tbsp	1.6
Dried, shelled, chopped: 1 cup	25.4
Dried, shelled, slivered: 1 cup	22.4
Dried, shelled, whole: 1 cup	27.7
Roasted, in oil: 1 cup	30.6
Beechnuts, in shell: 1 lb	56.2
Beechnuts, shelled: 1 lb	92.1
Brazil nuts, in shell: 1 cup	6.4
Brazil nuts, shelled: 1 oz (6-8 kernels)	3.1
Brazil nuts, shelled: 1 cup	15.3
Butternuts, in shell: 1 lb	5.3
Butternuts, shelled: 1 lb	38.1
Cashew nuts, roasted in oil: 1 cup	41
Cashew nuts, roasted in oil: 1 lb	132.9
Chestnuts, fresh	
in shell: 1 cup	40.9
in shell: 1 lb: 1 lb	154.7
Shelled: 1 cup	64.7
Shelled: 1 lb	191
Filberts, in shell: 1 lb	34.9
Filberts, shelled, chopped: 1 cup	19.2
Filberts, shelled, whole: 1 cup	22.5
Peanuts, roasted	
in shell: 10 jumbo nuts	3.7
in shell: 1 lb	62.6
Spanish and Virginia: 1 lb	225.9

GRAMS

Spanish and Virginia, chopped: 1 cup	27.1
Hickory nuts, shelled: 1 oz	3.8
Macadamia nuts, shelled: 1 oz	4.7
Pecans	
Chopped or pieces: 1 tbsp	1.1
Chopped or pieces: 1 cup	17.2
Halves: 10 large (451–550 per lb)	1.3
Halves: 10 jumbo (301–350 per lb)	2
Halves: 10 mammoth (250 or fewer per lb)	2.6
Pinenuts, pignolias, shelled: 1 oz	3.3
Pinenuts, piñon, shelled: 1 oz	5.8
Pistachio nuts, in shell: 1 lb	43.1
Pistachio nuts, shelled: 1 lb	86.2
Walnuts	
Black, in shell: 1 lb	14.8
Black, shelled, chopped or broken kernels: 1 tbsp	1.2
Black, shelled, chopped or broken kernels: 1 cup	18.5
Persian or English, in shell: 1 lb	32.2
Persian or English, shelled, halves: 1 cup	15.8
Persian or English: 10 large nuts	7.8
Persian or English, chopped: 1 tbsp	1.3

ROASTED AND FLAVORED

1 oz unless noted: (1 oz equals about ⅕ cup)

Almonds / **Granny Goose**	8
Almonds, dry roasted / **Planters**	6
Cashews / **Granny Goose**	7
Cashews / **Planters** Vacuum Can	8
Cashews, dry roasted / **Planters**	9
Cashews, unsalted / **Planters**	9
Mixed	
Planters Vacuum Can	6
Dry roasted / **Planters**	7
w peanuts / **Planters** Vacuum Can	6
Unsalted / **Planters**	7
Peanuts	
Planters Old Fashioned	5

	GRAMS
Safeway Party Pride	5
Cocktail / **Planters** Vacuum Can	5
Cocktail, unsalted / **Planters**	5
Dry roasted / **Planters**	6
Redskin Virginia / **Planters** Vacuum Can	5
Spanish / **Granny Goose**	4
Spanish / **Planters** Vacuum Can	5
Spanish, dry roasted / **Planters**	6
Virginia / **Granny Goose**	5
Pecans / **Granny Goose**	3
Pecans, dry roasted / **Planters**	5
Pistachios / **Granny Goose**	5
Pistachios, dry roasted / **Planters**	6
Sesame Nut Mix / **Planters**	8
Soy nuts / **Planters**	10
Sunflower nuts, unsalted / **Planters**	5
Tavern Nuts / **Planters**	6
Walnuts: ¼ cup shelled (about 5 unshelled) / **Diamond**	4

Olives

	GRAMS
10 olives	
Green	
Small	.5
Large	.5
Giant	.9
Ripe, black	
Ascolano: extra large	1.2
Ascolano: giant	1.8
Ascolano: jumbo	2.1
Manzanillo: small	.8
Manzanillo: medium	.9
Manzanillo: large	1
Manzanillo: extra large	1.2
Mission: small	.9
Mission: medium	1.1
Mission: large	1.3
Mission: extra large	1.5
Sevillano: giant	1.9
Sevillano: jumbo	2.2
Sevillano: collosal	2.8
Sevillano: supercollossal	3.3
Greek style: medium	1.7
Greek style: extra large	2.3

Pancakes, Waffles and Similar Breakfast Foods

GRAMS

See also Eggs

Breakfast, frozen, French toast w sausages: 1 entrée, 6¼ oz / **Swanson**	37
Breakfast, frozen, pancakes and sausages: 1 entrée, 6 oz / **Swanson**	50
Breakfast, frozen, scrambled eggs w sausage: 1 entrée, 6¼ oz / **Swanson**	17
French toast, frozen: 2 slices / **Aunt Jemima**	26
French toast w cinnamon, frozen: 2 slices / **Aunt Jemima**	27
Fritters, apple, frozen: 2 fritters (4 oz) / **Mrs. Paul's**	33
Fritters, corn, frozen: 2 fritters (4 oz) / **Mrs. Paul's**	30
Pancakes	
Batter, frozen: 3 cakes, 4-in diam / **Aunt Jemima**	42
Batter, frozen, blueberry: 3 cakes, 4-in diam / **Aunt Jemima**	42
Batter, frozen, buttermilk: 3 cakes, 4-in diam / **Aunt Jemima**	43
Mix, dry: 1 oz / **Health Valley**	22
Mix, dry, buckwheat: ½ cup / **Arrowhead Mills**	52
Mix, dry, buttermilk: ½ cup / **Fearn 7 Grain**	11
Mix, dry, buttermilk: 1 oz / **Health Valley**	22
Mix, dry, griddle lite: ½ cup / **Arrowhead Mills**	50
Mix, dry, multigrain: ½ cup / **Arrowhead Mills**	70

GRAMS

Mix, dry, triticale: ½ cup / **Arrowhead Mills**	53
Mix, dry, whole wheat: ¼ cup / **Elam's** 3 in 1	25
Mix, prepared: 3 cakes, 3-in diam / **Dia-Mel**	21
Mix, prepared: 5 cakes, 4-in diam / **Fearn** Low Sodium	49
Mix, prepared: 4 cakes, 4-in diam / **Fearn** Low Sodium 7 Grain	37
Mix, prepared: 5 cakes, 4-in diam / **Fearn** Rich Earth	47
Mix, prepared: 5 cakes, 4-in diam / **Fearn** Soy-O Triticale	43
Mix, prepared: 3 cakes, 4-in diam / **Golden Blend**	26
Mix, prepared: 3 cakes, 4-in diam / **Golden Blend** Complete	43
Mix, prepared: 3 cakes, 4-in diam / **Hungry Jack** Complete, bulk	39
Mix, prepared: 3 cakes, 4-in diam / **Hungry Jack** Complete, packets	35
Mix, prepared: 3 cakes, 4-in diam / **Hungry Jack** Extra Lights	30
Mix, prepared: 3 cakes, 4-in diam / **Panshakes**	43
Mix, prepared, blueberry: 3 cakes, 4-in diam / **Hungry Jack**	40
Mix, prepared, buttermilk: 3 cakes, 4-in diam / **Betty Crocker**	39
Mix, prepared, buttermilk: 3 cakes, 4-in diam / **Betty Crocker** Complete	41
Mix, prepared, buttermilk: 3 cakes, 4-in diam / **Hungry Jack**	29
Mix, prepared, buttermilk: 3 cakes, 4-in diam / **Hungry Jack** Complete, bulk	39
Mix, prepared, potato: 3 cakes, 3-in diam / **French's**	17
Pancakes and blueberry sauce, frozen: 7 oz / **Swanson**	70
Pancake-waffle mix	
Dry: ½ cup / **Aunt Jemima** Complete	46
Dry: ¼ cup / **Aunt Jemima** Original	22
Dry, buckwheat: ¼ cup / **Aunt Jemima**	21
Dry, buttermilk: ⅓ cup / **Aunt Jemima**	37

GRAMS

Dry, buttermilk: ½ cup / **Aunt Jemima** Complete	47
Dry, whole wheat: ⅓ cup / **Aunt Jemima**	29
Dry, whole wheat: ½ cup / **Elam's**	46
Mix, prepared: 5 cakes, 4-in diam / **Fearn** Soy-O	48
Mix, prepared, whole wheat: 5 cakes, 4-in diam / **Fearn** Soy-O	44
Waffles, frozen: 1 waffle	
Aunt Jemima Jumbo Original	15
Eggo Homestyle	16
Apple-cinnamon / **Aunt Jemima** Jumbo	15
Blueberry / **Aunt Jemima** Jumbo	15
Blueberry / **Eggo**	16
Buttermilk / **Aunt Jemima** Jumbo	15
Buttermilk / **Eggo**	15
Strawberry flavor / **Eggo**	18

Pastry

GRAMS

FROZEN AND REFRIGERATOR

Apple Criss Cross: 2 oz / **Pepperidge Farm**	24
Cobbler, apple: 4.3 oz / **Weight Watchers**	28
Cobbler, black cherry: 4.3 oz / **Weight Watchers**	27
Dumpling, apple: 3 oz / **Pepperidge Farm**	33
Fruit squares, apple: 1 square / **Pepperidge Farm**	27
Fruit squares, blueberry: 1 square / **Pepperidge Farm**	29
Fruit squares, cherry: 1 square / **Pepperidge Farm**	29
Strudel, apple: 3 oz / **Pepperidge Farm**	35
Turnovers: 1 turnover	
Apple / **Pepperidge Farm**	35
Apple / **Pillsbury**	23
Blueberry / **Pepperidge Farm**	32

GRAMS

Blueberry / **Pillsbury**	22
Cherry / **Pepperidge Farm**	32
Cherry / **Pillsbury**	24
Peach / **Pepperidge Farm**	34
Raspberry / **Pepperidge Farm**	37

TOASTER PASTRY

1 portion

Toaster pastry / **Town House**	35
Pop Tarts / **Kellogg's**	
Blueberry	36
Blueberry, frosted	38
Brown sugar cinnamon	33
Brown sugar cinnamon, frosted	34
Cherry	36
Cherry, frosted	37
Chocolate fudge, frosted	36
Chocolate vanilla, frosted	37
Concord grape, frosted	36
Dutch apple, frosted	36
Raspberry, frosted	36
Strawberry	37
Strawberry, frosted	38
Toaster Strudel / **Pillsbury**	
Blueberry	28
Cinnamon	26
Raspberry	27
Strawberry	27
Toastettes / **Nabisco**	
All varieties	35

Pickles and Relishes

	GRAMS
Capers: 1 tbsp / **Crosse & Blackwell**	0
Chow Chow Mustard: 1 tbsp / **Crosse & Blackwell**	0
Garden Mix: 1 oz / **Vlasic Hot & Spicy**	1
Onions	
Cocktail: 1 tbsp / **Crosse & Blackwell**	0–1
Cocktail, lightly spiced: 1 oz / **Vlasic**	1
Spiced: 1 oz / **Heinz**	0
Sweet: 1 oz / **Heinz**	9
Pepperoncini: 1 oz / **Vlasic** Mild Greek	1
Peppers	
Heinz rings or slices: 1 oz	1
Hot / **Heinz** Banana	1
Hot: 1 oz / **Vlasic** Banana Rings	1
Sweet: 1 oz / **Heinz** Mementos	1
Pickles, bread and butter	
Chips: 1 oz / **Vlasic**	6
Chunks: 1 oz / **Vlasic** Deli	6
Chunks: 1 oz / **Vlasic** Old Fashioned	6
Slices: 1 oz / **Heinz**	6
Sticks: 1 oz / **Vlasic** Butter Stix	5
Pickles, dill	
Chips: 1 oz / **Vlasic** Half-the-Salt Hamburger Chips	1
Spears: 1 oz / **Vlasic** Kosher	1
Spears: 1 oz / **Vlasic** Kosher Half-the-Salt	1
Gherkins: 1 oz / **Vlasic** Kosher	1
Whole: 1 / **Claussen** Kosher	1
Whole: 1 oz / **Vlasic** Kosher Baby	1
Whole: 1 oz / **Vlasic** Kosher Crunchy	1
Whole: 1 oz / **Vlasic** Kosher Crunchy Half-the-Salt	1
Whole: 1 oz / **Vlasic** Kosher Deli Dills	1
Whole: 1 oz / **Vlasic** No Garlic	1
Whole: 1 oz / **Vlasic** Original	1

GRAMS

Pickles, sweet	
Heinz: 1 oz	8
Chips: 1 oz / **Vlasic** Half-the-Salt	7
Cubes: 1 oz / **Heinz** Salad Cubes	7
Gherkins: 1 oz / **Heinz**	8
Mixed: 1 oz / **Heinz**	9
Slices: 1 slice / **Claussen** Sweet 'n Sour	0-1
Slices: 1 oz / **Heinz**	8
Slices: 1 oz / **Heinz** Cucumber Slices	5
Sticks: 1 oz / **Heinz** Cucumber Stix	6
Pimientos: 1 oz / **Dromedary**	2
Relishes: 1 oz	
Dill / **Vlasic**	1
Hamburg / **Vlasic**	9
Hamburger / **Heinz**	7
Hot Dog / **Heinz**	8
Hot Dog / **Vlasic**	8
India / **Heinz**	9
Picalilli / **Heinz**	7
Sweet / **Heinz**	9
Sweet / **Vlasic**	8
Watermelon rind, pickled: 1 tbsp / **Crosse & Blackwell**	9

Pies

GRAMS

HOME-BAKED

1 pie, 9-in diameter

Apple	360
Banana custard	280
Blackberry	325
Blueberry	330
Butterscotch	349

	GRAMS
Cherry	363
Chocolate chiffon	283
Chocolate meringue	305
Coconut custard	227
Custard	212
Lemon chiffon	284
Lemon meringue	317
Mince	389
Peach	361
Pecan	423
Pineapple	360
Pineapple chiffon	253
Pineapple custard	292
Pumpkin	223
Raisin	406
Rhubarb	361
Strawberry	229
Sweet potato	216

PIE CRUST, HOME-BAKED

1 pie shell	79

FROZEN

Apple	
Banquet: 3⅓ oz	37
Morton 24 oz: ⅙ pie	41
Mrs. Smith's 46 oz: ⅛ pie	56
Mrs. Smith's Lattice 36 oz: ⅛ pie	58
Mrs. Smith's Natural Juice 36¾ oz: ⅐ pie	52
Mrs. Smith's Old Fashioned 50 oz: ⅛ pie	64
Mrs. Smith's Streusel 41⅛ oz: ⅐ pie	67
Individual: 1 pie / **Banquet** 8 oz	88
Individual: 1 pie / **Morton** Great Little Desserts 8 oz	88
Banana: ⅙ pie / **Morton** 14 oz	19
Banana cream: 2⅓ oz / **Banquet**	21
Banana cream: ⅛ pie / **Mrs. Smith's** 24 oz	31
Banana cream, individual: 1 pie / **Morton** Great Little Desserts 3½ oz	27

GRAMS

Blackberry: 3⅓ oz / **Banquet**	40
Blueberry	
Banquet: 3⅓ oz	40
Morton 24 oz: ⅙ pie	39
Mrs. Smith's 46 oz: ⅛ pie	54
Individual: 1 pie / **Morton** Great Little	
Desserts 8 oz	86
Boston cream: ⅛ pie / **Mrs. Smith's** 36 oz	44
Cherry	
Banquet: 3⅓ oz	36
Morton 24 oz: ⅙ pie	42
Mrs. Smith's 46 oz: ⅛ pie	60
Mrs. Smith's Lattice 36 oz: ⅛ pie	59
Mrs. Smith's Natural Juice 36¾ oz: ⅐ pie	59
Individual: 1 pie / **Banquet**	87
Individual: 1 pie / **Morton** Great	
Little Desserts	87
Chocolate: ⅙ pie / **Morton** 14 oz	20
Chocolate cream: 2⅓ oz / **Banquet**	24
Chocolate cream: ⅛ pie / **Mrs. Smith's** 24 oz	35
Chocolate cream, individual: 1 pie / **Morton**	
Great Little Desserts 3½ oz	29
Coconut: ⅙ pie / **Morton** 14 oz	17
Coconut cream: 2⅓ oz / **Banquet**	22
Coconut cream: ⅛ pie / **Mrs. Smith's** 24 oz	33
Coconut cream, individual: 1 pie / **Morton** Great	
Little Desserts 3½ oz	25
Coconut custard: ⅛ pie / **Mrs. Smith's** 44 oz	40
Coconut custard, individual: 1 pie / **Morton**	
Great Little Desserts (6½ oz)	53
Dutch apple, individual: 1 pie / **Morton** Great	
Little Desserts 7¾ oz	94
Egg custard: ⅛ pie / **Mrs. Smith's** 44 oz	45
Lemon: ⅙ pie / **Morton** 14 oz	18
Lemon cream: 2⅓ oz / **Banquet**	23
Lemon cream: ⅛ pie / **Mrs. Smith's** 24 oz	32
Lemon cream, individual: 1 pie / **Morton**	
Great Little Desserts 3½ oz	27
Lemon meringue: ⅛ pie / **Mrs. Smith's** 36 oz	52
Mince: ⅙ pie / **Morton** 24 oz	46
Mincemeat: 3⅓ oz / **Banquet**	38

GRAMS

Peach
    Banquet: 3⅓ oz   35
    Morton 24 oz: ⅙ pie   39
    Mrs. Smith's 46 oz: ⅛ pie   53
    Individual: 1 pie / **Banquet** 8 oz   82
    Individual: 1 pie / **Morton** Great Little
        Desserts 8 oz   91
Pecan: 5 oz / **Howard Johnson's**   na
Pecan: ⅛ pie / **Mrs. Smith's** 36 oz   70
Pumpkin: 3⅓ oz **Banquet**   29
Pumpkin: ⅙ pie / **Morton** 24 oz   36
Pumpkin custard: ⅛ pie / **Mrs. Smith's** 46 oz   46
Strawberry cream: 2⅓ oz / **Banquet**   22

PIE MIXES

Boston cream: ⅛ pkg / **Betty Crocker** Classics   48

PIE CRUSTS AND PASTRY SHELLS

Pastry shells: 1 shell / **Stella O'Oro**   17
Patty shells: 1 shell / **Pepperidge Farm**   17
Pie crust
    Mix: ¹/₁₆ pkg / **Betty Crocker**   10
    Mix: 1⁷/₁₀ oz / **Flako**   25
    Mix and sticks: ⅙ of double crust pie /
        Pillsbury   25
    Refrigerated: ⅛ of double crust pie /
        Pillsbury All Ready   23
    Sticks: ⅛ stick / **Betty Crocker**   10
Pie shells, frozen: ⅛ (1 oz) / **Mrs. Smith's**   14
Puff pastry sheets, frozen: ¼ sheet /
    Pepperidge Farm   45

PIE FILLING

Canned, 4 oz unless noted

Apple

    Lucky Leaf   30
    Lucky Leaf Deluxe   35

	GRAMS
Musselman's	30
Musselman's Deluxe	35
Turnover filling, diced / **Lucky Leaf**	30
Turnover filling, diced / **Musselman's**	30
Apricot / **Lucky Leaf**	39
Apricot / **Musselman's**	39
Banana cream, mix: 1/6 pkg, prepared / **Jell-O**	17
Blackberry / **Lucky Leaf**	31
Blackberry / **Musselman's**	31
Black Raspberry / **Lucky Leaf**	143
Black Raspberry / **Musselman's**	143
Blueberry, cultivated / **Lucky Leaf**	31
Blueberry, cultivated / **Musselman's**	31
Boysenberry / **Lucky Leaf**	31
Boysenberry / **Musselman's**	31
Cherry / **Lucky Leaf**	29
Cherry / **Musselman's**	29
Coconut cream, mix: 1/6 pkg prepared / **Jell-O**	16
Gooseberry / **Lucky Leaf**	45
Gooseberry / **Musselman's**	45
Lemon	
Lucky Leaf	48
Musselman's	48
French / **Lucky Leaf**	42
French / **Musselman's**	42
Mix: 1/6 pkg, prepared / **Jell-O**	38
Mincemeat	
Crosse & Blackwell	114
Lucky Leaf	48
Musselman's	48
Condensed: 1/4 pkg / **Nonesuch**	50
w brandy and rum: 1/3 cup / **Nonesuch**	48
Peach / **Lucky Leaf**	37
Peach / **Musselman's**	37
Pineapple / **Lucky Leaf**	30
Pineapple / **Musselman's**	30
Pumpkin: 1 cup / **Libby's** plain	58
Pumpkin / **Lucky Leaf**	33
Pumpkin / **Musselman's**	33
Raisin / **Lucky Leaf**	34
Raisin / **Musselman's**	34

	GRAMS
Red Raspberry / **Lucky Leaf**	46
Red Raspberry / **Musselman's**	46
Strawberry / **Lucky Leaf**	30
Strawberry / **Musselman's**	30
Strawberry-rhubarb / **Lucky Leaf**	31
Strawberry-rhubarb / **Musselman's**	31
Vanilla creme / **Lucky Leaf**	32
Vanilla creme / **Musselman's**	32

PIE AND PASTRY SNACKS

1 piece

Apple pastry, dietetic / **Stella D'oro**	13
Apple pie	
Drake's	30
Hostess	45
Tastykake	52
French / **Tastykake**	72
Fried / **Dolly Madison**	59
Berry pie / **Hostess**	48
Blackberry pie / **Tastykake**	60
Blueberry pie / **Hostess**	49
Blueberry pie / **Tastykake**	62
Cherry pie / **Hostess**	55
Cherry pie / **Tastykake**	62
Cherry pie, fried / **Dolly Madison**	53
Coconut cream pie / **Tastykake**	44
Fig pastry, dietetic / **Stella D'oro**	14
Lemon pie / **Hostess**	53
Lemon pie / **Tastykake**	54
Peach pie / **Hostess**	53
Peach pie / **Tastykake**	48
Peach apricot pastry / **Stella D'oro**	14
Peach apricot pastry, dietetic / **Stella D'oro**	13
Pineapple pie / **Tastykake**	59
Prune pastry, dietetic / **Stella D'oro**	13
Pumpkin pie / **Tastykake**	55
Strawberry pie / **Hostess**	56
Strawberry-rhubarb pie / **Tastykake**	63
Tasty Klair pie / **Tastykake**	64

Pizza

	GRAMS
Canadian bacon	
Frozen: ¼ pizza / **Celeste** 19 oz	30
Frozen: 1 pizza / **Celeste** 8 oz	50
Frozen: ½ pizza / **Totino's** Party Pizza	40
Frozen: ⅓ pizza / **Totino's** My Classic	49
Cheese	
Frozen: 4 oz / **Buitoni** 6-slice	35
Frozen: 2 oz / **Buitoni**	20
Frozen: ¼ pizza / **Celeste** 19 oz	32
Frozen: 1 pizza / **Celeste** 7 oz	57
Frozen: 1 pizza / **Jeno's** 13 oz	108
Frozen: 1 pizza / **Jeno's** Deluxe 20 oz	171
Frozen: 1 piece (5³⁄₁₆ oz) / **Stouffer's** French Bread	43
Frozen: ½ pizza / **Totino's** Party Pizza	41
Frozen: ⅓ pizza / **Totino's** My Classic Deluxe	50
Frozen: 1 pkg (6 oz) / **Weight Watchers**	37
Frozen, English muffin pizza: ½ pkg / **Chef Boy-ar-dee** 13¼ oz	44
Frozen, English muffin pizza: 1 pizza / **Chef Boy-ar-dee** 6½ oz	48
Mix: ¼ pkg / **Chef Boy-ar-dee**	33
Mix: ⅛ pkg / **Chef-Boy-ar-dee** (2 pizzas)	31
Mix: ¼ pkg / **Chef Boy-ar-dee** Pizza in a Skillet	30
Combination	
Frozen: ¼ pizza / **Celeste** Chicago style 24 oz	36
Frozen: ¼ pizza / **Celeste** Deluxe 23.5 oz	37
Frozen: 1 pizza / **Celeste** Deluxe 9 oz	63
Frozen: ¼ pizza / **Celeste** Sicilian style 26 oz	45
Frozen: ¼ pizza / **Celeste** Suprema 24 oz	31
Frozen: 1 pizza / **Celeste** Suprema 10 oz	52
Frozen: ¼ pizza / **Celeste** Suprema wo meat 20 oz	31
Frozen: 1 pizza / **Celeste** Suprema wo meat 8 oz	49

	GRAMS
Frozen: 1 pizza / / **Jeno's** Deluxe 23 oz	165
Frozen: ⅓ pizza / **Totino's** My Classic	50
Frozen: 1 pkg / **Weight Watchers** 7.25 oz	38
Frozen: 6³⁄₁₆ oz / **Stouffer's** Deluxe French Bread	46
Hamburger, frozen: 1 pizza / **Jeno's**	114
Hamburger, frozen: 6⅛ oz / **Stouffer's** French Bread	39
Hamburger, frozen: ½ pizza / **Totino's** Party	41
Hamburger, mix: ¼ pkg / **Chef Boy-ar-dee**	42
Mexican style, frozen: ½ pizza / **Totino's** Party	31
Mushroom, frozen: 6 oz (1 piece) / **Stouffer's** French Bread	43
Nacho, frozen: ½ pizza / **Totino's** Party	34
Open face, frozen: 6½ oz / **Buitoni**	53
Pepperoni	
Frozen: ¼ pizza / **Celeste** 20 oz	35
Frozen: 1 pizza / **Celeste** 7.25	54
Frozen: ¼ pizza / **Celeste** Chicago style 24 oz	37
Frozen: ½ pizza / **Fox** Deluxe	36
Frozen / **Jeno's** 13 oz	114
Frozen: 5⅝ oz / **Stouffer's** French Bread	44
Frozen: ½ pizza / **Totino's** Party	40
Frozen: ⅓ pizza / **Totino's** My Classic	51
Frozen, English muffin pizza: ½ pkg / **Chef Boy-ar-dee** 14½ oz	48
Frozen, English muffin pizza: 1 pizza / **Chef Boy-ar-dee** 7¼ oz	50
Mix: ¼ pkg / **Chef Boy-ar-dee**	35
Mix: ⅛ pkg / **Chef Boy-ar-dee** 2-pizza size	34
Mix: ¼ pkg / **Chef Boy-ar-dee** Pizza in a Skillet	32
Sausage	
Frozen: ¼ pizza / **Celeste** 22 oz	35
Frozen: 1 pizza / **Celeste** 8 oz	60
Frozen: ¼ pizza / **Celeste** Chicago style	37
Frozen / **Jeno's** 13 oz	114
Frozen / **Jeno's** Deluxe 21 oz	159
Frozen: 6 oz (1 piece) / **Stouffer's** French Bread	44
Frozen: ½ pizza / **Totino's** Party	41

	GRAMS
Frozen: ⅓ pizza / **Totino's** My Classic	50
Frozen, English muffin: ½ pkg / **Chef Boy-ar-dee** 15½ oz	54
Frozen, English muffin: 1 pizza / **Chef Boy-ar-dee** 7¾ oz	54
Frozen, veal: 1 pkg / **Weight Watchers** 6¾ oz	35
Mix: ¼ pkg / **Chef Boy-ar-dee**	36
Mix: ¼ pkg / **Chef Boy-ar-dee** Pizza in a Skillet	33
w mushrooms, frozen: ¼ pizza / **Celeste** 24 oz	34
w mushrooms, frozen: 1 pizza / **Celeste** 9 oz	57
w mushrooms, frozen: 6½ oz (1 piece) / **Stouffer's** French Bread	40
w pepperoni: ½ pizza / **Totino's** Party	41
Vegetable, frozen: 1 pkg / **Weight Watchers** 7¼ oz	39
Pizza crust, mix: 1½ scoops / **Ragu** Pizza Quick	31

Popcorn

	GRAMS
Plain	
Unpopped: 1 oz	20
Air-or dry popped: 1 cup	5
Jiffy Pop: 1½ oz (4¾ cup popped)	21
Jolly Time large kernel: 1 cup popped	5
Jolly Time small kernel: 1 cup popped	11
Orville Redenbacher Gourmet: 4 cup popped	18
Popped w butter or oil, salt added: 1 cup	2.3
Popped w oil and salt	
Laura Scudder's: 1 oz	17
Orville Redenbacher Gourmet: 4 cup	21
Butter flavor, popped: 1½ oz (4¾ cup) / **Jiffy Pop**	24
Butter flavor, ready to eat: ½ oz (1½ cup) / **Wise**	8
Microwave	
Plain, popped: 4 cup / **Orville Redenbacher** Gourmet	16

	GRAMS
Plain, popped: 4 cup / **Pillsbury**	28
Plain, popped, no salt: 4 cup / **Pillsbury**	26
Butter flavor, popped: 4 cup / **Orville Redenbacher** Gourmet	17
Butter flavor, popped: 4 cup / **Pillsbury**	29
Cheese flavor: 1 oz / **Laura Scudder's**	17
Cheese flavor: ½ oz / **Wise Cheez**	7
Caramel corn: 1½ oz / **Laura Scudder's**	33
Cracker Jack: 1 oz (1¼ cup)	22
Screaming Yellow Zonkers: 1 oz	23

Pot Pies

	GRAMS
Frozen: 1 whole pie	
Beef	
Banquet 8 oz	47
Banquet Supreme 8 oz	38
Morton 8 oz	31
Stouffer's 10 oz	38
Swanson 8 oz	40
Swanson Chunky 10 oz	57
Swanson Hungry Man 16 oz	65
Chicken	
Banquet 8 oz	45
Banquet Supreme 8 oz	40
Morton 8 oz	33
Stouffer's 10 oz	40
Swanson 8 oz	39
Swanson Chunky 10 oz	56
Swanson Hungry Man 16 oz	64
Van de Kamp's 7½ oz	47
Steak burger / **Swanson** Hungry Man 16 oz	65
Tuna / **Banquet** 8 oz	48
Tuna / **Banquet** 8 oz	36

GRAMS

Turkey
Banquet 8 oz	41
Banquet Supreme 8 oz	41
Morton 8 oz	31
Stouffer's 10 oz	35
Swanson 8 oz	40
Swanson Chunky 10 oz	48
Swanson Hungry Man 16 oz	63

Poultry and Poultry Entrées

FRESH

GRAMS

Chicken, all cuts (fresh), raw or cooked, except organs	0
Duck, all cuts (fresh), raw or cooked, except organs	0
Goose, all cuts (fresh), raw or cooked, except organs	0
Turkey, all cuts (fresh), raw or cooked, except organs	0
Gizzard, chicken, cooked: 4 oz	.8
Gizzard, goose, cooked: 4 oz	0
Heart, chicken, cooked: 4 oz	.1
Heart, turkey, cooked: 4 oz	.2
Liver, chicken, cooked: 4 oz	3.5
Liver, goose, raw: 4 oz	6.1
Liver, turkey, cooked: 4 oz	3.5

CANNED, FROZEN, AND PROCESSED

See also, Dinners

Chicken, chunks or slices
Canned: 5 oz / **Health Valley**	0
Canned: 1½ oz / **Swanson**	0
Canned chunk style: 2½ oz / **Swanson** Mixin'	0

GRAMS

Canned, white chunk: 2½ oz / **Swanson**	0
Slices, breast: 2 slices / **Eckrich** Calorie Watcher	1
Slices, smoked: 1 oz / **Safeway**	0
Slices, frozen: 5 oz / **Morton** Boil-in-bag	7
Chicken à la King	
Canned: 5¼ oz / **Swanson**	9
Frozen: 5 oz / **Banquet** Cookin' Bag	10
Frozen: 9 oz / **Health Valley**	30
Frozen: 5 oz / **Morton** Boil-in-bag	8
Frozen: 9 oz / **Weight Watchers**	15
w biscuits, frozen: 9 oz / **Green Giant**	40
w rice, frozen: 9½ oz / **Stouffer's**	38
Chicken w barbecue sauce, frozen: 8 oz / **Light and Elegant**	31
Chicken w barbecue sauce, frozen: 1 pkg / **Green Giant** Entrée	45
Chicken w broccoli, rice and cheese sauce: 9½ oz / **Green Giant**	26
Chicken, creamed, frozen: 6½ oz / **Stouffer's**	6
Chicken crepes Marco Polo, frozen: 7 oz / **Health Valley**	23
Chicken croquettes, frozen: 6 oz / **Howard Johnson's**	19
Chicken Divan, frozen: 8½ oz / **Stouffer's**	14
Chicken and dumplings, canned: ½ can (7½ oz) / **Luck's**	18
Chicken and dumplings, canned: 7½ oz / **Swanson**	19
Chicken fillets Cacciatore, frozen: 11 oz / **Buitoni**	40
Chicken fillets Marsala, frozen: 11 oz / **Buitoni**	40
Chicken, fried, frozen	
Banquet: 6⅖ oz	20
Morton 32-oz size: 6.4 oz	33
Swanson Entrée: 7¼	30
Weight Watchers Entrée: 6¾	11
Assorted pieces: 3¼ oz / **Swanson**	13
Assorted pieces: 3¼ oz / **Swanson** Take-Out	10
Breast portions: 4⅖ oz / **Banquet**	14
Breast portions: 5½ oz / **Morton** 22 oz	30
Breast portions: 4½ oz / **Swanson**	20

GRAMS

Breast portions: 11¾ oz / **Swanson**
Hungry Man   51
Dark portions: 11 oz / **Swanson** Hungry Man   46
Thighs and drumsticks: 5 oz / **Banquet**   16
Thighs and drumsticks: 3¼ oz / **Swanson**   11
Nuggets: 3 oz / **Banquet**   14
Patties: 3 oz / **Banquet**   13
Sticks: 3 oz / **Banquet**   15
Chicken crepes: 8¼ oz / **Stouffer's**   19
Chicken, glazed, frozen: 8 oz / **Light and Elegant**   25
Chicken, glazed, frozen: 8½ oz / **Stouffer's**
Lean Cuisine   23
Chicken w herb butter: 1 pkg / **Green Giant**
entrée   30
Chicken Italian, frozen: 8 oz / **Light and Elegant**   19
Chicken Nibbles: 5 oz / **Swanson**   31
Chicken Nibbles: 3¼ oz / **Swanson**
Plump and Juicy   16
Chicken and noodles: 5¾ oz / **Stouffer's**   16
Chicken w noodles and vegetables: 9 oz / **Stouffer's**   38
Chicken Paprikash: 10½ oz / **Stouffer's**   32
Chicken w pea pods, rice: 10 oz / **Green Giant**   32
Chicken stew
Dia-Mel: 8 oz   19
Canned: 7 oz / **Ezo**   17
Canned: 7⅝ oz / **Swanson**   16
w dumplings, canned: 7¼ oz / **Heinz**   22
Chicken w vegetables and vermicelli: 12¾ oz /
Stouffer's Lean Cuisine   28
Turkey, slices and pieces
Breast, fresh, cooked: 1 oz / **Louis Rich**   0
Breast, barbecued: 1 oz / **Louis Rich**   0
Breast, smoked: 1 oz / **Louis Rich**   .6
Breast, oven-roasted: 1 slice / **Louis Rich**   .1
Breast, slices, fresh, cooked: 1 oz / **Louis Rich**   0
Breast, smoked: 1 slice / **Louis Rich**   .1
Breast, tenderloins, cooked: 1 oz / **Louis Rich**   0
Drumsticks, fresh, cooked: 1 oz / **Louis Rich**   0
Drumsticks, smoked: 1 oz / **Louis Rich**   .1
Ground, fresh: 1 oz cooked / **Louis Rich**   0
Slices, smoked: 1 slice / **Louis Rich**   .2

	GRAMS
Slices, smoked: 1 oz / **Eckrich** Calorie Watcher	2
Slices, smoked: 1 oz / **Safeway**	0
Slices, frozen w gravy: 5⅓ oz / **Banquet** Buffet Supper	4
Slices, frozen w gravy: 5 oz / **Banquet** Cookin' Bag	4
Slices, frozen: 12.3 oz / **Morton**	33
Slices, frozen: 5 oz / **Morton** Boil-in-bag	5
Slices, frozen: 8 oz / **Morton** Family Meal	8
Slices w wild rice, frozen: 9 oz / **Green Giant**	34
Wings, fresh, cooked: 1 oz / **Louis Rich**	0
Wings, smoked: 1 oz / **Louis Rich** Drumettes	.4
Turkey entrée, frozen: 8¾ oz / **Swanson**	27
Turkey entrée, frozen: 13¼ oz / **Swanson** Hungry Man	39
Turkey bologna: 1 slice / **Louis Rich**	.6
Turkey breakfast sausage, cooked: 1 oz / **Louis Rich**	0
Turkey casserole, frozen: 9¾ oz / **Stouffer's**	29
Turkey cotto salami: 1 slice / **Louis Rich**	.2
Turkey croquettes, frozen: 8 oz / **Morton** Family Meal	30
Turkey franks: 1 link / **Louis Rich**	.1
Turkey ham: 1 slice / **Louis Rich**	.4
Turkey ham, chopped: 1 slice / **Louis Rich**	.2
Turkey luncheon loaf: 1 slice / **Louis Rich**	.4
Turkey pastrami: 1 slice / **Louis Rich**	.4
Turkey pastry w ham and cheese: 1 pastry / **Pepperidge Farm** Deli's	23
Turkey smoked sausage: 1 oz / **Louis Rich**	.3
Turkey summer sausage: 1 slice / **Louis Rich**	.3
Turkey tetrazzini, frozen: 6 oz / **Stouffer's**	17
Turkey tetrazzini, frozen: 10 oz / **Weight Watchers**	28

Pretzels

	GRAMS
1 oz unless noted	
Charles, salted and unsalted	22
Estee: 5 pretzels	5
Mister Salty: 5 pretzels	20
Mister Salty Dutch: 2 pretzels	22
Mister Salty Little Shapes: 19 pretzels	22
Mister Salty Sticks	22
Pepperidge Farm Nugget Style: 25 pretzels	27
Pepperidge Farm Thin Sticks: 30 pretzels	28
Pepperidge Farm Tiny Twists: 15 pretzels	22
Planters Stick	22
Planters Twist	22
Rokeach Baldies or No Salt Dutch	20
Rokeach Party	23

Pudding

	GRAMS
½ cup unless noted; all mixes prepared with whole milk unless noted	
Banana	
Canned, ready to serve: 5 oz / **Del Monte** Pudding Cup	30
Canned, ready to serve: 5 oz / **Hunt's** Snack Pack	26
Canned, ready to serve / **Lucky Leaf**	24
Canned, ready to serve / **Musselman's**	24
Mix, prepared / **Royal**	27
Mix, prepared / **Royal** Instant	29
Mix, prepared / **Safeway**	31
Banana cream, mix, prepared / **Jell-O** Instant	30

	GRAMS
Butter pecan, mix, prepared / **Jell-O** Instant	29
Butterscotch	
Canned, ready to serve: 5 oz / **Del Monte** Pudding Cup	31
Canned, ready to serve: 5 oz / **Hunt's** Snack Pack	30
Canned, ready to serve / **Lucky Leaf**	26
Canned, ready to serve / **Musselman's**	26
Mix, prepared w nonfat milk / **Dia-Mel**	9
Mix, prepared w nonfat milk / **D-Zerta**	12
Mix, prepared w nonfat milk / **Estee**	13
Mix, prepared / **Jell-O**	30
Mix, prepared / **Jell-O** Instant	30
Mix, prepared / **My*T*Fine**	28
Mix, prepared / **Royal**	27
Mix, prepared / **Royal** Instant	29
Mix, prepared / **Safeway**	31
Chocolate	
Canned, ready to serve: 5 oz / **Del Monte** Pudding Cup	31
Canned, ready to serve: 5 oz / **Hunt's** Snack Pack	30
Canned, ready to serve / **Lucky Leaf**	27
Canned, ready to serve / **Musselman's**	27
Mix, prepared w nonfat milk / **Dia-Mel**	9
Mix, prepared w nonfat milk / **D-Zerta**	11
Mix, prepared w nonfat milk / **Estee**	13
Mix, prepared / **Jell-O**	28
Mix, prepared / **Jell-O** Instant	31
Mix, prepared / **My*T*Fine**	28
Mix, prepared / **Royal**	33
Mix, prepared / **Royal** Instant	35
Mix, prepared / **Safeway**	32
German, canned, ready to serve: 5 oz / **Hunt's** Snack Pack	35
Milk, mix, prepared / **Jell-O**	28
Milk, mix, prepared / **Jell-O** Instant	31
Chocolate almond, mix, prepared / **My*T*Fine**	27
Chocolate fudge	
Canned, ready to serve: 5 oz / **Del Monte** Pudding Cup	31

GRAMS

Canned, ready to serve: 5 oz / **Hunt's** Snack Pack	28
Canned, ready to serve / **Lucky Leaf**	25
Canned, ready to serve / **Musselman's**	25
Mix, prepared / **Jell-O** Instant	32
Mix, prepared / **My*T*Fine**	27
Chocolate marshmallow, canned, ready to serve: 5 oz / **Hunt's** Snack Pack	30
Coconut, mix, prepared / **Royal** Instant	30
Coconut cream, mix, prepared / **Jell-O** Instant	28
Coffee, mix, prepared / **Royal** Instant	29
Custard, mix, prepared / **Royal**	22
Dark 'N Sweet, mix, prepared / **Royal**	33
Dark 'N Sweet, mix, prepared / **Royal** Instant	35
Egg custard, golden, mix, prepared / **Jell-O** Americana	23
Flan, mix, prepared / **Royal**	22
Lemon	
Canned, ready to serve: 5 oz / **Hunt's** Snack Pack	36
Canned, ready to serve / **Lucky Leaf**	27
Canned, ready to serve / **Musselman's**	27
Mix, prepared / **Dia-Mel**	4
Mix, prepared / **Estee**	12
Mix, prepared / **Jell-O** Instant	31
Mix, prepared / **My*T*Fine**	30
Mix, prepared / **Royal** Instant	29
Mix, prepared / **Safeway**	31
Pineapple cream, mix, prepared / **Jell-O** Instant	30
Pistachio, mix, prepared / **Jell-O** Instant	30
Pistachio, mix, prepared / **Safeway**	30
Plum, canned, ready to serve: 4 oz / **Crosse & Blackwell**	62
Rice	
Canned, ready to serve: 5 oz / **Hunt's** Snack Pack	27
Canned, ready to serve / **Lucky Leaf**	20
Canned, ready to serve / **Musselman's**	20
Mix, prepared / **Jell-O** Americana	30

GRAMS

Tapioca
    Canned, ready to serve: 5 oz / **Del Monte**
       Pudding Cup   30
    Canned, ready to serve: 5 oz / **Hunt's**
       Snack Pack   27
    Canned, ready to serve / **Lucky Leaf**   20
    Canned, ready to serve / **Musselman's**   20
    Chocolate, mix, prepared / **Jell-O** Americana   28
    Chocolate, mix, prepared / **Royal**   33
    Vanilla, mix, prepared / **Jell-O** Americana   27
    Vanilla, mix, prepared / **My*T*Fine**   28
    Vanilla, mix, prepared / **Royal**   27
Vanilla
    Canned, ready to serve: 5 oz / **Del Monte**
       Pudding Cup   32
    Canned, ready to serve: 5 oz / **Hunt's**
       Snack Pack   31
    Canned, ready to serve / **Lucky Leaf**   25
    Canned, ready to serve / **Musselman's**   25
    Mix, prepared w nonfat milk / **Dia-Mel**   9
    Mix, prepared w nonfat milk / **D-Zerta**   12
    Mix, prepared w nonfat milk / **Estee**   13
    Mix, prepared / **Jell-O**   27
    Mix, prepared / **Jell-O** Instant   29
    Mix, prepared / **My*T*Fine**   28
    Mix, prepared / **Royal**   27
    Mix, prepared / **Royal** Instant   29
    Mix, prepared / **Safeway**   31
    French, mix, prepared / **Jell-O**   30
    French, mix, prepared / **Jell-O** Instant   30

Rice and Rice Dishes

RICE, PLAIN

	GRAMS
Brown, long grain, parboiled: 1 cup cooked	50
White, instant: 1 cup cooked	40
White, long grain: 1 cup cooked	50
White, parboiled: 1 cup cooked	41

RICE DISHES

Frozen

w broccoli in cheese sauce: ½ cup / **Green Giant** Originals	19
French Style: 3.6 oz / **Birds Eye**	25
Chinese Style, fried rice: 3.6 oz / **Birds Eye**	23
w herb butter sauce / **Green Giant** Originals: ½ cup	21
Italian w spinach and cheese: ½ cup / **Green Giant** Originals	21
Italian: 3.6 oz / **Birds Eye**	28
Medley: ½ cup / **Green Giant** Originals	20
Oriental style: 3.6 oz / **Birds Eye**	27
w peas and mushrooms: 2.3 oz / **Birds Eye**	23
Pilaf: ½ cup / **Green Giant** Originals	23
Spanish: 3.6 oz / **Birds Eye**	26
Wild rice and white long grain: ½ cup / **Green Giant** Rice Originals	23

CANNED OR MIXES

Beef flavor, mix, prepared w margarine or butter: ½ cup / **Lipton** Rice and Sauce	27
Beef flavor, mix: ⅙ pkg dry / **Beef Rice-a-Roni**	27

189

	GRAMS
Beef flavor, mix, prepared w butter: ½ cup / **Minute**	258
Chicken flavor, mix, prepared w margarine or butter: ½ cup / **Lipton** Rice and Sauce	26
Chicken flavor, mix: ⅓ pkg dry / **Rice-a-Roni**	33
Chicken flavor, mix, prepared w butter: ½ cup / **Minute**	25
Florentine, mix: ½ cup / **Uncle Ben's**	22
Florentine, mix, prepared w butter or margarine: ½ cup / **Uncle Ben's**	22
Fried, mix, prepared w oil: ½ cup / **Minute**	25
Herb and butter, mix, prepared w butter or margarine: ½ cup / **Lipton** Rice and Sauce	25
Pilaf, mix, prepared w butter or margarine: ½ cup / **Uncle Ben's** Original	23
Pilaf, mix, brown rice: ½ cup / **Pritikin**	19
Spanish, mix, prepared w butter or margarine: ½ cup / **Lipton** Rice and Sauce	26
Spanish, canned: 7¼ oz / **Heinz**	26
Spanish, canned: 8 oz / **Heinz**	27
Spanish, mix: ⅙ pkg dry / **Rice-a-Roni**	26
Spanish, mix: ½ cup / **Pritikin**	20
Wild and white long grain, mix, prepared w butter: ½ cup / **Minute**	25
Wild and white long grain, mix, prepared: ½ cup / **Uncle Ben's**	21
Wild and white long grain, mix, prepared w butter or margarine: ½ cup / **Uncle Ben's**	21

Rolls, Buns and Bagels

	GRAMS
1 roll, bun or bagel unless noted	
Bagels, frozen	
Egg / **Lender's**	29
Garlic / **Lender's**	32

	GRAMS
Onion / **Lender's**	31
Onion, mini / **Lender's** Bagelettes	14
Plain / **Lender's**	30
Plain, mini / **Lender's**	13
Poppy seed / **Lender's**	29
Pumpernickel / **Lender's**	31
Raisin 'n honey / **Lender's**	40
Raisin 'n wheat / **Lender's**	39
Rye / **Lender's**	30
Sesame seed / **Lender's**	31

Buns for sandwiches

Arnold Dutch Egg Sandwich Buns	22
Arnold Francisco Sandwich Rolls	30
Arnold Soft Sandwich	18
w poppyseeds / **Arnold** Soft Sandwich	18
w poppyseeds / **Pepperidge Farm**	22
w sesame seeds / **Arnold** Soft Sandwich	19
w sesame seeds / **Pepperidge Farm**	23
Wheat, Cracked, **Pepperidge Farm**	25

Hamburger

Arnold 8's	21
Butternut	14
Colonial	28
Eddy's	14
Kilpatrick's	28
Millbrook	14
Pepperidge Farm	21
Rainbo	28
Sweetheart	14
Weber's	14
Wonder	22

Hot Dog

Arnold 6's	20
Butternut	14
Colonial	28
Eddy's	14
Kilpatrick's	28
Millbrook	14
Pepperidge Farm	23
Rainbo	28
Sweetheart	14

GRAMS

Weber's	14
Wonder	22
Mustard bran / **Pepperidge Farm**	21
Onion w poppy seeds / **Pepperidge Farm**	26
Submarine rolls / **Earth Grains**: ½ roll	36
Croissants	
Pepperidge Farm	19
Pepperidge Farm Tray	19
Pepperidge Farm Petite	14
Sara Lee	19
Almond / **Pepperidge Farm**	21
Apple / **Sara Lee**	36
Cheese / **Sara Lee**	19
Chocolate / **Pepperidge Farm**	25
Chocolate / **Sara Lee**	30
Cinnamon / **Pepperidge Farm**	28
Cinnamon nut raisin / **Sara Lee**	43
Raisin / **Pepperidge Farm**	24
Strawberry / **Sara Lee**	33
Walnut / **Pepperidge Farm**	21
Wheat 'n honey / **Sara Lee**	18

DINNER AND SOFT ROLLS

1 roll

Arnold Francisco French Style	31
Arnold Francisco Sourdough French	16
Arnold Francisco Sourdough French Brown and Serve	17
Arnold Party Rounds 12's	10
Arnold Party Rounds 24's	10
Butternut Brown 'n Serve	11
Earth Grains Wheat	22
Eddy's Brown 'n Serve	11
Home Pride	14
Millbrook Brown 'n Serve	11
Pepperidge Farm	10
Pepperidge Farm Butter Crescent	13
Pepperidge Farm Finger w poppy seeds	8
Pepperidge Farm Finger w sesame seeds	9
Pepperidge Farm Golden Twist	14

GRAMS

Pepperidge Farm Hearth	10
Pepperidge Farm Old Fashioned	7
Pepperidge Farm Parker House	9
Pepperidge Farm Party	5
Pepperidge Farm Party w poppy seeds	22
Pepperidge Farm Soft Family	18
Sweetheart Brown 'n Serve	11
Weber's Brown'n Serve	11
Wonder	17
Wonder Gem Style	13
Wonder Buttermilk	13
Wonder Half & Half	12
Wonder Home Bake	13
Wonder Pan	17
Mix, prepared / **Pillsbury** Hot Roll Mix	17

REFRIGERATOR

1 roll

Merico Crescent	12
Pillsbury Butterflake	16
Pillsbury Country White, Bakery Style	20
Pillsbury Crescent	11
Pillsbury Parkerhouse	13
Pillsbury Weiner Wrap	10
Pillsbury Weiner Wrap, cheese	10

HARD ROLLS

1 roll

Club / **Pepperidge Farm**	20
French	
Earth Grains	19
Pepperidge Farm	19
Pepperidge Farm Brown 'n Serve 2:	
½ roll	36
Pepperidge Farm Brown 'n Serve 3:	
½ roll	24
Wonder Brown 'n Serve	13
Sourdough / **Earth Grains**	19

	GRAMS
Kaiser / **Earth Grains**	37
Kaiser / **Wonder**	82
Onion / **Earth Grains**	35
Popovers, mix / **Flako**: 1-oz mix	20
Popovers, mix / **Flako**: 1 popover	25

SWEET ROLLS

1 roll

Bear Claws / **Earth Grains**	27
Cherry / **Dolly Madison**	33
Cinnamon	
Dolly Madison	28
Earth Grains	29
Refrigerated / **Merico**	18
Refrigerated / **Pillsbury** Pipin' Hot	27
Butter flavored, refrigerated / **Merico**	15
w icing, refrigerated / **Hungry Jack**	
Butter Tastin'	18
w icing, refrigerated / **Pillsbury**	17
Danish	
Apple / **Earth Grains**	26
Apple / **Hostess**	43
Apple / **Pepperidge Farm**	28
Apple, refrigerated / **Pillsbury** Pipin' Hot	33
Apple, individual / **Sara Lee**	17
Apple / **Tastykake**	38
Apple / **Tastykake** Morning Fresh	47
Blueberry / **Pepperidge Farm**	30
Blueberry / **Tastykake**	41
Butterhorn / **Hostess**	39
Caramel w nuts, refrigerated / **Pillsbury**	19
Cheese / **Pepperidge Farm**	35
Cheese, individual / **Sara Lee**	13
Cheese / **Tastykake**	33
Cheese / **Tastykake** Morning Fresh	34
Cherry / **Earth Grains**	26
Cherry / **Pepperidge Farm**	29
Cherry / **Tastykake**	44
Cherry / **Tastykake** Morning Fresh	48
Cinnamon, refrigerated / **Merico**	21

GRAMS

      Cinnamon, raisin, refrigerated, w icing /
        Pillsbury   19
      Lemon / **Tastykake**   40
      Orange, refrigerated / **Merico**   18
      Orange, refrigerated, w icing / **Pillsbury**   19
      Raisin, refrigerated / **Merico**   21
      Raspberry / **Hostess**   48
Honey buns / **Hostess**   49
Honey buns, frozen / **Morton**   31
Honey buns, frozen, mini / **Morton**   18

Salad Dressings

Bottled unless noted: 1 tbsp unless noted

A & P	2
Bama	3
Estee, all types	1–2
Mrs. Filbert's	2
NuMade	2
Nutri-Dyne Elwood Zero Dressing: ½ oz	0
P & Q	3
Scotch Buy	3
Avocado: 1 oz / **Health Valley**	2
Bacon and tomato / **NuMade**	2
Bacon and tomato French / **Henri's**	5
Blue cheese	
Dia-Mel	0–1
Good Seasons	0–1
Good Seasons Thick 'n Creamy	0–1
Henri's	3
Henri's Reduced Calorie	4
NuMade Chunky	1
Weight Watchers	2
Wish-Bone Chunky	0–1
Wish-Bone Lite Chunky	3
Mix, prepared / **Hain** Natural No Oil	1
Mix, prepared / **Weight Watchers**	1
Buttermilk	
Good Seasons	1
Wish-Bone	2
Mix, prepared / **Hain** Natural No Oil	2
Buttermilk Farms / **Henri's**	1
Buttermilk and onion / **Hidden Valley Ranch**	2

GRAMS

Caesar
NuMade	1
Pfeiffer	1
Pfeiffer Low-Cal	2
Wish-Bone	0–1
Mix, prepared / **Hain** Natural No Oil	0
Cheddar and bacon / **Wish-Bone**	1
Chopped chive / **Henri's**	1

Cucumber, creamy
Dia-Mel	0–1
NuMade	1
Weight Watchers	2
Wish-Bone	1
Wish-Bone Lite	1
Cucumber and onion / **Henri's**	5
Cucumber and onion / **Henri's** Reduced Calorie	5
Dill: ½ oz / **Nutri-Dyne** Elwood	0
Dill / **Weight Watchers**	1
Dill, creamy / **Henri's**	2

French
Dia-Mel	0
Good Seasons	3
Good Seasons Old Fashioned	1
Good Seasons Riviera	3
Good Seasons Thick 'n Creamy	2
Henri's	3
Henri's Hearty Beefsteak	4
Henri's Sweet 'n Saucy	5
Henri's Reduced Calorie	6
NuMade Savory	2
NuMade Reduced Calorie	2
Nutri-Dyne Elwood: ½ oz	0
Pfeiffer	7
Pfeiffer Low-Cal	5
Pritikin	0
Weight Watchers	2
Wish-Bone Deluxe	2
Wish-Bone Sweet 'n Spicy	3
Wish-Bone Lite	2
Wish-Bone Lite Sweet 'n Spicy	4
Garlic / **Wish-Bone**	2

  GRAMS

Herbal / **Wish-Bone**	2
Mix, prepared / **Hain** Natural No Oil	3
Mix, prepared / **Weight Watchers**	1
Garden Herb / **Hidden Valley Ranch**	2
Garlic, creamy	
Dia-Mel	0
Henri's	3
Henri's Reduced Calorie	5
Wish-Bone	0–1
Garlic and cheese, mix, prepared / **Hain**	
Natural No Oil	1
Green goddess / **NuMade**	1
Herb: 1 oz / **Health Valley**	2
Herb / **Weight Watchers**	1
Herb, mix, prepared / **Hain** Natural No Oil	1
Italian	
Dia-Mel	0
Good Seasons	1
Good Seasons Thick 'n Creamy	1
NuMade	1
NuMade Reduced Calorie	1
Nutri-Dyne Elwood: ½ oz	0
Pfeiffer Chef	1
Pfeiffer Low-Cal	3
Pritikin	0
Wish-Bone	1
Wish-Bone Lite	1
Wish-Bone Robusto	1
Weight Watchers	1
Mix, prepared / **Good Seasons** Low Calorie	2
Mix, prepared / **Hain** Natural No Oil	1
Mix, prepared / **Weight Watchers**	0
Creamy / **Dia-Mel**	0
Creamy / **Weight Watchers**	1
Creamy / **Wish-Bone**	1
Creamy / **Wish-Bone** Lite	1
Creamy, mix, prepared / **Weight Watchers**	1
Italian, Herbal / **Wish-Bone**	1
Onion / **Good Seasons**	1
Onion and chive / **Wish-Bone** Lite	3
Ranch Original / **Hidden Valley** Ranch	2

	GRAMS
Red wine vinegar / **Dia-Mel**	0
Red wine vinegar and oil / **NuMade**	4
Russian	
Henri's	4
Nutri-Dyne Elwood: ½ oz	0
Pfeiffer	4
Pfeiffer Low-Cal	4
Pritikin	0
Wish-Bone	6
Wish Bone Lite	5
Mix, prepared / **Weight Watchers**	1
Russian/Thousand Island / **Weight Watchers**	1
Salad Life Cheese and Herbs / **Health Valley**	1
Slaw dressing / **Henri's**	4
Smoky Bits / **Henri's**	4
Sour cream and bacon / **Wish-Bone**	1
Tahiti / **Dia-Mel**	0-1
Tas-tee / **Henri's**	4
Thousand Island	
Dia-Mel	0-1
Good Seasons Thick 'n Creamy	2
Henri's	3
Henri's Reduced Calorie	4
NuMade Reduced Calorie	2
Pfeiffer	4
Pfeiffer Low-Cal	4
Weight Watchers	2
Wish-Bone	2
Wish-Bone Lite	3
Wish-Bone Southern Recipe	3
w bacon / **Wish-Bone**	2
Mix, prepared / **Hain** Natural No Oil	2
Mix, prepared / **Weight Watchers**	1
Whipped / **Dia-Mel**	0-1
Whipped / **Weight Watchers**	3
Yogonaise / **Henri's** Reduced Calorie	2
Yogowhip / **Henri's** Reduced Calorie	2
Yogurt buttermilk / **Dia-Mel**	0-1

Sauces

	GRAMS
A la King, mix, prepared: 1 cup / **Durkee**	14
Barbecue, bottled or canned: 1 tbsp unless noted	
Chris' & Pitt's	4
Estee	4
French's Cattlemen's Regular	5
French's Cattlemen's Smoky	5
Heinz Regular	4
Heinz Hickory Smoke	5
Hunt's All Natural Hickory	6
Hunt's All Natural Original	5
Nutri-Dyne Elwood: ½ oz	1
Hot / **Heinz**	5
Hot / **Hunt's** All Natural Hot & Zesty	6
Mushroom / **Heinz**	5
Onion / **Heinz**	5
Onion / **Hunt's** All Natural	5
Barbecue, mix, dry: 1 oz / **Nutri-Dyne** Chef Otto	19
Brown, mix, dry: 1 oz / **Nutri-Dyne** Chef Otto	16
Burrito salsa: ¼ cup / **Del Monte**	4
Cheese: 1 oz unless noted	
Land O Lakes Original	2
Cheddar / **Land O Lakes**	2
Cheddar / **Land O Lakes** LaChedda	3
Cheddar, canned / **Lucky Leaf**	3
Cheddar, canned / **Musselman's**	3
Cheddar, mild, canned / **Lucky Leaf**	2
Cheddar, mild, canned / **Musselman's**	2
Cheddar, sharp, canned / **Lucky Leaf**	1
Cheddar, sharp, canned / **Musselman's**	1
Nacho, canned / **Lucky Leaf**	3
Nacho, canned / **Musselman's**	3
Mix, dry / **Nutri-Dyne** Chef Otto	17
Mix, prepared w milk: 1 cup / **Durkee**	25
Mix, prepared: ¼ cup / **French's**	7
Chili: ¼ cup / **Del Monte**	17
Chili: 1 tbsp / **Heinz**	4

GRAMS

Chile hot dog w beef, canned: 1 oz /
   Chef Boy-ar-dee   4
Cocktail: 1 tbsp / **Estee**   3
Cream, mix, dry: 1 oz / **Nutri-Dyne** Chef Otto   17
Dill, creamy, mix for fish: 1 pkg / **Durkee**
   Roastin' Bag   4
Enchilada: ¼ cup
   Green chili, canned / **Old El Paso**   4
   Hot, canned / **Del Monte**   5
   Hot, canned / **Old El Paso**   4
   Mild, canned / **Del Monte**   5
   Mild, canned / **Old El Paso**   4
   Mix, prepared / **Durkee**   3
57 Sauce: 1 tbsp / **Heinz**   3
Green chile salsa, mild: ¼ cup / **Del Monte**   3
Hard: 1 tbsp / **Crosse & Blackwell**   8
Hollandaise, mix, prepared: ¾ cup / **Durkee**   11
Hollandaise, mix, prepared: 3 tbsp / **French's**   2
Italian, mix, dry: 1 oz / **Nutri-Dyne** Chef Otto   24
Lemon-butter, mix, prepared: 1 tbsp /
   Weight Watchers   1
Meat marinade, mix, prepared: ½ cup / **Durkee**   9
Mexican: 4 oz / **Pritikin**   8
Pizza, in can or jar: ¼ cup unless noted
   Contadina Original Quick & Easy   5
   Ragu Pizza Quick: 3 tbsp   6
   Ragu Pizza Quick Chunky: 3 tbsp   6
   w cheese: ¼ can (2.63 oz) / **Chef Boy-ar-dee**   7
   w cheese / **Contadina**   5
   w cheese: ¼ jar (3.88 oz) / **Chef Boy-ar-dee**   10
   w pepperoni / **Contadina**   5
   w pepperoni: ¼ can (2.6 oz) / **Chef Boy-ar-dee**   6
   w sausage: ¼ can (2.6 oz) / **Chef Boy-ar-dee**   5
   w tomato chunks / **Contadina**   5
Portovista, in jar
   Chef Boy-ar-dee: 3½ oz   11
   w meat: 3½ oz / **Chef Boy-ar-dee**   11
   w mushrooms: 3½ oz / **Chef Boy-ar-dee**   11
Salsa picante, hot: ¼ cup / **Del Monte**   4
Salsa picante, hot and chunky: ¼ cup / **Del Monte**   3
Salsa roja, mild: ¼ cup: / **Del Monte**   4

	GRAMS
Sauce for potatoes, scalloped, mix, dry: ⅙ pkg / **French's**	5
Sauce for potatoes, au gratin, mix, dry: ⅙ pkg / **French's**	8
Sauce for potatoes, sour cream & chives, mix, dry: ⅙ pkg / **French's**	6
Seafood cocktail: ¼ cup / **Del Monte**	17
Sloppy Joe: 5 tbsp / **Hunt's** Manwich Original	10
Sloppy Joe: 5 tbsp / **Hunt's** Manwich Mexican	9
Sour cream, mix, prepared: 2½ tbsp / **French's**	5
Spaghetti	
Canned: ¼ can (3¾ oz) / **Chef Boy-ar-dee**	12
Canned: 4 oz / **Hain** Naturals	14
Canned: 4 oz / **Hunt's** No Salt	13
in jar: ¼ jar (4 oz) / **Chef Boy-ar-dee** 16 oz	11
in jar: ⅐ jar (4.14 oz) / **Chef Boy-ar-dee** 29 oz	11
in jar: 4 oz / **Prego**	20
in jar: 4 oz / **Prego** No Salt	10
in jar: 4 oz / **Pritikin**	12
in jar: 4 oz / **Ragu**	11
in jar: 4 oz / **Ragu** Extra Thick and Zesty	15
in jar: 4 oz / **Ragu** Homestyle	12
in jar: 4 oz / **Ragu** Marinara	12
in jar: 1/3 cup / **Weight Watchers**	9
Mix, prepared: 2½ cups / **Durkee**	52
Mix, prepared: 2¼ cup / **Durkee** Extra Thick & Rich	55
Mix, prepared: 5 oz / **French's** Italian Style	15
Mix, prepared: 7 oz (⅞ cup) / **French's** Thick Homemade Style	24
Mix: ⅕ pkg / **McCormick**	5
Mix, prepared: 1 oz / **Spatini**	4
w ground beef, in jar: ¼ jar (4 oz) **Chef Boy-ar-dee** 16 oz	14
w ground beef, in jar: ⅐ jar (4.14 oz) **Chef Boy-ar-dee** 29 oz	14
w meat, canned: 4 oz / **Chef Boy-ar-dee**	12
w meat, canned: ¼ can (3¾ oz) / **Chef Boy-ar-dee** Original	13
Meat-flavored, in jar: 4 oz / **Prego**	21

GRAMS

Meat-flavored, in jar: 4 oz / **Ragu**	11
Meat-flavored, in jar: 4 oz / **Ragu** Extra Thick and Zesty	14
Meat-flavored, in jar: 4 oz / **Ragu** Homestyle	12
Meat-flavored, in jar: ⅓ oz / **Weight Watchers**	9
w mushrooms, canned: 4 oz / **Chef Boy-ar-dee**	14
w mushrooms, canned: ¼ can (3¾ oz) / **Chef Boy-ar-dee** Original	13
w mushrooms, canned: 4 oz / **Hain** Naturals	14
w mushrooms, in jar: 4 oz / **Chef Boy-ar-dee**	11
w mushrooms, in jar: 4 oz / **Prego**	21
w mushrooms, in jar: 4 oz / **Pritikin**	12
w mushrooms, in jar: 4 oz / **Ragu**	9
w mushrooms, in jar: 4 oz / **Ragu** Extra Thick and Zesty	13
w mushrooms, in jar: 4 oz / **Ragu** Homestyle	12
w mushrooms, in jar: ⅓ cup / **Weight Watchers**	9
w mushrooms, mix, prepared: 2⅔ cup / **Durkee**	48
w mushrooms, mix, prepared: 5 oz / **French's**	13
w mushrooms and cheese, canned: 4 oz / **Health Valley** Bellissimo Regular or No Salt	8
Sparerib, mix w roasting bag: 1 pkg / **Durkee** Roastin' Bag	37
Stroganoff, mix, prepared: 1/3 cup / **French's**	11
Sweet and sour: 4 oz / **Contadina**	30
Sweet and sour, mix, prepared: 1 cup / **Durkee**	45
Sweet and sour, mix, prepared: ½ cup / **French's**	14
Taco	
Hot: ¼ cup / **Del Monte**	4
Hot: 2 tbsp / **Old El Paso**	2
Mild: ¼ cup / **Del Monte**	4
Mild: 2 tbsp / **Old El Paso**	2
Teriyaki, mix, prepared: 2 tbsp / **French's**	7
Tomato, canned	
A & P: ½ cup	9
Contadina: ½ cup	9
Contadina Italian style: ½ cup	8
Del Monte: 1 cup	16
Del Monte No Salt: 1 cup	16

	GRAMS
Health Valley Natural: ½ cup	6
Health Valley No Salt: 1 cup	10
Hunt's: 4 oz	7
Hunt's Italian: 4 oz	11
Hunt's No Salt Added: 4 oz	8
Hunt's Special: 4 oz	8
Town House: 8 oz	18
w bits: 4 oz / **Hunt's**	7
w cheese: 4 oz / **Hunt's**	8
Herb: 4 oz / **Hunt's**	11
w mushrooms: 4 oz / **Hunt's**	6
w onions: 1 cup / **Del Monte**	23
w onions: 4 oz / **Hunt's**	9
White, mix, prepared w milk: 1 cup / **Durkee**	23

Seasonings

	GRAMS
1 tsp unless noted	
Ac'cent Flavor Enhancer	0
Bacon, imitation, crumbled: 1 tbsp	
Bac*Os	2
Durkee Bacon Bits	3
Durkee Bacon Chips	4
Lawry's Baconion	6
Libby's Bacon Crumbles	2
McCormick Bacon Chips	2
Barbeque / **French's**	1
Brown Seasoning & Broth: ⅛ pkg / **G. Washington's**	1
Brown Seasoning & Broth: ⅛ pkg /	
G. Washington's Kosher for Passover	1
Chili powder / **Lawry's**	1
Garlic concentrate: 1 tbsp / **Lawry's**	1
Golden Seasoning & Broth: ⅛ pkg /	
G. Washington's	1

GRAMS

Golden Seasoning & Broth: ⅛ pkg /	
G. Washington's Kosher for Passover	1
Herb blend / **Lawry's**	1
Lemon and Pepper / **French's**	1
Lemon and Pepper / **McCormick**	0–1
Lemon pepper marinade / **Lawry's**	1
Meat marinade: ⅛ pkg **French's**	2
Meat tenderizer / **French's**	0
Meat tenderizer, seasoned / **French's**	0
Meat tenderizer / **McCormick**	0–1
Meat tenderizer, seasoned / **McCormick**	0–1
Mrs. Dash	2
Mrs. Dash Low-Pepper, No Garlic	3
Onion Seasoning: ⅛ pkg / **G. Washington's**	2
Pepper, seasoned / **French's**	1
Pepper, seasoned / **Lawry's**	2
Pizza seasoning / **French's**	1
Potato Toppers: 1 tbsp / **Libby's**	4
Salad Crispins, American, Italian or French	2
Salad Crispins, Country or Swiss	2
Salad Crispins, Home	2
Salad Crunchies: 1 tbsp / **Libby's**	4
Salad Onions, instant: 1 tbsp / **French's**	3
Salad seasoning / **French's**	1
Salad Supreme / **McCormick**	0–1
Salt	
Butter flavor, imitation / **French's**	0
Celery / **French's**	0
Garlic / **French's**	1
Garlic-flavored / **Lawry's**	1
Garlic, parslied / **French's**	1
Hickory smoke / **French's**	0
Onion / **French's**	1
Onion-flavored / **Lawry's**	1
Salt 'N Spice / **McCormick**	0–1
Seasoned / **Lawry's** Seasoned Salt-Free	0–1
Seasoning salt / **French's**	1
Substitute / **Dia-Mel** Salt-It	0
Substitute / **Estee** Salt-Free	0
Seafood seasoning / **French's**	0
Season-All / **McCormick**	0–1

	GRAMS
Soup greens: 2½-oz jar	43
Stock base, beef flavor / **French's**	2
Stock base, chicken flavor / **French's**	1
Vegetable flakes, dehydrated / **French's**	1
Vegetable Seasoning & Broth: ⅛ pkg /	
G. Washington's	2

SEASONING MIXES

	GRAMS
Beef	
Lawry's Beef Ole: 1¼ oz pkg	24
Stew, mix, dry: 1 pkg / **Durkee**	22
Stew, mix, prepared: 1 cup / **Durkee**	17
Stew: ⅙ pkg / **French's**	5
Stew: 1⅔ oz pkg / **Lawry's**	24
Chili: ⅙ pkg / **McCormick**	3
Chili, Texas, mix, dry: 1 pkg / **Durkee**	23
Chili, Texas, mix, prepared: 1 cup / **Durkee**	38
Chili con carne, mix, dry: 1 pkg / **Durkee**	33
Chili con carne, mix, prepared: 1 cup / **Durkee**	31
Chili con carne: 1⅝ oz pkg / **Lawry's**	23
Chili-O: ⅙ pkg / **French's**	5
Chop suey, mix, dry: 1 pkg / **Durkee**	19
Chop suey, mix, prepared: ½ cup / **Durkee**	6
Enchilada: ¼ pkg / **French's**	5
Fried rice, mix, dry: 1 oz / **Durkee**	11
Fried rice, mix, prepared: 1 cup / **Durkee**	47
Ground beef	
Mix, dry: 1 pkg / **Durkee**	18
Mix, prepared: 1 cup / **Durkee**	9
w onions, mix, dry: 1 pkg / **Durkee**	13
w onions, mix, prepared: 1 cup / **Durkee**	7
w onions, mix, dry: ¼ pkg / **French's**	6
Hamburger, mix, dry: 1 pkg / **Durkee**	15
Hamburger, mix, prepared: 1 cup / **Durkee**	8
Hamburger, mix, dry: ¼ pkg / **French's**	5
Lemon butter, for fish, mix: 1 pkg / **Durkee**	
Roastin' Bag	17
Meatball, mix, dry: ¼ pkg / **French's**	7
Meatball, Italian, mix, dry: 1 pkg / **Durkee**	9
Meatball, Italian, mix, prepared: / **Durkee**	5

GRAMS

Meatloaf
- **Bells:** 4½ oz dry   15
- **Bells:** 4½ oz prepared   15
- **Contadina:** 1 rounded tbsp   7
- **French's:** ⅛ pkg   5
- **Nutri-Dyne** Chef Otto: 1 oz dry   16

Mrs. Dash Crispy Coating Mix: ¼ env   10

Sloppy Joe
- Mix, dry: 1 pkg / **Durkee**   29
- Mix, prepared: ½ cup / **Durkee**   12
- Mix, dry: ⅛ pkg / **French's**   4
- Mix, dry: ⅙ pkg / **McCormick**   4
- Italian, mix, dry: 1 pkg / **Durkee**   12
- Italian, mix, prepared: ½ cup / **Durkee**   10

Super Slaw: ½ cup prepared / **Libby's**   11

Taco
- Mix, dry: 1 pkg / **Durkee**   15

Mix, prepared: 1 cup / **Durkee**   8
- Mix: ⅙ pkg / **French's**   4
- Mix: ¹⁄₁₀ pkg / **McCormick**   2
- Mix: 1 pkg / **Old El Paso**   21

Soft Drinks

Some companies report their diet drinks as having less than 1 gram of carbohydrate; for convenience, we have reported these as having 1 gram. Others round off to 0 and a few report the count with a decimal. The difference is infinitesimal.

6 fl ounces unless noted

Birell, non-alcoholic beverage	8.5
Bitter lemon / **Canada Dry**	20
Bitter lemon / **Schweppes**	20
Black cherry / **Cragmont** Diet	0

GRAMS

Black cherry / **Shasta**	22
Black cherry / **Shasta** Sugar free	0
Bubble Up	19
Bubble Up Sugar Free	0
Cherry	
Cola / **Cragmont** Diet	0
Crush	25
Shasta	18.5
Shasta Sugar Free	0
Chocolate / **No-Cal**	0
Club soda / **Schweppes**	0
Club soda / **Shasta**	0
Coffee / **No-Cal**	0
Cola	
Coca-Cola	19
Coca-Cola Caffeine Free	20
diet Coke	0
diet Coke Caffeine Free	0
Cragmont Diet	0
Diet-Rite	.1
New Natural / **Health Valley**	20
Like	20
Like Sugar Free	0
No-Cal	0
Pepsi-Cola	19
Diet Pepsi	.2
Pepsi Free	19
Diet Pepsi Free	.2
Pepsi Light	1
RC 100 Caffeine Free	19
Diet RC Caffeine Free	.1
Royal Crown	19
Shasta	20
Shasta Sugar Free	1
Cream soda	
Cragmont Diet	1
Crush, red/brown	21
No-Cal	0
Shasta	21
Shasta Sugar Free	1
Diet Skipper / **Cragmont**	1

GRAMS

Dr. Pepper	18
Dr. Pepper Sugar Free	.2
Fresca	0
Fruit punch / **Shasta**	23
Ginger ale	
Cragmont Diet	.1
Canada Dry	16
Fanta	16
Health Valley	18
No-Cal	0
Schweppes	16
Schweppes Sugar Free	0
Shasta	16
Shasta Sugar Free	1
Ginger beer / **Schweppes**	17
Ginseng root beer / **Health Valley**	25
Grape	
Canada Dry	24
Crush	25
Fanta	22
Hi-C	20
Nehi	22
Schweppes	24
Shasta	24
Shasta Sugar Free	1
Grapefruit	
Cragmont Diet	1
Shasta	22
Shasta Sugar Free	1
Grapefruit, lime / **No-Cal**	0
Iced tea / **Shasta**	16.5
Lemon / **Hi-C**	18
Lemon / **Schweppes**	15.6
Lemon-lime	
Cragmont Diet	1
Health Valley	14.7
No-Cal	0
Shasta	19.5
Shasta Sugar Free	1
Mandarin lime / **Health Valley**	17.4
Mello Yello	22

	GRAMS
Mineral water / **Schweppes**	0
Mountain Dew	22
Mr Pibb	19
Mr Pibb Sugar Free	.2
Orange	
Cragmont Diet	1
Crush	25
Crush Sugar Free	1
Fanta	23
Hi-C	20
Nehi	23
No-Cal	0
Schweppes Sparkling	22
Shasta	23.5
Shasta Sugar Free	1
Pineapple / **Crush**	25
Punch / **Hi-C**	20
Red Cherry / **No-Cal**	0
Red creme / **Schweppes**	21
Rondo / **Schweppes**	19
Root beer	
A & W	21
A & W Sugar Free	1
Canada Dry Barrelhead	20
Cragmont Diet	1
Dad's	21
Dad's Diet	1
Fanta	20
Health Valley Old Fashioned	18
Health Valley Sarsaparilla	19
Hires	19
Hires Sugar Free	1
Nehi	22
No-Cal	0
Ramblin'	23
Ramblin' Sugar Free	.2
Schweppes	19
Shasta	20
Shasta Sugar Free	1
7 Up	18
Diet 7 Up	0

	GRAMS
Sprite	18
Sprite, Diet	0
Strawberry	
Crush	22
Nehi	22
No-Cal	0
Shasta	19.5
Shasta Sugar Free	1
Sun-Drop	23
Sun-Drop Sugar Free	1
Tab	.2
Teem	18.7
Tonic	
Cragmont Diet	1
Schweppes	16
Schweppes Sugar Free	0
Shasta	16
Vichy/Water / **Schweppes**	0
Wild Berry / **Health Valley**	17

Soups

	GRAMS
Prepared according to package directions, unless noted	
Asparagus, cream of, canned: 8 fl oz / **Campbell's**	11
Bean, canned	
Health Valley Chunky: 4 fl oz	14
Health Valley Old Fashioned: 4 fl oz	13
Health Valley Old Fashioned No Salt: 4 fl oz	12
w bacon: 8 fl oz / **Campbell's**	21
Black bean: 8 fl oz / **Campbell's**	17
Black bean w sherry: ½ can /	
Crosse & Blackwell	18
Chowder, pinto bean: 8½ fl oz / **Luck's**	
Country	34

GRAMS

w ham: 11 fl oz / **Campbell's** Soup for One
   Old Fashioned   30
w ham, ready to serve: 11 fl oz / **Campbell's**
   Chunky Old Fashioned   37
w ham: 8½ fl oz / **Luck's** Country
   Old Fashioned   30
w ham: 9½ fl oz / **Progresso**   30
w ham and onions: 8½ fl oz / **Luck's** Country   28
w sausage: 8½ fl oz / **Luck's** Country   25
Bean barley stew, mix: 1.6 oz dry / **Fearn**   30
Blackbean creole, mix: 1.9 oz dry / **Fearn**   28
Beef, canned
   Campbell's: 8 fl oz   10
   Campbell's Chunky: 10¾ fl oz   23
   Progresso: 9½ fl oz   19
   Cannelloni, mini, w vegetables: 8¼ fl oz /
      Chef Boy-ar-dee Soup di Pasta   28
   Mushroom: 10¾ fl oz / **Campbell's**
      Chunky Low Sodium   23
   Noodle: 8 fl oz / **Campbell's**   7
   Noodle: 8 fl oz / **Campbell's** Homestyle   8
   Ravioli w vegetables: 8¼ fl oz /
      Chef Boy-ar-dee Soup di Pasta   25
   Stroganoff style: 10¾ fl oz / **Campbell's**
      Chunky   28
   Vegetable: 9½ fl oz / **Progresso**   19
   Vegetable: 10½ fl oz / **Progresso**   21
Beef flavor, mix: 7 fl oz / **Lipton** Cup-A-Soup
  Lots-A-Noodles   21
Beef flavor, mix: 6 fl oz / **Lipton** Cup-A-Soup   1
Beef vegetable noodle, mix: 8 fl oz / **Lipton** Hearty   14
Borscht, canned or in jars
   Manischewitz: 8 fl oz   20
   Manischewitz Low Calorie: 8 fl oz   4
Bouillon
   Beef, cube: 1 cube / **Herb-Ox**   0–1
   Beef, instant: 1 tsp / **Lite-Line** Low Sodium   2
   Beef, instant: 1 tsp / **Wyler's**   1
   Chicken, cube: 1 cube / **Herb-Ox**   0–1
   Chicken, cube: 1 cube / **Wyler's**   1
   Chicken, instant: 1 tsp / **Lite-Line** Low Sodium   2

	GRAMS
Onion, cube: 1 cube / **Herb-Ox**	1
Onion, instant: 1 tsp / **Wyler's**	1
Vegetable, cube: 1 cube / **Herb-Ox**	0–1
Broth	
Beef, canned: 8 fl oz / **Campbell's**	1
Beef, canned: 8 fl oz / **College Inn**	1
Beef, canned: 4 fl oz / **Health Valley**	1
Beef, canned: 4 fl oz / **Health Valley** No Salt	1
Beef, canned: 7¼ fl oz / **Swanson**	1
Beef, mix: 1 packet / **Herb-Ox**	1
Beef, mix: 1 packet / **Herb-Ox** Low Sodium	2
Beef, mix: 1 packet / **Weight Watchers**	2
Chicken, canned: 8 fl oz / **Campbell's**	3
Chicken, canned: 1 can / **Campbell's**	
Low Sodium	3
Chicken, canned: 8 fl oz / **College Inn**	0
Chicken, canned: 4 fl oz / **Health Valley**	0
Chicken, canned: 4 fl oz / **Health Valley**	
No Salt	1
Chicken, canned: 6⅞ fl oz / **Pritikin**	0
Chicken, canned: 7¼ fl oz / **Swanson**	2
Chicken, mix: 1 packet / **Herb-Ox**	2
Chicken, mix: 1 packet / **Herb-Ox** Low Sodium	2
Chicken, mix: 6 fl oz / **Lipton** Cup-A-Broth	4
Chicken, mix: 1 packet / **Weight Watchers**	2
Chicken and noodles, canned: 8 fl oz /	
Campbell's	8
Chicken and rice, canned: 8 fl oz / **Campbell's**	8
Onion, mix: 1 packet / **Herb-Ox**	2
Onion, mix: 1 packet / **Weight Watchers**	2
Scotch, canned: 8 fl oz / **Campbell's**	9
Vegetable, mix: 1 packet / **Herb-Ox**	2
Celery, cream of, canned: 8 fl oz / **Campbell's**	8
Celery, cream of, canned: 10 fl oz / **Rokeach**	12
Celery, cream of, canned, prepared w milk:	
10 fl oz / **Rokeach**	19
Cheddar cheese, canned: 8 fl oz / **Campbell's**	10
Chickarina w tiny meatballs, canned: 9½ fl oz /	
Progresso	8
Chicken	
Alphabet, canned: 8 fl oz / **Campbell's**	10

GRAMS

Cream of, canned: 8 fl oz / **Campbell's**	9
Cream of, mix: 6 fl oz / **Estee**	8
Cream of, mix: 6 fl oz / **Lipton** Cup-A-Soup	9
Cream of, mix: 7 fl oz / **Lipton** Cup-A-Soup Lots-A-Noodles	22
'n Dumplings, canned: 8 fl oz / **Campbell's**	9
Flavor, mix: 7 fl oz / **Lipton** Cup-A-Soup Lots-A-Noodles	23
Flavor, mix: 6 fl oz / **Lipton** Cup-A-Soup Trim	1
Gumbo, canned: 8 fl oz / **Campbell's**	8
Hearty, mix: 6 fl oz / **Lipton** Country Style Cup-A-Soup	10
Home style, canned: 9½ fl oz / **Progresso**	8
Home style, canned: 10½ fl oz / **Progresso**	9
Mushroom, creamy, canned: 8 fl oz / **Campbell's**	9
Noodle, canned: 8 fl oz / **Campbell's**	8
Noodle, canned: 10¾ / **Campbell's** Chunky	20
Noodle, canned: 8 fl oz / **Campbell's** Homestyle	8
w noodles, canned: 1 can / **Campbell's** Low Sodium	17
and noodles, canned: 11 fl oz / **Campbell's** Soup for One	14
Noodle: 8 fl oz / **Dia-Mel**	7
Noodle, canned: 9½ fl oz / **Progresso**	10
Noodles, canned: 10½ fl oz / **Progresso**	11
Noodle, mix: 8 fl oz / **Lipton**	9
Noodle w meat, mix: 6 fl oz / **Lipton** Cup-A-Soup	6
NoodleO's, canned: 8 fl oz / **Campbell's**	9
Old Fashioned, canned: 10¾ fl oz / **Campbell's** Chunky	21
w pasta, meatballs, and chicken, canned: 8 fl oz / **Chef Boy-ar-dee** Soup di Pasta	14
Ravioli, mini, canned: 8¼ fl oz / **Chef Boy-ar-dee** Soup di Pasta	19
w ribbon pasta, canned: 7¼ fl oz / **Pritikin**	8
Rice, canned: ½ can / **Campbell's** Chunky 19 oz can	15
w rice, canned: 8 fl oz / **Campbell's**	7
Rice, mix: 6 fl oz / **Lipton** Cup-A-Soup	7

GRAMS

Rice w vegetables, canned: 9½ fl oz / **Progresso**	22
and stars, canned: 8 fl oz / **Campbell's**	7
Supreme, mix: 6 fl oz / **Lipton** Country Style Cup-A-Soup	11
Vegetable, canned: 8 fl oz / **Campbell's**	8
Vegetable, canned: ½ can / **Campbell's** chunky 19-oz can	19
Vegetable, canned: 1 can / **Campbell's** Chunky Low Sodium	20
Vegetable, canned: 11 fl oz / **Campbell's** Soup for One	13
Vegetable, canned: 7¼ fl oz / **Pritikin**	12
Vegetable, mix: 6 fl oz / **Lipton** Cup-A-Soup	7
Chili beef, canned: 8 fl oz / **Campbell's**	17
Chili beef, canned / **Campbell's** Chunky	37
Chix w vegetables and pasta, canned: 8¼ fl oz / **Chef Boy-ar-dee** Soup di Pasta	16
Clam chowder, canned	
Health Valley: 4 fl oz	10
Health Valley Chunky, Regular or No Salt: 4 fl oz	9
Health Valley No Salt: 4 fl oz	9
Manhattan style / **Campbell's**: 8 fl oz	11
Manhattan style / **Campbell's** Chunky: 10¾ oz	24
Manhattan style / **Crosse & Blackwell**: ½ can	9
Manhattan style / **Doxsee**: 6 fl oz	9
Manhattan style / **Progresso**: 9½ fl oz	21
Manhattan style / **Snow's**: 7½ fl oz	9
New England / **Campbell's**; 8 fl oz	11
New England, prepared w milk / **Campbell's**: 8 fl oz	17
New England / **Campbell's** Chunky: 10¾ oz	17
New England / **Campbell's** Soup for One: 11 fl oz	19
New England, prepared w milk / **Campbell's** Soup for One: 11 fl oz	24
New England / **Crosse & Blackwell**: ½ can	14
New England / **Doxsee**: 6 fl oz	12
New England / **Hain** Naturals: 9½ fl oz	23

GRAMS

New England, prepared w milk: 7½ fl oz /
   Snow's   13
New England, frozen pouch: 8 fl oz /
   Stouffer's   19
Consomme, beef, canned: 8 fl oz / **Campbell's**   2
Consomme, Madrilene, clear, canned: ½ can /
  Crosse & Blackwell   4
Consomme, Madrilene, red, canned: ½ can /
  Crosse & Blackwell   5
Corn chowder, New England, canned,
  prepared w milk: 7½ fl oz / **Snow's**   18
Escarole in chicken broth, canned: 9½ fl oz /
  Progresso   3
Fish chowder, New England, canned,
  prepared w milk: 7½ fl oz / **Snow's**   11
Gazpacho, canned: ½ can / **Crosse & Blackwell**   1
Ham and butter bean, canned: 10¾ oz /
  Campbell's Chunky   33
Lentil
  Canned: 9½ fl oz / **Hain** Naturals regular or
    No Salt   30
  Canned: 4 fl oz / **Health Valley** regular or
    No Salt   12
  Canned: 9½ fl oz / **Progresso**   26
  Canned: 10½ fl oz / **Progresso**   28
  Minestrone, mix: 1.9 oz dry / **Fearn**   31
Macaroni and bean, canned: 9½ fl oz / **Progresso**   30
Meatball alphabet, canned: 8 fl oz / **Campbell's**   11
Minestrone
  Canned: 8 fl oz / **Campbell's**   11
  Canned: ½ can / **Campbell's** Chunky
    19-oz can   21
  Canned: ½ can / **Crosse & Blackwell**   18
  Canned: 9½ fl oz / **Hain** Naturals
    regular or No Salt   33
  Canned: 4 fl oz / **Health Valley**   1
  Canned: 4 fl oz / **Health Valley** Chunky   12
  Canned: 4 fl oz / **Health Valley** No Salt   13
  Canned: 4 fl oz / **Health Valley**
    No Salt Chunky   13

GRAMS

Canned: 7⅜ fl oz / **Pritikin**	19
Canned: 10½ fl oz / **Progresso**	27
Mix: 6 fl oz / **Manischewitz**	9
Beef, canned: 9½ fl oz / **Progresso**	19
Chicken, canned: 9½ fl oz / **Progresso**	15
w meatballs and pasta, canned 8¼ fl oz / **Chef Boy-ar-dee** Soup di Pasta	17

Mushroom

Canned: 9½ fl oz / **Hain** Naturals	16
Canned: 4 fl oz / **Health Valley** Regular or No Salt	8
Beef flavor, mix: 8 fl oz / **Lipton**	7
Beefy, canned: 8 fl oz / **Campbell's**	5
Bisque, canned: ½ can / **Crosse & Blackwell**	8
Cream of, canned: 8 fl oz / **Campbell's**	9
Cream of, canned: / **Campbell's** Low Sodium	16
Cream of, canned: 11 fl oz / **Campbell's** Soup for One	14
Cream of, canned: 10 fl oz / **Rokeach**	13
Cream of, prepared w milk: 10 fl oz / **Rokeach**	20
Cream of, mix: 6 fl oz / **Lipton** Cup-A-Soup	9
Cream of, mix: 6 fl oz / **Nutri-Dyne** Med-Diet	20
Cream of, mix: 6 fl oz / **Estee**	9
Golden, canned: 8 fl oz / **Campbell's**	10
Golden w chicken broth, mix: 8 fl oz / **Lipton**	8

Noodle

Mix: 8 fl oz / **Lipton** Giggle Noodle	12
Mix: 8 fl oz / **Lipton** Ring-O-Noodle	9
Mix: 6 fl oz / **Lipton** Cup-A-Soup Ring	9
w beef flavor, mix: 6 fl oz / **Lipton** Cup-A-Soup	8
w chicken, canned: 8 fl oz / **Campbell's** Curly	9
w chicken broth, mix: 8 fl oz / **Lipton**	10
w ground beef, canned: 8 fl oz / **Campbell's**	10
w vegetables and chicken broth, mix: 8 fl oz / **Lipton** Hearty	12

Onion

Mix: 8 fl oz / **Lipton**	6
Mix: 6 fl oz / **Lipton** Cup-A-Soup	5
Beefy, mix: 8 fl oz / **Lipton**	5
Cream of, canned: 8 fl oz / **Campbell's**	12

GRAMS

Cream of, canned, prepared w milk and water: 8 fl oz / **Campbell's**	15
French, canned: 8 fl oz / **Campbell's**	9
French, canned: 1 can / **Campbell's** Low Sodium	7
French, canned: 9½ fl oz / **Progresso**	9
Golden, w chicken broth, mix: 8 fl oz / **Lipton**	10
Mushroom, mix: 8 fl oz / **Lipton**	7
Oriental style, mix: 7 fl oz / **Lipton** Cup-A-Soup Lots-A Noodles	20
Oyster stew, canned: 8 fl oz / **Campbell's**	5
Oyster stew, canned, prepared w milk: 8 fl oz / **Campbell's**	10
Pea, green, canned: 8 fl oz / **Campbell's**	11
Pea, green, mix: 6 fl oz / **Lipton** Cup-A-Soup	16
Pea, split	
Canned: 1 can / **Campbell's** Low Sodium	37
Canned: 9½ fl oz / **Hain** Naturals	37
Canned: 9½ fl oz / **Hain** Naturals No Salt	40
Canned: 4 fl oz / **Health Valley**	15
Canned: 4 fl oz / **Health Valley** Chunky	10
Canned: 4 fl oz / **Health Valley** No Salt	14
Canned: 4 fl oz / **Health Valley** No Salt Chunky	11
Mix: 1.8 oz dry / **Fearn**	26
Mix: 6 fl oz / **Manischewitz**	9
w ham, canned: 10¾ fl oz / **Campbell's** Chunky	33
w ham, frozen pouch: 8¼ fl oz / **Stouffer's**	27
w ham and bacon, canned: 8 fl oz / **Campbell's**	24
Pea, Virginia, mix: 6 fl oz / **Lipton** Country Style Cup-A-Soup	18
Pepper pot, canned: 8 fl oz / **Campbell's**	9
Potato	
Cream of, canned: 8 fl oz / **Campbell's**	11
Cream of, canned, prepared w milk and water: 8 fl oz / **Campbell's**	14
Old-Fashioned, canned: 4 fl oz / **Health Valley**	11
Old-Fashioned, canned: 4 fl oz / **Health Valley** No Salt	9

GRAMS

Seafood chowder, **New England,** canned, prepared w milk: 7½ fl oz / **Snow's**	11
Shrimp bisque, canned: ½ can / **Crosse & Blackwell**	7
Shrimp, cream of, canned: 8 fl oz / **Campbell's**	8
Shrimp, cream of, canned, prepared w milk: 8 fl oz / **Campbell's**	13
Sirloin burger, canned: 10¾ fl oz / **Campbell's** Chunky	23
Spinach, cream of, frozen pouch: 8 fl oz / **Stouffer's**	17
Steak and potato, canned: 10¾ fl oz / **Campbell's** Chunky	24

Tomato

Canned: 8 fl oz / **Campbell's**	17
Canned, prepared w milk: 8 fl oz / **Campbell's**	22
Canned: 9½ fl oz / **Hain** Naturals	23
Canned: 9½ fl oz / **Hain** Naturals No Salt	23
Canned: 4 fl oz / **Health Valley**	7
Canned: 4 fl oz / **Health Valley** No Salt	6
Canned: 10 fl oz / **Rokeach**	20
Canned, prepared w milk: 10 fl oz / **Rokeach**	27
Mix: 6 fl oz / **Estee**	10
Mix: 6 fl oz / **Lipton** Cup-A-Soup	17
Mix: 6 fl oz / **Nutri-Dyne** Med-Diet	21
Beefy, mix: 6 fl oz / **Lipton** Cup-A-Soup Trim	2
Bisque, canned: 8 fl oz / **Campbell's**	23
w macaroni shells, canned: 10½ fl oz / **Progresso**	24
w meatballs and pasta, canned: 8¼ fl oz / **Chef Boy-ar-dee** Soup di Pasta	21
Onion, mix: 8 fl oz / **Lipton**	15
Rice, canned: 8 fl oz / **Campbell's** Old Fashioned	22
Rice, canned: 10 fl oz / **Rokeach**	25
Royale, canned: 11 fl oz / **Campbell's** Soup for One	35
w tomato pieces, canned: 1 can / **Campbell's** Low Sodium	30
w tomato pieces, canned: 7¼ fl oz / **Pritikin**	14
Vegetable, mix: 6 fl oz / **Estee**	13

GRAMS

Vegetable, mix: 7 fl oz / **Lipton** Cup-A-Soup Lots-A-Noodles	21
Vegetable noodle, mix: 8 fl oz / **Lipton** Hearty	15
Turkey noodle, canned: 8 fl oz / **Campbell's**	8
Turkey vegetable, canned: 8 fl oz / **Campbell's**	8
Vegetable	
Canned: 8 fl oz / **Campbell's**	12
Canned: 10¾ fl oz / **Campbell's** Chunky	23
Canned: 8 fl oz / **Campbell's** Old Fashioned	9
Canned: 11 fl oz / **Campbell's** Soup for One	18
Canned: 4 fl oz / **Health Valley**	9
Canned: 4 fl oz / **Health Valley** Chunky	7
Canned: 4 fl oz / **Health Valley** No Salt	10
Canned: 4 fl oz / **Health Valley** No Salt Chunky	10
Canned: 8½ fl oz / **Luck's** Country	17
Canned: 7⅜ fl oz / **Pritikin**	14
Mix: 6 fl oz / **Manischewitz**	9
Beef, canned: 8 fl oz / **Campbell's**	8
Beef, canned: 10¾ oz / **Campbell's** Chunky	20
Beef, canned: 1 can / **Campbell's** Chunky Low Sodium	19
Beef, canned: 8¼ fl oz / **Chef Boy-ar-dee** Soup di Pasta	19
Beef, mix: 6 fl oz / **Lipton** Cup-A-Soup	8
Beef and Bacon, canned: 11 fl oz / **Campbell's** Soup for One Burly	20
w beef stock, mix: 8 fl oz / **Lipton**	9
Chicken, canned: 9½ fl oz / **Hain** Naturals Regular or No Salt	15
Country, canned: 8¼ fl oz / **Chef Boy-ar-dee** Soup di Pasta	18
Country, mix: 8 fl oz / **Lipton**	14
Cream of, mix: 6 fl oz / **Estee**	14
Garden, mix: 7 fl oz / **Lipton** Cup-A-Soup Lots-A-Noodles	23
Harvest, mix: 6 fl oz / **Lipton** Country Style Cup-A-Soup	20
Herb, mix: 6 fl oz / **Lipton** Cup-A-Soup Trim	1
Italian, canned: 8¼ fl oz / **Chef Boy-ar-dee** Soup di Pasta	16

GRAMS

	GRAMS
Mediterranean, canned: ½ can / **Campbell's** Chunky 19-oz can	24
Soup for dip, mix: 8 oz / **Lipton**	8
Spanish style, canned: 8 fl oz / **Campbell's**	10
Spring, mix: 6 fl oz / **Lipton** Cup-A-Soup	7
Vegetarian, canned: 8 fl oz / **Campbell's**	12
Vegetarian, canned: 9½ fl oz / **Hain** Naturals	25
Vegetarian, canned: 9½ fl oz / **Hain** Naturals No Salt	25
Vichysoisse, cream of, canned: ½ can / **Crosse & Blackwell**	5
Won ton, canned: 8 fl oz / **Campbell's**	5

Spaghetti and Spaghetti Dishes

	GRAMS
Spaghetti, plain, enriched, cooked firm, "al dente": 1 cup	39
Spaghetti, plain, enriched, cooked, tender stage: 1 cup	32
Spaghetti, in tomato sauce, canned	
Franco-American UFOs: 7½ oz	35
Franco-American UFOs w meteors: 7½ oz	31
w beef: 7½ oz / **Chef Boy-ar-dee** Spaghetti 'n Beef 15-oz can	25
w beef: 7-oz can / **Ezo**	25
w beef: 7 oz can / **Ezo** Spaghetti 'N Beef	25
w cheese: 7½ oz / **Chef Boy-ar-dee** 15-oz can	31
w cheese: 8 oz / **Chef Boy-ar-dee** 40-oz can	30
w cheese: 7⅜ oz / **Franco-American**	36
w cheese sauce: 7½ oz / **Franco-American** SpaghettiOs	33
w cheese: 7¾ oz / **Heinz**	30

GRAMS

w frankfurters: 7⅜ oz / **Franco-American**
SpaghettiOs   26
w meat sauce: 7½ oz / **Franco-American**   26
w meat sauce: 7½ oz / **Heinz**   21
w meatballs: 7½ oz / **Chef Boy-ar-dee**
15-oz can   29
w meatballs: 8 oz / **Chef Boy-ar-dee** 40-oz can   30
w meatballs: 8½ oz / **Chef Boy-ar-dee**
Spaghetti & Meatballs 25½-oz can   30
w meatballs: 8 oz / **Dia-Mel**   24
w meatballs: 7-oz can / **Enzo**   26
w meatballs: 7⅜ oz / **Franco-American**   27
w meatballs: 7⅜ oz / **Franco-American**
SpaghettiOs   25
w meatballs: 7½ oz / **Lido Club** Spaghetti
Rings & Little Meat Balls   26
Spaghetti w sauce, frozen
Banquet Casserole: 8 oz   35
Light and Elegant: 10¼ oz   40
Morton Casserole: 8 oz   31
Stouffer's: 14 oz   62
Stouffer's Lean Cuisine: 11½ oz   38
w breaded veal: 8¼ oz / **Swanson Entrée**   29
Spaghetti and sauce, mixes
Chef Boy-ar-dee Dinner w meat sauce
(19½ oz): ¼ pkg   42
Chef Boy-ar-dee Dinner w meat sauce:
(26 oz): ⅛ pkg   43
Chef Boy-ar-dee Spaghetti and Meatball
Dinner (21¼ oz): ¼ pkg   43
Chef Boy-ar-dee Dinner w mushroom sauce:
(19½ oz): ¼ pkg   41
Hamburger Helper: 1/5 pkg   31
Kraft Dinner: ¾ cup prepared   31
Kraft Dinner, American Style: 1 cup prepared   44
Kraft Tangy Italian Style: 1 cup prepared   42

Spices

1 teaspoon	GRAMS
Allspice	1.4
Anise seed	1.1
Basil, ground	.9
Bay leaf	.5
Caraway seed	1.1
Cardamom, ground	1.4
Celery seed	.9
Chervil, dried	.3
Chili powder	1.5
Cinnamon, ground	2
Cloves, ground	1.3
Coriander leaf, dried	.4
Coriander seed	1
Cumin seed	1
Curry powder	1.2
Dill seed	1.2
Dill weed	.6
Fennel seed	1.1
Fenugreek seed	2.2
Garlic powder	2.1
Ginger, ground	1.3
Mace, ground	.9
Marjoram, dried	.4
Mustard seed	1.2
Nutmeg, ground	1.1
Onion powder	1.7
Oregano, ground	1
Paprika	1.2
Parsley, dried	.2
Pepper, black	1.4
Pepper, red or cayenne	1.1
Pepper, white	1.7
Poppy seed	.7
Rosemary, dried	.8
Saffron	.5

	GRAMS
Sage, ground	.5
Savory, ground	1
Sesame seeds	.3
Tarragon, ground	.9
Thyme, ground	.9
Turmeric, ground	1.5

Spreads

	GRAMS
1 oz = about ¼ cup	
Chicken, canned: 1 oz / **Swanson**	2
Chicken, canned: ½ can (2.4 oz) / **Underwood** Chunky	3
Chicken salad, canned: ¼ can / **Carnation** Spreadables	4
Ham, deviled, canned: 1½ oz / **Libby's**	0
Ham salad, canned: ¼ can / **Carnation** Spreadables	4
Liverwurst, canned: ½ can (2.4 oz) / **Underwood**	3
Pâté, liver, canned: ½ can (2.4 oz) / **Underwood** Sell's	3
Peanut butter: 1 tbsp unless noted	
Bama Creamy	4
Bama Crunchy	3
Country Pure Chunky: about 1 oz / **Safeway**	6
Country Pure Creamy: about 1 oz / **Safeway**	6
Dia-Mel	3
Jif Creamy	3
Jif Crunchy	3
Laura Scudder's Homogenized	3
Laura Scudder's Old Fashioned	2
NuMade Chunky: about 1 oz	5
NuMade Creamy: about 1 oz	5
Real Roast Chunky / **Safeway**: about 1 oz	6
Real Roast Creamy / **Safeway**: about 1 oz	6

	GRAMS
Skippy Creamy	2
Skippy Super Chunk	2
Goober Grape / **Smucker's**	9
Potted meat, canned: 1.83 oz / **Libby's**	0
Sandwich spread: 1 tbsp unless noted	
NuMade (whole egg)	4
NuMade (egg yoke)	4
Oscar Mayer: 1 oz	3
Tuna salad, canned: ¼ can (1.9 oz) / **Carnation** Spreadables	3
Turkey salad, canned: ¼ can / **Carnation** Spreadables	3

Sugar and Sweeteners

	GRAMS
Honey, strained or extracted: 1 tbsp	17
Honey, strained or extracted: 1 cup	279
Fructose: 1 tsp	3
Sugar	
Brown, not packed: 1 cup	140
Brown, packed: 1 cup	212
Maple: 1 oz	25
Powdered, unsifted: 1 cup	119
Powdered, unsifted: 1 tbsp	8
White, granulated: 1 cup	199
White, granulated: 1 tbsp	12
White, granulated: 1 tsp	4
Sugar, cinnamon: 1 tsp / **French's**	4
Sugar substitute, granulated	
Equal: 1 pkt	1
Equal: 1 tablet	.5
Weight Watchers: 1 pkt	1
Sweetener, artificial: 6 drops / **Dia-Mel** Sweet 'n It	0

Syrups

	GRAMS
Pancake and waffle	
Aunt Jemima: 1 fl oz	26
Aunt Jemima Lite: 1 fl oz	15
Cary's Lite: 1 tbsp	8
Cary's Low Calorie: 1 tbsp	2
Golden Griddle: 1 tbsp	13
Karo: 1 tbsp	15
Log Cabin, buttered: 1 tbsp	13
Log Cabin Country Kitchen	13
Log Cabin Maple-Honey	14
Mrs. Butterworth's: 1 tbsp	13
Nutri-Dyne Elwood: ½ oz	1
Corn, dark: 1 tbsp / **Karo**	15
Corn, light: 1 tbsp / **Karo**	15
Fruit: 2 tbsp / **Smucker's**	26
Maple, pure: 1 tbsp	15
Molasses, unsulphured: 1 tbsp / **Grandma's**	15
Sorghum: 1 tbsp	14

Tea

Brewed, plain

Ice tea, canned, lemon-flavored: 8 fl oz / **Lipton**	20
Ice tea, canned, lemon-flavored, sugar free: 8 fl oz / **Lipton**	0
Ice tea, instant: 8 fl oz unless noted	
Crystal Light, sugar free	0
Lipton	0
Lemon-flavored / **Lipton**, sugar free	0
Lemon-flavored / **Nestea**	0
Lemon-flavored w nutrasweet / **Lipton**	0
Lemon-flavored w sugar / **Lipton**	16
Lemon-flavored w sugar: 6 fl oz / **Nestea**	17
Lemon-flavored w sugar / **Wyler's**	21

Thickeners

Cornstarch: 1 tbsp	
Argo	8.3
Duryea's	8.3
Kingsford's	8.3
Potato starch: 1 oz / **Manischewitz**	24

Toppings

	GRAMS
1 tbsp unless noted	
Blueberry / **Dia-Mel**	
Butterscotch / **Smucker's**	16
Caramel / **Smucker's**	16
Chocolate	
Dia-Mel	1
Hershey's	9
Smucker's	14
Fudge / **Hershey's**	7
Fudge / **Smucker's**	16
Hot caramel / **Smuckers**	14
Hot fudge / **Smucker's**	9
Peanut butter caramel / **Smucker's**	15
Pecans in syrup / **Smucker's**	14
Pineapple / **Smucker's**	16
Strawberry / **Smucker's**	15
Swiss milk chocolate fudge / **Smucker's**	16
Smucker's Magic Shell: 4 tsp	11
Walnuts in syrup / **Smucker's**	14
Whipped	
Nondairy, frozen / **Cool Whip**	1
Nondairy, frozen / **Cool Whip** Extra Creamy	1
Nondairy, frozen / **Dover Farms**	1
Mix, prepared / **Dream Whip**	1
Mix, prepared / **D-Zerta**	0
Mix, prepared / **Estee**	0–1

$\mathbf{V}$egetables

FRESH

	GRAMS
Amaranth, raw, leaves: 1 lb	29.5
Artichoke: 1 medium	12
Asparagus	
Raw: 1 lb	22.7
Raw, cut (1½–2 in): 1 cup	6.8
Cooked, cut (1½–2 in), drained: 1 cup	5.2
Spears, cooked, drained: 1 small	1.4
Spears, cooked, drained: 1 medium	2.2
Spears, cooked, drained: 1 large	3.6
Bamboo shoots, raw, 1-in pieces: 1 lb	23.6
Barley, pearled, light: 1 cup	157.6
Barley, pearled, Pot or Scotch: 1 cup	154.4
Bean curd (tofu): 1 piece (2½ x 2¾ x 1 in)	2.9
Beans	
Great Northern, cooked, drained: 1 cup	38.2
Lima, immature (green), raw: 1 cup	34.3
Lima, immature (green), cooked, drained: 1 cup	33.7
Lima, mature, cooked, drained: 1 cup	48.6
Mung, mature, dry, raw: 1 cup	126.6
Mung, mature, dry, raw: 1 lb	273.5
Mung, sprouted seeds, raw: 1 cup	6.9
Mung, sprouted seeds, cooked, drained: 1 cup	6.5
Pea (navy), cooked, drained: 1 cup	40.3
Pinto, dry, raw: 1 cup	121
Pinto or calico or red Mexican, dry, raw: 1 lb	288.9
Red, dry, cooked: ½ cup	21.4
Red, dry, raw: ½ cup	61.9
Red, kidney, cooked, drained: 1 cup	39.6
Snap, green, raw, cut: 1 cup	7.8

GRAMS

Snap, green, cooked, drained: 1 cup	6.8
Snap, yellow or wax, raw, cut: 1 cup	6.6
Snap, yellow or wax, cooked, drained: 1 cup	5.8
White, dry, raw: 1 lb	278.1
Beets, common, red, raw, peeled, diced: 1 cup	13.4
Beets, common, red, peeled, cooked, drained, whole (2-in diam): 2 beets	7.2
Beets, common, red, peeled, cooked, drained, diced or sliced: 1 cup	12.2
Beet greens, common, edible leaves and stems, raw: 1 lb	20.9
Beet greens, common, edible leaves and stems, cooked, drained: 1 cup	4.8
Broadbeans, raw, immature seeds: 1 lb	80.7
Broadbeans, raw, mature seeds, dry: 1 lb	264
Broccoli	
Stalks, raw: 1 lb	26.8
Cooked, drained: 1 small stalk	6.3
Cooked, drained: 1 medium stalk	8.1
Cooked, drained: 1 large stalk	12.6
Cooked, drained, ½-in pieces: 1 cup	7
Cooked, drained, whole or cut: 1 lb	20.4
Brussels sprouts, cooked: ½ cup	5
Brussels sprouts, raw: 9 med	8.3
Cabbage	
Raw: 1 lb	24.5
Raw, ground: 1 cup	8.1
Raw, shredded coarsely or sliced: 1 cup	3.8
Raw, shredded finely or chopped: 1 cup	4.9
Chinese, raw: 1 lb	20.9
Chinese, raw, 1-in pieces: 1 cup	2.3
Red, raw: 1 lb	31.3
Red, raw, shredded coarsely or sliced: 1 cup	4.8
Red, raw, shredded finely or chopped: 1 cup	6.2
Savoy, raw: 1 lb	20.9
Savoy, raw, shredded coarsely or sliced: 1 cup	3.2
Spoon, raw, 1-in pieces: 1 cup	2
Spoon, cooked, drained, 1-in pieces: 1 cup	4.1
Carrots	
Raw: 1 carrot (2⅞ oz)	7
Raw: 1 lb	44

GRAMS

Raw, grated or shredded: 1 cup	10.7
Raw, strips: 1 oz (6–8 strips)	2.7
Cooked, drained, diced: 1 cup	10.3
Cooked, drained, sliced crosswise: 1 cup	11

Cauliflower
Raw: 1 head (1.9 lb)	44.7
Raw, flowerbuds, whole: 1 cup	5.2
Raw, flowerbuds, sliced: 1 cup	4.4
Raw, flowerbuds, chopped: 1 cup	6
Cooked, drained: 1 cup	5.1

Celeriac, raw: 4 to 6 roots	8.5

Celery
Raw: 1 lb	17.7
Raw, large outer stalk (8-in long, 1½-in wide): 1 stalk	1.6
Raw, small inner stalk (5-in long, ¾-in wide): 3 stalks	2
Raw, chopped or diced: 1 cup	4.7
Cooked, diced: 1 cup	4.7

Chard, Swiss, raw: 1 lb	20.9
Chard, Swiss, cooked, drained, leaves: 1 cup	5.8
Chayote, raw: ½ medium squash	7.1
Chickpeas or garbanzos, mature seeds, dry, raw: 1 cup	122
Chickpeas or garbanzos, mature seeds, dry, raw: 1 lb	276.7
Chicory, Witloof, raw: 1 head (5–7-in long)	1.7
Chicory, Witloof, raw: 1 lb	14.5
Chickory, Witloof, raw, chopped, ½-in pieces: 1 cup	2.9
Chives, raw, chopped: 1 tbsp	.2

Collards
Raw, leaves w stems: 1 lb	32.7
Raw, leaves wo stems: 1 lb	34
Cooked, drained, leaves w stems: 1 cup	7.1
Cooked, drained, leaves wo stems: 1 cup	9.7

Corn, sweet, raw, white and yellow, husked: 1 lb	55.1
Corn, sweet, white and yellow, cooked, drained, kernels only: 1 cup	31
Corn, sweet, white and yellow, cooked, drained, on cob: 1 ear (5 x 1¾ in)	16.2

GRAMS

Cowpeas (including blackeye peas)	
Immature, raw: 1 cup blackeye peas	31.6
Immature, cooked, drained: 1 cup	
blackeye peas	29.9
Mature seeds, dry, cooked, drained: 1 cup	34.5
Young pods w seeds, raw: 1 lb	43.1
Young pods w seeds, cooked, drained: 1 lb	31.8
Cress, garden, raw, trimmed: 5–8 sprigs	.5
Cress, garden, raw, trimmed: ½ lb	12.4
Cucumbers	
Raw, unpeeled, whole: 1 small	5.8
Raw, unpeeled, whole: 1 large	10.2
Raw, unpeeled, sliced: 1 cup	3.6
Raw, peeled, whole: 1 small	5.1
Raw, peeled, whole: 1 large	9
Dandelion greens, raw: 1 lb	41.7
Dandelion greens, cooked, drained: 1 cup	6.7
Dock or sorrel, raw: ½ lb	8.9
Eggplant, cooked, drained, diced: 1 cup	8.2
Endive, raw: 1 lb	18.6
Endive, raw, small pieces: 1 cup	2.1
Fennel leaves, raw, trimmed: ½ lb	10.7
Garlic, cloves, raw: 1 clove	.9
Hyacinth beans, raw, young pods, ½-in pieces:	
1 cup	6.6
Hyacinth beans, raw, mature, dry: 1 lb	276.7
Kale, leaves wo stems, raw: 1 lb	40.8
Kale, cooked, drained: 1 cup	6.7
Kohlrabi, raw, diced: 1 cup	9.2
Kohlrabi, cooked, drained: 1 cup	8.7
Leeks, raw: 3 leeks (5-in long)	11.2
Lentils, mature seeds, dry, whole, raw: 1 cup	114.2
Lentils, mature seeds, cooked, drained: 1 cup	38.6
Lettuce	
Butternut (Boston types and Bibb): 1 head	4.1
Butternut (Boston types and Bibb), chopped	
or shredded: 1 cup	1.4
Cos or romaine: 1 lb	15.9
Cos or romaine, chopped or shredded: 1 cup	1.9
Crisphead (including Iceberg):	
1 wedge (¼ head)	3.9

	GRAMS
Crisphead (including Iceberg): 1 head	15.6
Crisphead (including Iceberg), chopped or shredded: 1 cup	1.6
Looseleaf varieties, chopped or shredded: 1 cup	1.9
Mushrooms: 1 lb	20
Mushrooms, sliced, chopped or diced: 1 cup	3.1
Mustard greens, raw: 1 lb	25.4
Mustard greens, cooked, drained: 1 cup	5.6
Mustard spinach, raw: 1 lb	17.7
Mustard spinach, cooked, drained: 1 cup	5
New Zealand spinach, raw: 1 lb	14.1
New Zealand spinach, cooked, drained: 1 cup	3.8
Okra, crosscut slices, cooked, drained: 1 cup	9.6
Onions	
Raw: 1 lb	39.5
Raw, chopped: 1 cup	14.8
Raw, chopped or minced: 1 tbsp	.9
Raw, sliced: 1 cup	10
Cooked, drained, whole or sliced: 1 cup	13.7
Young green: 2 medium or 6 small	3.2
Young green, chopped: 1 tbsp	.5
Young green, chopped or sliced: 1 cup	8.2
Parsley, raw: 10 sprigs (2½-in long)	.9
Parsley, raw, chopped: 1 tbsp	.3
Parsnips, raw: 1 lb	67.5
Parsnips, cooked, drained: 1 large parsnip	23.8
Parsnips, cooked, drained, diced: 1 cup	23.1
Peas	
Green, immature, raw: 1 cup	20.9
Green, immature, raw: 1 lb	65.3
Cooked, drained: 1 cup	19.4
Mature, dry, split, cooked: 1 cup	41.6
Peppers, chili, green, raw: ½ lb	15
Peppers, chili, red w seeds: ½ lb	39.4
Peppers, chili, red wo seeds: ½ lb	26.2
Pepper, hot, red, wo seeds, dried: 1 tbsp	8
Peppers, sweet	
Green, raw, whole: 1 small (about 5 per lb)	3.5
Green, raw, whole: 1 large (about 2¼ per lb)	7.9
Green, chopped or diced: 1 cup	7.2
Green, cooked, drained: 1 large	6.1

GRAMS

Red, raw, whole: 1 small (about 5 per lb)	5.2
Red, raw, whole: 1 large (about 2¼ per lb)	11.6
Red, chopped or diced: 1 cup	10.7
Pokeberry (poke), shoots, cooked, drained: 1 cup	5.1
Potatoes	
Baked in skin: 1 potato (2⅓ x 4¾ in)	32.8
Boiled in skin: 1 potato (2⅓ x 4¾ in)	38.9
Boiled in skin: 1 potato, round, 2½-in diam	23.3
Boiled in skin, diced or sliced: 1 cup	22.5
Peeled, boiled: 1 potato (2⅓ x 4¾ in)	32.6
Peeled, boiled: 1 potato, round, 2½-in diam	19.6
Peeled, boiled, diced or sliced: 1 cup	22.5
French fried: 10 strips, 2–3½-in long	18
Fried from raw: 1 cup	55.4
Mashed w milk and butter or margarine: 1 cup	25.8
Pumpkin, pulp: 8 oz	10.3
Purslane leaves and stems, raw: ½ lb	8.6
Radishes, raw, whole: 10 medium	1.6
Radishes, raw, whole: 10 large	2.9
Radishes, raw, sliced: 1 cup	4.1
Rutabagas, raw, sliced: 1 cup	15.4
Rutabagas, cooked, drained, cubed or sliced: 1 cup	13.9
Shallot bulbs, raw, chopped: 1 tbsp	1.7
Soybeans	
Mature seeds, dry, cooked: 1 cup	19.4
Sprouted seeds, raw: 1 cup	5.6
Sprouted seeds, cooked, drained: 1 cup	4.6
Spinach, raw: 1 lb	19.5
Spinach, raw, chopped: 1 cup	2.4
Spinach, leaves, cooked, drained: 1 cup	6.5
Squash	
Acorn, baked: ½ squash	24.6
Acorn, baked, mashed: 1 cup	28.7
Butternut, baked, mashed: 1 cup	35.9
Butternut, boiled, mashed: 1 cup	25.5
Crookneck and straightneck, yellow, raw, sliced: 1 cup	5.6
Crookneck and straightneck, yellow, raw: 1 lb	19.5
Crookneck and straightneck, yellow, cooked, sliced: 1 cup	5.6

	GRAMS
Crookneck and straightneck, yellow, cooked, mashed: 1 cup	7.4
Hubbard, baked, mashed: 1 cup	24
Hubbard, boiled, mashed: 1 cup	16.9
Hubbard, boiled, diced: 1 cup	16.2
Scallop varieties, white and pale green, raw, sliced: 1 cup	6.6
Scallop varieties, white and pale green, raw: 1 lb	23.1
Summer, all varieties, cooked, sliced: 1 cup	5.6
Summer, all varieties, cooked, cubed or diced: 1 cup	6.5
Summer, all varieties, cooked, mashed: 1 cup	7.4
Winter, all varieties, cooked, baked, mashed: 1 cup	31.6
Winter, all varieties, cooked, boiled, mashed: 1 cup	22.5
Zucchini and Cocozelle, green, raw, sliced: 1 cup	4.7
Zucchini and Cocozelle, green raw: 1 lb	16.3
Zucchini and Cocozelle, green, cooked, sliced: 1 cup	4.5
Zucchini and Cocozelle, green, cooked, mashed: 1 cup	6
Sweet potatoes, baked in skin: 1 potato (5 x 2 in)	37
Sweet potatoes, boiled in skin: 1 potato (5 x 2 in)	39.8
Sweet potatoes, mashed: 1 cup	67.1
Tofu (bean curd): 1 piece (2½ x 2¾ x 1 in)	2.9
Tomatoes, raw: 1 small (3½ oz)	4.3
Tomatoes, raw: 1 large (4¾ oz)	5.8
Tomatoes, boiled: 1 cup	13.3
Turnips, raw: 1 cup	8.6
Turnips, cooked, drained, cubed: 1 cup	7.6
Turnips, mashed: 1 cup	11.3
Turnip greens, raw: 1 lb	22.7
Turnip greens, cooked, drained: 1 cup	5.2
Water chestnut, Chinese, raw: 1 lb	66.4
Watercress, raw, whole: 1 cup	1.1
Watercress, raw, finely chopped: 1 cup	3.8

CANNED AND FROZEN

GRAMS

All vegetables are ½ cup unless noted; 3.3 ounces are usually about ½ cup.

Artichoke hearts, frozen: 3 oz (5 or 6 hearts) / **Birds Eye** Deluxe	7
Asparagus, canned	
Cut / **Green Giant**	2
Spears and tips / **Del Monte**	3
Spears / **Le Sueur**	4
Tipped / **Del Monte**	3
Asparagus, frozen	
Cut: 3.3 oz / **Bel-Air**	4
Cut: 3.3 oz / **Birds Eye**	4
Cut, in butter sauce / **Green Giant**	6
Spears: 3.3 oz / **Bel-Air**	4
Spears: 3.3 oz / **Birds Eye**	4
Beans, baked, canned, pea: 8 oz / **B & M**	49
Beans, baked, canned, red kidney: 8 oz / **B & M**	50
Beans, baked, canned, yellow eye: 8 oz / **B & M**	50
Beans, baked style, canned	
Campbell's Home Style: 8 oz	48
Campbell's Old Fashioned: 8 oz	49
Van Camp: 8 oz	52
Van Camp Brown Sugar: 8 oz	51
w frankfurters: 8 oz / **Van Camp** Beanee Weenee	32
w frankfurters: 8 oz / **Van Camp** Chilee Weenee	29
w frankfurters: 7¾ oz / **Heinz** Beans 'n' Franks	34
w pork: 8 oz / **Campbell's**	44
w pork: 8 oz / **Heinz**	46
w pork: 4 oz / **Hunt's**	26
w pork: 8 oz / **Van Camp**	41
w pork and molasses / **Libby's**	25
w pork and molasses / **Seneca**	25
w pork and tomato sauce / **A & P**	25
w pork and tomato sauce / **Libby's**	25
w pork and tomato sauce / **Seneca**	25
Vegetarian / **A & P**	25

	GRAMS
Vegetarian: 8 oz / **Heinz**	43
Vegetarian / **Libby's**	25
Vegetarian / **Seneca**	25
Vegetarian: 8 oz / **Van Camp**	42
Beans, barbecue: 7⅞ oz / **Campbell's**	43
Beans, black turtle, canned: 8 oz / **Progresso**	37
Beans, cannellini (white kidney), canned: 8 oz / **Progresso**	30
Beans, fava, canned: 8 oz / **Progresso**	31
Beans, great northern, canned, w pork: 7¼ oz / **Luck's** 29 oz	32
Beans, great northern, canned, w pork: 7½ oz / **Luck's** 15 oz	35
Beans, great northern, canned: 7 oz / **Luck's** 7 oz	28
Beans, green, canned	
Cut / **A & P** Regular or No Salt	4
Cut / **Del Monte** Regular or No Salt	4
Cut / **Green Giant**	3
Cut / **Libby's** Regular or No Salt	4
Cut / **Seneca** Regular or No Salt	4
Cut, w pork: 8 oz / **Luck's**	24
French style / **A & P** Regular or No Salt	4
French style / **Del Monte** Regular or No Salt	4
French style / **Libby's** Regular or No Salt	4
French style / **Seneca** Regular or No Salt	4
French style, cut / **Green Giant**	3
French style, seasoned / **Del Monte**	4
Italian, cut / **Del Monte**	6
Kitchen cut / **Green Giant**	3
Whole / **A & P**	4
Whole / **Del Monte**	4
Whole / **Libby's** Regular or No Salt	4
Whole / **Seneca** Regular or No Salt	4
Beans, green, frozen	
Cut: 3 oz / **A & P**	6
Cut: 3 oz / **Bel-Air**	6
Cut: 3 oz / **Birds Eye**	6
Cut / **Green Giant**	4
Cut / **Green Giant** Harvest Fresh	
French style: 3 oz / **A & P**	6
French style: 3 oz / **Bel-Air**	6

	GRAMS
French style: 3 oz / **Birds Eye**	6
French style: about 3½ oz / **Health Valley**	5
French style, in butter sauce / **Green Giant**	6
French style, w toasted almonds: 3 oz / **Birds Eye**	8
Italian: 3 oz / **Bel-Air**	7
Italian: 3 oz / **Birds Eye**	7
Whole: 3 oz / **Bel-Air**	5
Whole: 3 oz / **Birds Eye** Deluxe	5
in cream sauce w mushrooms / **Green Giant**	10
w corn, carrots, and pearl onions: 3.2 oz / **Birds Eye** Farm Fresh	10
w cauliflower and carrots: 3.2 oz / **Birds Eye** Farm Fresh	6
Beans, kidney, red, canned	
A & P	20
Hunt's: 4 oz	21
Luck's Special Cook: 7½ oz	31
Progresso: 8 oz	34
Van Camp: 8 oz	35
Light: 8 oz / **Van Camp**	35
Seasoned w pork: 7½ oz / **Luck's**	30
Beans, kidney, New Orleans style, canned: 8 oz / **Van Camp**	34
Beans, lima, canned	
A & P	15
Del Monte	14
Libby's Regular or No Salt	15
Seneca Regular or No Salt	15
w ham: 7½ oz / **Dennison's**	33
Giant, seasoned w pork: 7½ oz / **Luck's** 15-oz can	34
Giant, seasoned w pork: 7 oz / **Luck's** 7-oz can	30
Small, seasoned w pork: 7½ oz / **Luck's**	33
Beans, lima, frozen	
Green Giant	19
Green Giant Harvest Fresh	19
Baby: 3.3 oz / **A & P**	24
Baby: 3.3 oz / **Bel-Air**	24
Baby: 3½ oz / **Health Valley**	25
Fordhook: 3.3 oz / **A & P**	19

GRAMS

Fordhook: 3.3 oz / **Bel-Air**	19
Fordhook: 3.3 oz / **Birds Eye**	19
Tiny: 3.3 oz / **Birds Eye** Deluxe	21
In butter sauce / **Green Giant**	20
Beans, navy, canned, seasoned w pork: 7½ oz / **Luck's**	33
Beans, October, canned, seasoned w pork: 7¼ oz / **Luck's** 29 oz can	32
Beans, October, canned w pork: 7½ oz / **Luck's** 15 oz can	31
Beans, pinto, canned	
Progresso: 8 oz	31
Seasoned w pork: 7¼ oz / **Luck's** 29-oz can	30
Seasoned w pork: 7 oz / **Luck's** 15-oz can	30
Seasoned w pork: 7 oz / **Luck's** 7-oz can	29
w onions, seasoned w pork: 7½ oz / **Luck's**	33
and great northern, seasoned w pork: 7¼ oz / **Luck's** 29 oz can	29
and great northern, seasoned w pork: 7½ oz / **Luck's** 15 oz can	30
Beans, red, canned / **A & P**	23
Beans, red, canned: 8 oz / **Van Camp**	38
Beans, Roman, canned: 8 oz / **Progresso**	36
Beans, wax, canned	
Cut / **A& P**	5
Cut / **Del Monte**	4
Cut / **Libby's** Regular or No Salt	5
Cut / **Seneca** Regular or No Salt	5
French / **Del Monte**	4
Beans, western style, canned: 8 oz / **Van Camp**	35
Beans, yelloweye, canned, seasoned w pork: 7½ oz / **Luck's**	31
Bean salad, canned / **Green Giant** Three Bean	18
Beets, canned	
Cut / **Libby's** Regular or No Salt	8
Cut / **Seneca** Regular or No Salt	8
Diced / **Libby's** Regular or No Salt	8
Diced / **Seneca** Regular or No Salt	8
Harvard / **Libby's** Regular or No Salt	20
Harvard / **Seneca** Regular or No Salt	20
Pickled, crinkle sliced / **Del Monte**	19

Pickled, sliced / **Libby's** Regular or No Salt	18
Pickled, sliced / **Seneca** Regular or No Salt	18
Pickled, sliced, w onions / **Libby's** Regular or No Salt	18
Pickled, sliced, w onions / **Seneca** Regular or No Salt	18
Pickled, whole / **Libby's** Regular or No Salt	18
Pickled, whole / **Seneca** Regular or No Salt	18
Shoestring / **Libby's** Regular or No Salt	6
Shoestring / **Seneca** Regular or No Salt	6
Sliced / **A & P**	9
Sliced / **A & P** No Salt	8
Sliced / **Del Monte** Regular or No Salt	8
Sliced / **Libby's** Regular or No Salt	8
Sliced / **Seneca** Regular or No Salt	8
Whole / **A & P**	9
Whole / **Del Monte**	8
Whole / **Libby's** Regular or No Salt	8
Whole / **Seneca** Regular or No Salt	8
Broccoli, frozen	
Baby spears: 3.3 oz / **Birds Eye** Deluxe	5
Chopped: 3.3 oz / **A & P**	5
Chopped: 3.3 oz / **Bel-Air**	5
Chopped: 3.3 oz / **Birds Eye**	5
Cut: 3.3 oz / **A & P**	5
Cut: 3.3 oz / **Bel-Air**	5
Cut: 3.3 oz / **Birds Eye**	4
Cut / **Green Giant**	2
Cut / **Green Giant** Harvest Fresh	4
Florets: 3.3 oz / **Birds Eye** Deluxe	5
Mini-spears / **Green Giant** Frozen Like Fresh	3
Spears: 3.3 oz / **A & P**	5
Spears: 3.3 oz / **Bel-Air**	5
Spears, cut: 3.3 oz / **Bel-Air**	5
Spears: 3.3 oz / **Birds Eye**	5
Spears / **Green Giant** Harvest Fresh	4
Spears: 3½ oz / **Health Valley**	5
w almonds: 3.3 oz / **Birds Eye**	6
In butter sauce / **Green Giant**	5
w carrots / **Green Giant** Fanfare	5

GRAMS

w carrots and pasta twists: 3.3 oz / **Birds Eye**
Blue Ribbon   11
w carrots and water chestnuts: 3.2 oz /
Birds Eye Farm Fresh   6
w cauliflower / **Green Giant** Medley   10
w cauliflower / **Green Giant** Supreme   4
w cauliflower: 3.2 oz / **Kohl's** Blend   4
w cauliflower and carrots: 3.2 oz / **Birds Eye**
Farm Fresh   5
w cauliflower and carrots in cheese sauce:
5 oz / **Birds Eye**   12
w cauliflower and carrots in cheese sauce /
Green Giant   8
w cauliflower and red peppers: 3.3 oz /
Birds Eye Deluxe   5
w cheese sauce: 5 oz / **Birds Eye**   13
w cheese sauce / **Green Giant**   8
w cheese sauce (white cheddar) / **Green Giant**   7
w cheese sauce: 4½ oz / **Stouffer's**   8
w corn and red peppers: 3.2 oz / **Birds Eye**
Farm Fresh   11
w green beans, pearl onions, and red peppers:
3.2 oz / **Birds Eye** Farm Fresh   5
w water chestnuts: 3.3 oz / **Birds Eye**   6
Brussels sprouts, frozen
    A & P: 3.3 oz   7
    Bel-Air: 3.3 oz   7
    Birds Eye: 3.3 oz   7
    Green Giant   5
    Baby: 3.3 oz / **Birds Eye**   7
    In butter sauce / **Green Giant**   9
    w cauliflower and carrots: 3.2 oz / **Birds Eye**
    Farm Fresh   6
    w cheese sauce: 4½ oz / **Birds Eye**   13
    w cheese sauce / **Green Giant**   13
Butterbeans, canned / **A & P**   20
Butterbeans, canned: 7½ oz / **Luck's**   29
Butterbeans, canned: 8 oz / **Van Camp**   30
Carrots, canned
    Diced / **Del Monte**   7

Diced / **Libby's** Regular or No Salt	5
Diced / **Seneca** Regular or No Salt	5
Sliced / **A & P**	6
Sliced / **A & P** No Salt	6
Sliced / **Del Monte**	7
Sliced / **Libby's** Regular or No Salt	5
Sliced / **Seneca** Regular or No Salt	5
Whole / **Del Monte**	7

Carrots, frozen

A & P: 3.3 oz	9
Bel-Air: 3.3 oz	9
Birds Eye Deluxe: 3.3 oz	9
Baby, w sweet peas and pearl onions: 3.3 oz / **Birds Eye** Deluxe	10
Crinkle cut, in butter sauce / **Green Giant**	16

Cauliflower, frozen

A & P: 3.3 oz	5
Bel-Air: 3.3 oz	5
Birds Eye: 3.3 oz	5
Green Giant	3
Kohl's: 3 oz	4
w almonds / **Birds Eye:** 3.3 oz	5
w carrots / **Green Giant** Bonanza	7
w cheese sauce: 5 oz / **Birds Eye**	12
w cheese sauce / **Green Giant**	10
w cheese sauce (white cheddar) / **Green Giant**	7
w green beans / **Green Giant** Festival	3
w green beans and corn: 3.2 oz / **Birds Eye** Farm Fresh	8

Chick peas (garbanzos), canned / **A & P**	17
Chick peas (garbanzos), canned: 8 oz / **Progresso**	32
Collard greens, canned, seasoned w pork: 7½ oz / **Luck's**	7
Collard greens, frozen: 3.3 oz / **Bel-Air**	4

Corn, golden, canned

Cream style / **A & P**	25
Cream style / **Del Monte**	18
Cream style / **Del Monte** No Salt	20
Cream style / **Green Giant**	21
Cream style / **Libby's** Regular or No Salt	16
Cream style / **Seneca** Regular or No Salt	16

GRAMS

Shoepeg / **Green Giant**	18
Whole kernel / **A & P**	20
Whole kernel / **A & P** No Salt	20
Whole kernel / **A & P** Vacuum-Packed	25
Whole kernel / **Del Monte**	17
Whole kernel / **Del Monte** No Salt	18
Whole kernel / **Del Monte** Vacuum-Packed	22
Whole kernel / **Del Monte** Vacuum-Packed No Salt	22
Whole kernel / **Green Giant** Vacuum-Packed	20
Whole kernel / **Le Sueur**	18
w peppers / **Mexicorn**	18
Corn, golden, frozen	
On cob: 1 ear / **A & P**	28
On cob: 2 ears / **A & P** Cob Treats	28
On cob: 1 ear / **Bel-Air**	29
On cob: 2 ears / **Bel-Air** Short Ears	30
On cob: 1 ear / **Birds Eye**	29
On cob: 1 ear / **Birds Eye** Big Ears	37
On cob: 2 ears / **Birds Eye** Little Ears	30
On cob: 1 ear / **Green Giant** Nibblers	16
On cob: 1 ear / **Green Giant** Niblet Ears	30
On cob: 4½ oz / **Ore-Ida**	31
Whole kernel: 3.3 oz / **A & P**	18
Whole kernel: 3.3 oz / **Bel-Air**	20
Whole kernel: 3.3 oz / **Birds Eye**	20
Whole kernel, sweet: 3.3 oz / **Birds Eye** Deluxe	20
Whole kernel / **Green Giant** Harvest Fresh Niblets	22
w broccoli / **Green Giant** Bounty	11
w butter sauce / **Green Giant** Niblets	18
Cream style / **Green Giant**	25
w cream sauce / **Green Giant** Niblets	18
w green beans and pasta curls: 3.3 oz / **Birds Eye**	15
w white corn / **Green Giant** Niblets and White Corn	16
Corn, white	
Cream style, canned / **Del Monte**	21
Whole kernel, canned / **Del Monte**	16

GRAMS

Whole kernel, canned / **Green Giant** Vacuum-Packed	20
Whole kernel, canned / **Libby's** Regular or No Salt	18
Whole kernel, canned / **Seneca** Regular or No Salt	18
In butter sauce, frozen / **Green Giant**	19
Eggplant parmigiana, frozen: 11 oz / **Mrs. Paul's**	40
Eggplant sticks, fried, frozen: 3½ oz / **Mrs. Paul's**	29
Green peppers, frozen, diced: 1 oz / **Bel-Air**	1
Green peppers, frozen, stuffed: ½ pkg / **Green Giant**	15
Hominy, golden, canned: 8 oz / **Van Camp**	27
Hominy, golden, canned, w red and green peppers: 8 oz / **Van Camp:**	27
Hominy, white, canned: 8 oz / **Van Camp**	28
Kale, frozen, cut leaf: 3.3 oz / **Bel-Air**	5
Mixed, canned	
A & P (Eastern label)	8
A & P (Western label)	9
A & P No Salt	9
Del Monte	7
Libby's Regular or No Salt	9
P & Q Chunky	8
Seneca Regular or No Salt	9
Mixed, frozen	
A & P: 3.3 oz	13
A & P California Blend: 3.3 oz	5
Bel-Air: 3.3 oz	13
Bel-Air Rancho Fiesta Style: 3.3 oz	12
Birds Eye: 3.3 oz	13
Green Giant	10
Green Giant Harvest Fresh	13
Health Valley: 3½ oz	60
Bavarian style beans and spaetzl: 3.3 oz / **Birds Eye**	11
w butter sauce / **Green Giant**	12
Chinese style: 3.3 oz / **Birds Eye**	8
Chinese style: 3.3 oz / **Birds Eye** Stir-Fry	7
Chinese style / **Green Giant**	7
Far Eastern style: 3.3 oz / **Birds Eye**	8

GRAMS

Italian blend: 3.3 oz / **A & P** 8
Italian style: 3.3 oz / **Birds Eye** 11
Japanese style: 3.3 oz / **Birds Eye** 10
Japanese style: 3.3 oz / **Birds Eye** Stir-Fry 6
Japanese style / **Green Giant** 8
Mexicana style: 3.3 oz / **Birds Eye** 16
New England style: 3.3 oz / **Birds Eye** 14
w onion sauce: 2.6 oz / **Birds Eye** 11
Oriental blend: 3.3 oz / **A & P** 5
San Francisco style: 3.3 oz / **Birds Eye** 11
Winter blend: 3.3 oz / **A & P** 6
Mushrooms, canned
    B in B: 2 oz 3
    Green Giant: 2 oz 2
    Libby's Regular or No Salt: ¼ cup 4
    Seneca Regular or No Salt: ¼ cup 4
    In butter sauce: 2 oz / **Green Giant** 4
Mushrooms, frozen, in butter sauce / **Green Giant** .. 5
Mustard greens, canned: 1 cup / **Town House** 4
Mustard greens, frozen, chopped: 3.3 oz / **Bel-Air** .. 3
Okra, frozen
    Cut: 3.3 oz / **Bel-Air** 6
    Cut: 3.3 oz / **Birds Eye** 6
    Whole: 3.3 oz / **Bel-Air** 7
    Whole: 3.3 oz / **Birds Eye** 7
Onions, frozen
    Chopped: 1 oz / **Bel-Air** 2
    Chopped: 2 oz / **Ore-Ida** 4
    Pearl: 3.3 oz / **Birds Eye** Deluxe 8
    Small, whole: 4 oz / **Birds Eye** 10
    Small, w cream sauce: 3 oz / **Birds Eye** 11
Onion rings, fried, frozen: 2¼ oz / **Mrs. Paul's** .. 20
Onion rings, fried, frozen: 2 oz / **Ore-Ida**
    Onion Ringers 17
Peas, black-eye, canned
    A & P 20
    Progresso: 8 oz 29
    Seasoned w pork: 7¼ oz / **Luck's** 29-oz can .. 28
    Seasoned w pork: 7½ oz / **Luck's** 15-oz can .. 25
    Seasoned w pork: 7 oz / **Luck's** 7-oz can 27
    w corn, seasoned w pork: 7½ oz / **Luck's** 33

GRAMS

Peas, black-eye, frozen: 3.3 oz / **Bel-Air**	23
Peas, Crowder, canned, seasoned w pork: 7½ oz / **Luck's**	24
Peas, field, canned, w snaps, seasoned w pork: 7½ oz / **Luck's**	27
Peas, green, canned	
A & P	15
A & P No Salt	12
Del Monte	10
Del Monte No Salt	11
Del Monte Small	9
Green Giant	11
Le Sueur	11
Le Sueur Mini	11
Libby's Regular or No Salt	12
Seneca Regular or No Salt	12
Seasoned / **Del Monte**	11
w carrots / **Del Monte**	10
w carrots / **Kohl's**	20
w carrots / **Libby's** Regular or No Salt	10
w carrots / **Seneca** Regular or No Salt	10
w onions / **Green Giant**	11
w snaps, seasoned w pork: 7½ oz / **Luck's**	26
Peas, green, frozen	
A & P: 3.3 oz	13
Bel-Air: 3.3 oz	13
Birds Eye: 3.3 oz	13
Birds Eye Deluxe Tiny: 3.3 oz	11
Green Giant	10
Green Giant Harvest Fresh	14
Health Valley: 3½ oz	60
In butter sauce / **Green Giant**	14
w carrots: 3.3 oz / **A & P**	11
w carrots: 3.3 oz / **Bel-Air**	11
w carrots and pearl onions: 3.2 oz / **Birds Eye** Farm Fresh	11
w cream sauce: 2.6 oz / **Birds Eye**	14
w cream sauce / **Green Giant**	12
w cauliflower / **Green Giant** Medley	7
w onions: 3.3 oz / **Birds Eye**	13

w onions and carrots, in butter sauce / **Le Sueur**	11
w onions and cheese sauce: 5 oz / **Birds Eye**	18
w pea pods and water chestnuts in butter sauce / **Green Giant**	10
w potatoes, in cream sauce: 2.6 oz / **Birds Eye**	15
Potatoes, canned	
A & P	11
Del Monte	10
Libby's	11
Seneca	11
Potatoes, frozen	
Au gratin: 3¹³⁄₁₆ oz / **Stouffer's**	13
French-fried: 3½ oz / **A & P**	25
French-fried: 3½ oz / **A & P** Crinkle Cut	25
French-fried: 3½ oz / **A & P** Potato Morsels	23
French-fried: 3½ oz / **A & P** Shoestrings	24
French-fried: 3 oz / **Bel-Air** Crinkle Cut	20
French-fried: 3 oz / **Bel-Air** Shoestrings	20
French-fried: 2.8 oz / **Birds Eye** Cottage Fries	17
French-fried: 3 oz / **Birds Eye** Crinkle Cuts	18
French-fried: 3 oz / **Birds Eye** French Fries	17
French-fried: 3.3 oz / **Birds Eye** Shoestrings	20
French-fried: 2½ oz / **Birds Eye** TastiFries	17
French-fried: 3 oz / **Ore-Ida** Cottage Fries	21
French-fried: 3 oz / **Ore-Ida** Country Style Dinner Fries	20
French-fried: 3 oz / **Ore-Ida** Crispers!	25
French-fried: 3 oz / **Ore-Ida** Crispy Crowns	18
French-fried: 3 oz / **Ore-Ida** Golden Crinkles	20
French-fried: 3 oz / **Ore-Ida** Golden Fries	21
French-fried: 3 oz / **Ore-Ida** Pixie Crinkles	22
French-fried: 3 oz / **Ore-Ida** Shoestrings	24
Fried: 3½ oz / **A & P** Steak Fries	24
Fried: 2 oz / **Bel-Air** Patties	13
Fried: 2 oz / **Bel-Air** Steak Fries	18
Fried: 3.2 oz / **Birds Eye** Tiny Taters	22
Fried: 2½ oz / **Ore-Ida** Golden Patties	17
Fried: 3 oz / **Ore-Ida** Tater Tots	21

GRAMS

Fried, w bacon flavor: 3 oz / **Ore-Ida** Tater Tots	21
Fried, w onions: 3 oz / **Ore-Ida** Tater Tots	21
Hash browns: 3½ oz / **A & P**	17
Hash browns: 4 oz / **Bel-Air**	19
Hash browns: 4 oz / **Birds Eye**	17
Hash browns: 3 oz / **Birds Eye** Shredded	13
Hash browns: 3 oz / **Ore-Ida** Shredded	29
Hash browns: 3 oz / **Ore-Ida** Southern Style	17
O'Brien: 3 oz / **Ore-Ida**	17
w onions: 3 oz / **Ore-Ida** Crispy Crowns	19
Puffs: 2½ oz / **Birds Eye** TastiPuffs	19
Scalloped: 4 oz / **Stouffer's**	14
Stuffed: 1 potato / **Larry's** Deluxe	27
Stuffed, w cheese topping: 5 oz / **Green Giant**	33
Stuffed, w cheese: 1 potato / **Larry's** Deluxe	23
Stuffed, w chives: 1 potato / **Larry's** Deluxe	24
Stuffed, w sour cream and chives: 5 oz / **Green Giant**	31
w peas in bacon cream sauce / **Green Giant**	15
Sliced: 3 oz / **Bel-Air**	20
Sliced: 3 oz / **Ore-Ida**	17
Sliced: 3 oz / **Ore-Ida** Home Style Potato Planks	18
Sliced: 3 oz / **Ore-Ida** Potato Thins	18
Sliced, in butter sauce / **Green Giant**	14
Wedges: 3 oz / **Birds Eye** Farm Style	18
Wedges: 3 oz / **Ore-Ida** Home Style	17
Whole, peeled: 3.2 oz / **Birds Eye**	13
Whole, peeled: 3 oz / **Ore-Ida**	17
Potatoes, mix, prepared	
Au gratin / **Betty Crocker**	21
Au gratin / **French's** Tangy	25
Au gratin: ¾ cup / **Libby's** Potato Classics	22
Chicken 'n herb / **Betty Crocker**	19
Creamed, oven / **Betty Crocker**	22
Creamed, saucepan / **Betty Crocker**	23
Hash browns w onions / **Betty Crocker**	22
Hickory smoke cheese / **Betty Crocker**	21
Julienne / **Betty Crocker**	17
Mashed / **Betty Crocker** Potato Buds	15

	GRAMS
Mashed / **French's** Big Tate	16
Mashed / **French's** Idaho	16
Mashed / **Hungry Jack**	17
Mashed / **Idaho** Naturally	20
Mashed / **Mr. Spud**	20
Mashed: 4 oz / **Town House**	14
Scalloped / **Betty Crocker**	19
Scalloped / **French's** Crispy Top	25
Scalloped: ¾ cup / **Libby's** Potato Classics	24
Scalloped, cheese / **French's**	25
Sour cream and chives / **French's**	24
Potatoes, sweet, canned, in syrup / **Kohl's**	31
Pumpkin, canned / **Del Monte**	9
Pumpkin, canned / **Libby's** Solid Pack: 1 cup	20
Ratatouille, frozen: 5 oz / **Stouffer's**	9
Salad greens, canned, seasoned w pork: 7½ oz / **Luck's**	7
Sauerkraut, canned or in jar	
A & P	5
Claussen	3
Del Monte	6
Libby's	5
Seneca	5
Vlasic Old Fashioned: 1 oz	1
Spinach, canned	
A & P	3
Del Monte Regular or No Salt	4
Libby's Regular or No Salt	4
Seneca Regular or No Salt	4
Spinach, frozen	
Chopped: 3.3 oz / **A & P**	4
Chopped: 3.3 oz / **Birds Eye**	3
Chopped: 3.3 oz / **Birds Eye**	3
Chopped: 3½ oz / **Health Valley**	20
Creamed: 3 oz / **Birds Eye**	5
Creamed / **Green Giant**	8
Creamed: 4½ oz / **Stouffer's**	9
Leaf: 3.3 oz / **A & P**	4
Leaf: 3.3 oz / **Bel-Air**	4
Leaf: 3.3 oz / **Birds Eye**	4
Leaf: 3½ oz / **Health Valley**	20

GRAMS

Leaf, in butter sauce / **Green Giant**	6
Mushroom casserole: 7½ oz / **Health Valley**	9
Souffle: 4 oz / **Stouffer's**	12
w water chestnuts: 3.3 oz / **Birds Eye**	5
Squash, cooked, frozen: 4 oz / **Bel-Air**	11
Squash, cooked, frozen: 4 oz / **Birds Eye**	11
Squash, cooked, frozen: 4 oz / **Kohl's**	11
Squash, yellow, sliced, frozen: 3.3 oz / **Bel-Air**	4
Stew vegetables, frozen: 4 oz / **A & P**	13
Stew vegetables, frozen: 3.3 oz / **Kohl's**	10
Stew vegetables, frozen: 3 oz / **Ore-Ida**	12
Succotash, canned / **Libby's** Regular or No Salt	22
Succotash, canned / **Seneca** Regular or No Salt	22
Succotash, frozen: 3.3 oz / **Bel-Air**	19
Tomato paste, canned	
A & P: 6 oz (¾ cup)	35
Contadina: 6 oz	35
Del Monte: ¾ cup	34
Del Monte No Salt: 6 oz	34
Hunt's: 2 oz	11
Hunt's No Salt: 2 oz	11
Town House: ⅔ cup	35
Italian: 2 oz / **Contadina**	12
Italian: 2 oz / **Hunt's**	11
Italian w mushrooms: 2 oz / **Contadina**	12
Tomato puree, canned / **A & P**	14
Tomato puree, canned / **Contadina**	11
Tomato puree, canned: 4 oz / **Hunt's**	10
Tomatoes, canned	
Baby sliced / **Contadina**	10
Italian style / **Contadina**	5
Kosher: 1 oz / **Claussen**	1
Stewed / **A & P**	8
Stewed / **Contadina**	9
Stewed / **Del Monte**	8
Stewed / **Del Monte** no salt	8
Stewed: 4 oz / **Hunt's**	8
Stewed: 4 oz / **Hunt's** no salt	8
Stewed / **Town House**	9
Wedges / **Del Monte**	8
Whole / **A & P**	6

GRAMS

Whole / **Contadina**	6
Whole / **Del Monte**	5
Whole: 4 oz / **Hunt's**	5
Whole: 4 oz / **Hunt's** No Salt	5
Whole / **Town House**	6
Turnip greens, canned, w diced turnips: 7½ oz / **Luck's**	6
Turnip greens, frozen, chopped: 3.3 oz / **Bel-Air**	4
Turnip greens, frozen, chopped, w diced turnips: 3.3 oz / **Bel-Air**	3
Yams	
Canned / **Town House**	24
Frozen, candied: 4 oz / **Mrs. Paul's**	44
Frozen, candied, w apples: 4 oz / **Mrs. Paul's**	36
Frozen, w apples: 5 oz / **Stouffer's**	31
Zucchini	
Canned, in tomato sauce / **Del Monte**	8
Frozen, baby sliced: 3.3 oz / **Birds Eye** Deluxe	3
Frozen, crinkle cut: 3.3 oz / **Bel-Air**	3
Frozen, sticks, in light batter: 3 oz / **Mrs. Paul's**	23

VEGETABLES IN PASTRY

1 piece

Asparagus w mornay sauce / **Pepperidge Farm** Vegetable in Pastry	18
Broccoli w cheese / **Pepperidge Farm** Vegetable in Pastry	19
Cauliflower and cheese sauce / **Pepperidge Farm** Vegetable in Pastry	20
Green beans w mushroom sauce / **Pepperidge Farm** Vegetable in Pastry	20
Mexican style / **Pepperidge Farm** Vegetable in Pastry	21
Mushrooms Dijon / **Pepperidge Farm** Vegetable in Pastry	19
Oriental Garden / **Pepperidge Farm** Vegetable in Pastry	19
Ratatouille w cheese / **Pepperidge Farm** Vegetable in Pastry	18

GRAMS

Spinach almondine / **Pepperidge Farm**
   Vegetable in Pastry   19
Zucchini Provencal / **Pepperidge Farm**
   Vegetable in Pastry   21

Vegetable Juices

GRAMS

6-fluid-ounce glass unless noted

Tomato
   A & P   7
   Campbell's   8
   Hunt's   7
   Hunt's No Salt   7
   Libby's   8
   Town House: 5½ fl oz   8
   Welch's   7
Tomato cocktail / **Snap-E-Tom**   7
Vegetable cocktail
   Town House   8
   V-8   8
   V-8 No Salt   9
   V-8 Spicy Hot   8

Wines and Distilled Spirits

All straight liquors—gin, rum, vodka, whiskey,
  bourbon, brandy, tequila, etc: any
  amount, all brands   Trace

4 fl oz unless noted

Almonetta: 3½ fl oz / **Manischewitz**	10
Barbera / **Sebastiani** Vineyards (1978)	3
Beaujolais, Gamay / **Almaden**	0–1
Blackberry: 3½ fl oz / **Manischewitz**	25
Bordeaux	
Red / **B&G** Margaux	0–1
Red / **B&G** Prince Noir	0–1
Red / **B&G** St. Emilion	1
White / **B&G** Graves	1
White / **B&G** Haut Sauternes	12
White / **B&G** Prince Blanc	1
White / **B&G** Sauternes	10
Burgundy	
Almaden Monterey	0–1
Almaden Mountain	1
Charles Fournier American	4
Charles Fournier Personal Selection Superieur	4
Manischewitz: 3½ fl oz	2
Sebastiani Mountain	3
Red / **B&G** Beaujolais St. Louis	0–1
Red / **B&G** Nuits St. George	1
Red / **B&G** Pommard	0–1
Red / **Gallo**	0–1
Red / **Gallo** Hearty	0–1
Sparkling / **Henry Marchant** American	7
White / **B&G** Chablis	0–1
White / **B&G** Pouilly Fuisse	0–1

GRAMS

White / **B&G** Puligny Montrachet	0–1
Cabernet Pfeffer / **Almaden**	0–1

Cabernet Sauvignon
Almaden	0–1
Sebastiani Country	3
Sebastiani Vineyards (1980)	3
Sebastiani Vineyards (1981)	3
Wine Cellars of Ernest and Julio Gallo	0

Catawba
Pink / **Mountain Lake**	14
Red / **Mountain Lake**	13
White / **Mountain Lake**	13

Chablis
Almaden Monterey	1
Almaden Mountain	1
Charles Fournier American	4
Charles Fournier Personal Selection Superieur	4
Gallo Chablis Blanc	0–1
Manischewitz: 3½ fl oz	2
Sebastiani Mountain	3
Pink / **Gallo**	1

Champagne
Almaden Blanc de Blancs	1
Almaden Eye of the Partridge	1
Almaden LeDomaine Brut	3
Almaden LeDomaine Extra Dry	4
Almaden Vintage Brut	2
Almaden Vintage Extra Dry	4
Charles Fournier Special Selection American Blanc de Blancs	3
Charles Fournier Special Selection American Blanc de Noirs	3
Gold Seal New York State Brut	4
Gold Seal New York State Extra Dry	7
Gold Seal New York State Naturel	3
Henri Marchant American Brut	5
Henri Marchant American Extra Dry	7
Henri Marchant American Naturel	3
Mum's Cordon Rouge Brut	2
Mum's Extra Dry	7
Pierre Corbeau American Brut	4

GRAMS

Pierre Corbeau American Extra Dry | 7
Pink / **Gold Seal** New York State | 7
Pink / **Henri Marchant** American | 7

Chardonnay
    Almaden | 0–1
    Charles Fournier (1982) | 2
    Charles Fournier (1981) | 3
    Sebastiani Country | 3
    Sebastiani Vineyards (1982) | 3
    Sebastiani Vineyards (1983) | 2
    Wine Cellars of Ernest and Julio Gallo | 0

Chenin Blanc
    Almaden | 2
    Sebastiani Country | 3
    Sebastiani Vineyards (1984) | 3
    Wine Cellars of Ernest and Julio Gallo | 0–1

Cherry: 3½ fl oz **Manischewitz** | 25
Claret, red / **Almaden** Mountain | 0–1
Cold Duck / **Henri Marchant** | 7
Colombard, French / **Almaden** | 2
Colombard, French / **Sebastiani** Country | 3
Colombard, French / **Wine Cellars of Ernest and Julio Gallo** | 0–1

Concord
    Manischewitz: 3½ fl oz | 25
    Cream red: 3½ fl oz / **Manischewitz** | 25
    Cream white: 3½ fl oz / **Manischewitz** | 10
    Medium dry: 3½ fl oz / **Manischewitz** | 5
    Pink: 3½ fl oz / **Manischewitz** | 10
    Red / **Gold Seal** | 14

Elderberry: 3½ fl oz / **Manischewitz** | 25
Fumé Blanc / **Almaden** | 0–1
Fumé Blanc / **Sebastiani** Country | 2
Gamay Rose / **Sebastiani** Country | 3
Gewurtztraminer / **Almaden** | 2
Gewurtztraminer / **Sebastiani** Vineyards (1984) | 3
Gewurtztraminer / **Wine Cellars of Ernest and Julio Gallo** | 0–1
Green Hungarian / **Sebastiani** Vineyards (1984) | 3
Labrusca, red / **Gold Seal** | 14
Loganberry: 3½ fl oz / **Manischewitz** | 25

Maison Blanc / **Almaden**	0–1
Maison Rouge / **Almaden**	0–1
Moselle / **Julius Kayser's** Graacher Himmelreich	3
Moselle / **Julius Kayser's** Piesporter Reisling	2
Moselle / **Julius Kayser's** Zeller Schwarze Katz	4
Pina Coconetta: 3½ fl oz / **Manischewitz**	10
Pinot Noir / **Almaden**	0–1
Pinot Noir / **Sebastiani Vineyards** Blanc (1984)	3
Pinot St. George / **Almaden**	0–1

Port

Almaden Solera	12
Gallo	3
White / **Gallo**	3

Rhine

Alamaden Mountain	5
Charles Fournier American	5
Gallo	1
Julius Kayser's Liebfraumilch Glockenspiel	2
Julius Kayser's Bereich Nierstein	1
Sebastiani Mountain	3

Riesling

Almaden California	2
Charles Fournier Personal Selection Dry	4
Charles Fournier Personal Selection Johannisberg (1980 Late Harvest)	7
Sebastiani Vineyards Johannisberg	3
Wine Cellars of Ernest and Julio Gallo Johannisberg	0–1

Rosé

Almaden Carafe	2
Almaden Gamay	2
Almaden Grenache	1
Almaden Mountain Nectar Vin	4
Charles Fournier American Vin	5
Charles Fournier Personal Selection Superieur	4
Gallo Vin Rosé	0–1
Sebastiani Mountain Vin	3
Wine Cellars of Ernest and Julio Gallo	0–1
Red / **Gallo**	2
Sauterne / **Almaden** Mountain	0–1
Sauterne / **Charles Fournier** American Dry	6

GRAMS

Sauvignon Blanc / **Almaden**	1
Sauvignon Blanc / **Sebastiani** Vineyards (1982)	3
Sauvignon Blanc / **Wine Cellars of Ernest and Julio Gallo**	0–1
Sherry	
Gallo	1
Cocktail / **Almaden**	2
Cream / **Almaden**	14
Cream / **Gallo** Livingston Cellars	3
Golden / **Almaden**	7
Very Dry / **Gallo** Livingston Cellars	0–1
Strawberry Coconetta: 3½ fl oz / **Manischewitz**	10
Vermouth	
Dry / **Gallo**	0–1
Sweet / **Gallo**	5
Wine Coolers: 3½ fl oz / **Manischewitz**	10
Zinfandel	
Almaden	0–1
Sebastiani Country	3
Sebastiani Vineyards (1980)	3
Sebastiani Vineyards (1981)	3
Wine Cellars of Ernest and Julio Gallo	0
White / **Sebastiani** Country	3

$\mathbf{Y}$east

	GRAMS
Bakers: 1 oz	3.1
Brewer's, debittered: 1 tbsp	3.1
Brewer's, debittered: 1 oz	10.9
Dry, active: ¼ oz pkg / **Fleischmann's**	3
Dry, active, in jar: ¼ oz / **Fleischmann's**	3
Fresh, active: .6 oz pkg / **Fleischmann's**	2
Household: .5 oz / **Fleischmann's**	2

Yogurt

	GRAMS
8 ounces equals ⅞ to 9/10 of a cup	
All flavors: 3½ oz / **Colombo**	24
All flavors: 1 cup / **Lucerne** Low-Fat	46
Apple cinnamon: 6 oz / **Yoplait** Breakfast	40
Berries: 6 oz / **Yoplait** Breakfast	39
Blueberry: 6 oz / **Weight Watchers** European Style Nonfat	27
Blueberry: 8 oz / **Weight Watchers** Nonfat	29
Cherry: 1 cup / **Dannon**	49
Cherry vanilla: 8 oz / **Borden**	54
Citrus fruits: 6 oz / **Yoplait** Breakfast	43
Coffee: 1 cup / **Dannon**	32
Coffee: 1 cup / **Friendship** Low-Fat	35
Coffee: 6 oz / **Yoplait** Custard Style	30
Fruit: 1 cup / **Friendship** Low-Fat	44

Fruit flavors, all varieties: 6 oz / **Y.E.S., Yogurt Extra Smooth** 33

Fruit flavors: 6 oz / **Yoplait** Custard Style 32

Fruit flavors: 6 oz / **Yoplait** Original 32

Lemon: 8 oz / **Borden** 69

Lemon: 1 cup / **Dannon** 32

Orchard fruits: 6 oz / **Yoplait** Breakfast 40

Peach: 1 cup / **Dannon** 49

Pineapple: 8 oz / **Borden** 51

Plain

    Dannon: 1 cup 17

    Friendship: 1 cup 15

    Lite-Line: 8 oz 24

    Lucerne: 1 cup 17

    Weight Watchers European Style: 6 oz 12

    Weight Watchers Nonfat: 8 oz 14

    Yoplait Original: 6 oz 14

    w honey: 6 oz / **Yoplait** Custard Style 23

Raspberry: 6 oz / **Weight Watchers** European Style Nonfat 27

Raspberry: 8 oz / **Weight Watchers** Nonfat 29

Strawberry

    Borden: 8 oz 46

    Dannon: 1 cup 49

    Meadow Gold Sundae style: 1 cup 49

    Weight Watchers European Style Nonfat: 6 oz 27

    Weight Watchers Nonfat: 8 oz 29

Tropical fruits: 6 oz / **Yoplait** Breakfast 43

Vanilla: 1 cup / **Dannon** 32

Vanilla: 1 cup / **Friendship** Low-Fat 35

Vanilla: 6 oz / **Yoplait** Custard Style 30

FROZEN YOGURT

Regular: 1 cup

    Blueberry / **Danny** 42

    Chocolate / **Danny** 32

    Piña Colada / **Danny** 44

    Raspberry / **Danny** 42

    Strawberry / **Danny** 42

    Vanilla / **Danny** 33

	GRAMS
Soft, all varieties: 3½ oz / **Danny-Yo**	21
Bars: 1 bar	
Boysenberry, carob-coated / **Danny**	15
Chocolate, chocolate-coated / **Danny**	12
Chocolate, uncoated / **Danny**	10
Piña Colada, uncoated / **Danny**	14
Raspberry, chocolate-coated / **Danny**	15
Strawberry, chocolate-coated / **Danny**	15
Vanilla, chocolate-coated / **Danny**	11
Vanilla, uncoated / **Danny**	11

Fast Foods

Fast Foods

ARBY'S

ARTHUR TREACHER'S FISH & CHIPS

BURGER CHEF

GRAMS

Cheeseburger	28
Cheeseburger, Double	28
Chicken club	33
Fisherman's filet	41
Fries, Large: 1 serving	36
Fries, Regular: 1 serving	26
Hamburger	27
Hash Rounds: 1 serving	26
Mushroom Burger	34
Scrambled Eggs and Bacon Platter	50
Scrambled Eggs and Sausage Platter	50
Shake, Chocolate	72
Shake, Vanilla	60
Sunrise w Bacon	30
Sunrise w Sausage	30
Super Shef	35
Top Shef	29
Turnover, Apple	38

BURGER KING

Apple pie	32
Bacon Double Cheeseburger	36
Cheeseburger	30
Cheeseburger, Double	32
Chicken Sandwich	52
French Fries, Regular: 1 serving	25
Hamburger	29
Onion Rings, Regular: 1 serving	29
Shake, Chocolate: 10 oz	57
Shake, Vanilla: 10 oz	52
Veal Parmigiana	65
Whaler	57
Whaler w Cheese	58
Whopper	50
Whopper w Cheese	52
Whopper, Double Beef	52
Whopper, Double Beef w Cheese	54
Whopper Junior	31
Whopper Junior w Cheese	32

CARL'S JR.

	GRAMS
Bacon: 2 strips	0
California Roast Beef Sandwich	34
Carrot cake: 1 piece	44
Charbroiler Chicken Sandwich	55
Charbroiler Steak	0
Charbroiler Steak Sandwich	54
Cheese Sandwich, American	1
Cheese Sandwich, Swiss	1
Chicken Breasts: 2 pieces	0
Crispirito	55
Eggs, scrambled: 1 serving	1
English Muffin w Butter and Jelly	34
Famous Star Hamburger	38
Filet of Fish Sandwich	61
French Fries, Regular: 1 serving	25
Garlic Bread: 1 serving	18
Ground Beef: 1 serving	0
Happy Star Hamburger	33
Hashed Brown Potatoes: 2	26
Hot Cakes w Syrup and Butter: 1 serving	80
Hot Chocolate: 1 serving	20
Old Time Star Hamburger	45
Omelette, Bacon 'N Cheese	2
Omelette, California	3
Omelette, Cheese	2
Onion Rings: 1 serving	39
Onion Ring Garnish: 1 serving	13
Potato, Baked	33
Potatoes, Wedge Cut: 1 serving	32
Salad, Regular	33
Salad Dressing, Blue Cheese: 2 oz	2
Salad Dressing, Low-Cal Italian: 2 oz	0
Salad Dressing, Thousand Island: 2 oz	8
Sausage: 1 patty	0
Shake, Regular	90
Sunrise Sandwich w Bacon	28
Sunrise Sandwich w Sausage	28
Super Star Hamburger	38
Sweet Roll w Butter	57
Tartar Sauce: ¾ oz	39

	GRAMS
Top Sirloin Steak	0
Trout w Lemon Garlic Butter	0
Turnover, Apple	45
Western Bacon Cheeseburger	42
Zucchini: 1 serving	32

CHURCH'S FRIED CHICKEN

Chicken	
Dark Meat: 1 average portion	7
White Meat: 1 average portion	10
Chicken Snack	
Chicken: 1 large piece	9
Dinner Roll: 1	15
Cole Slaw: 3 oz	6
Corn on the Cob: 9 oz buttered	29
French Fries: 3 oz	31
Jalapeno Pepper: 1	1
Pie, Apple: 3 oz	31
Pie, Pecan: 3 oz	44

DAIRY QUEEN / BRAZIER

Banana Split	103
Buster Bar	41
Chicken Sandwich	46
Cone, Large	57
Cone, Regular	38
Cone, Small	22
Cone, Dipped, Chocolate, Large	64
Cone, Dipped, Chocolate, Regular	42
Cone, Dipped, Chocolate, Small	25
Dilly Bar	21
Double Delight	69
DQ Sandwich	24
Fish Sandwich	41
Fish Sandwich w Cheese	39
Float	82
Freeze	89
French Fries, Large: 1 serving	40
French Fries, Regular: 1 serving	25

	GRAMS
Hamburger, Double	33
Hamburger, Double w Cheese	34
Hamburger, Single	33
Hamburger, Single w Cheese	33
Hamburger, Triple	33
Hamburger, Triple w Cheese	34
Hot Dog	21
Hot Dog w Cheese	21
Hot Dog w Chili	23
Hot Dog, Super	44
Hog Dog, Super w Cheese	45
Hot Dog, Super w Chili	47
Hot Fudge Brownie Delight	85
Malt, Chocolate, Large	187
Malt, Chocolate, Regular	134
Malt, Chocolate, Small	91
Mr. Misty Float	74
Mr. Misty Freeze	91
Mr. Misty Kiss	17
Mr. Misty, Large	84
Mr. Misty, Regular	63
Mr. Misty, Small	48
Onion Rings: 1 serving	31
Parfait	76
Peanut Buster Parfait	94
Shake, Chocolate, Large	168
Shake, Chocolate, Regular	120
Shake, Chocolate, Small	82
Strawberry Shortcake	100
Sundae, Chocolate, Large	78
Sundae, Chocolate, Regular	56
Sundae, Chocolate, Small	33

HARDEE'S

Bacon Cheeseburger	42
Bacon and Egg Biscuit	30
Biscuit	35
Biscuit w Egg	35
Cheeseburger	28
Chicken Fillet	42

	GRAMS
Cookie, Big	33
Fisherman Fillet	47
French Fries, Large: 1 serving	44
French Fries, Small: 1 serving	28
Ham Biscuit	37
Ham Biscuit w Egg	37
Ham and Cheese Sandwich, Hot	37
Hamburger	29
Hashrounds: 1 serving	20
Hot Dog	26
Milkshake	63
Mushroom 'N' Swiss	43
Roast Beef Sandwich	36
Roast Beef Sandwich, Big	33
Sausage Biscuit	34
Sausage Biscuit w Egg	34
Steak Biscuit	40
Steak Biscuit w Egg	41
Turkey Club	32
Turnover, Apple	37

JACK IN THE BOX

Bacon Cheeseburger Supreme	44
Bacon Croissant	27
Breakfast Jack	30
Cheeseburger	32
Chicken Strips Dinner	65
Chicken Supreme	39
Croissant Supreme	27
French Fries: 1 serving	27
Hamburger	30
Ham Croissant	24
Jumbo Jack	38
Jumbo Jack w Cheese	45
Moby Jack	39
Nachos, Cheese: 1 serving	49
Nachos, Supreme: 1 serving	66
Onion Rings: 1 serving	39
Pancake Breakfast	79
Pita Pocket Supreme	30

	GRAMS
Sausage Croissant	28
Scrambled Eggs Breakfast	55
Shake, Chocolate	59
Shake, Strawberry	63
Shake, Vanilla	54
Shrimp Dinner	77
Shrimp Salad Supreme	10
Sirloin Steak Dinner	75
Swiss and Bacon Burger	31
Taco, Regular	16
Taco, Super	21
Taco Salad	10
Turnover, Apple	45

KENTUCKY FRIED CHICKEN

Chicken Breast Filet Sandwich	34
Chicken Dinner, Extra Crispy: 2 pieces of chicken w mashed potatoes, gravy, cole slaw and roll	
Combination	58
Dark	55
White	60
Chicken Dinner, Original Recipe: 2 pieces of chicken w mashed potatoes, gravy, cole slaw and roll	
Combination	48
Dark	46
White	48
Cole slaw: 1 serving	13
Corn: 5½-in piece	31
Gravy: 1 serving	1
Individual Chicken Pieces, Extra Crispy	
Drumstick	5
Keel	14
Side Breast	14
Thigh	13
Wing	9
Individual Chicken Pieces, Original Recipe	
Drumstick	3
Keel	7
Side Breast	7

GRAMS

Thigh	7
Wing	4
Kentucky Fries: 1 serving	28
Mashed potatoes: 1 serving	12
Roll	11

LONG JOHN SILVER'S SEAFOOD SHOPPES

Catfish Fillet: 1 piece	13
Catfish Fillet Dinner	86
Chicken Plank: 1 piece	7
Chicken Planks: 4 pieces w Fryes	59
Chicken Plank Dinner w Slaw	70
Chicken Sandwich	48
Clam Chowder: 6 fl oz	15
Clams, Breaded: 1 serving	58
Clams, Fried, w Fryes, Slaw: 1 serving	100
Cole Slaw: 3½-oz serving drained on fork	11
Corn on the Cob: 1 ear	29
Fish, Baked, w sauce: 5½-oz serving	0
Fish, Baked, w sauce, slaw, mixed vegetables	19
Fish w Batter: 1 piece	11
Fish, Kitchen-Breaded: 1 piece	8
Fish Dinner	92
Fish Dinner, Kitchen-Breaded, 2-piece	74
Fish Dinner, Kitchen-Breaded, 3-piece	82
Fish & Chicken	72
Fish & Fryes, 2-piece	53
Fish & Fryes, 3-piece	64
Fish & More	81
Fish Sandwich	45
Fish Sandwich Platter	87
Fryes, Bigger Better: 3-oz serving	31
Hush Puppies: 2 pieces	18
Oyster, Breaded: 1 piece	6
Oysters w Fryes, Slaw	77
Peg Leg w Batter: 1 piece	4
Peg Legs w Fryes	50
Pie, Apple: 4-oz serving	43
Pie, Cherry: 4-oz serving	46
Pie, Lemon Meringue: 3½-oz serving	37

GRAMS

Pie, Pecan: 4-oz serving	59
Pie, Pumpkin: 4-oz serving	34
Sauce, Seafood: 1.2 oz	9
Sauce, Tartar: 1 oz	5
Scallop w Batter: 1 piece	4
Scallops w Fryes, Slaw	68
Seafood Combo, Chilled	27
Seafood Platter	85
Seafood Salad: 5.8-oz serving	19
Seafood Salad w Lettuce, Tomato, Crackers	34
Shrimp, Battered: 1 piece	3
Shrimp, Battered, w Fryes, Slaw	59
Shrimp, Breaded: 4.7-oz serving	33
Shrimp, Breaded, Platter	93
Shrimp, chilled: 1 piece	0–1
Shrimp Dinner, chilled	19
Treasure Chest	71
Vegetables, mixed: 4-oz serving	8
Children's Menu	
1 Piece Fish, Fryes	42
2 Chicken Planks, Fryes	45
3 Peg Legs, Fryes	42
1 Piece Fish, 1 Peg Leg, Fryes	46

McDONALD'S

Big Mac	40
Cheeseburger	29
Chicken McNuggets: 1 serving	15
Cone (soft ice cream)	30
Cookies, Chocolaty Chip: 2½-oz serving	44
Cookies, McDonaldland: 2½-oz serving	48
Egg McMuffin	31
Eggs, Scrambled	2
English muffin w Butter	29
Filet-O-Fish	37
Fries, Regular: 1 serving	26
Hamburger	29
Hash Brown Potatoes: 1 serving	14
Hotcakes w Butter and Syrup	93
Pie, Apple	29

GRAMS

Pie, Cherry	32
Quarter Pounder	32
Quarter Pounder w Cheese	32
Sauce, Barbeque (for McNuggets): 1 serving	13
Sauce, Honey (for McNuggets): 1 serving	12
Sauce, Hot Mustard (for McNuggets): 1 serving	10
Sauce, Sweet and Sour (for McNuggets): 1 serving	15
Sausage: 1 serving	0–1
Shake, Chocolate	65
Shake, Strawberry	62
Shake, Vanilla	59
Sundae, Caramel	52
Sundae, Hot Fudge	46
Sundae, Strawberry	46

PIZZA HUT

Serving size: one-half of a 10-inch pizza (3 slices)

Thin 'N Crispy Pizza	
Beef	51
Pork	51
Cheese	54
Pepperoni	45
Supreme	51
Thick 'N Chewy Pizza	
Beef	73
Pork	71
Cheese	71
Pepperoni	68
Supreme	74

PONDEROSA

Baked Fish	12
Baked Fish w potato, garnishes, roll, butter, or margarine, tartar sauce	92
Chicken Strips	16
Chicken Strips w baked potato, garnishes, roll, butter or margarine	89
Chopped Beef	0

GRAMS

Chopped Beef w baked potato, garnishes, roll, butter or margarine	74
Chopped Beef, Big	0
Chopped Beef, Big, w baked potato, garnishes, roll, butter or margarine	74
Double Deluxe	37
Double Deluxe w garnishes, fries	67
Filet Mignon	0–1
Filet Mignon w baked potato, garnishes, roll, butter or margarine	74
Filet of Sole Dinner	85
Filet of Sole Sandwich	47
Filet of Sole Sandwich w Fries	77
Ham 'n Cheese	48
Ham 'n Cheese w Fries	79
Imperial Prime Rib	0
Imperial Prime Rib w baked potato, garnishes, roll, butter or margarine	74
King Prime Rib	0
King Prime Rib w baked potato, garnishes, roll, butter or margarine	74
New York Strip	0–1
New York Strip w baked potato, garnishes, roll, butter or margarine	74
Prime Rib	74
Prime Rib w baked potato, garnishes, roll, butter or margarine	76
Ribeye	0
Ribeye w baked potato, garnishes, roll, butter or margarine	74
Ribeye & Shrimp	6
Ribeye & Shrimp w baked potato, garnishes, roll, butter or margarine, cocktail sauce	97
Salad Bar: 1-oz serving each item	
Bean sprouts	2
Beets	1
Broccoli	2
Cabbage, Red	2
Carrots	3
Cauliflower	2
Celery	1

GRAMS

Chickpeas (garbanzos)	17
Cucumber	1
Green Pepper	1
Lettuce	1
Mushrooms	1
Onions, White	3
Radish	1
Tomato	1
Salad dressings: 1 oz	
Blue Cheese	2
Creamy Italian	3
Low Calorie	1
Oil-Vinegar	1
Sweet 'n Tart	9
Thousand Island	7
Shrimp Dinner	101
Sirloin	0
Sirloin w baked potato, garnishes, roll, butter or margarine	74
Sirloin Tips	0–1
Sirloin Tips w baked potato, garnishes, roll, butter or margarine	74
Steakhouse Deluxe	37
Steakhouse Deluxe w Fries	67
Super Sirloin	0
Super Sirloin w baked potato, garnishes, roll, butter or margarine	74
T-Bone	0
T-Bone w baked potato, garnishes, roll, butter or margarine	74
Children's Items	
Chicken Strips	8
French Fries	30
Gelatin: ½ cup	24
Hot Dog	21
Pudding, Butterscotch	27
Pudding, Chocolate	27
Pudding, Vanilla	28
Square Shooter	21
Whipped Topping: ¼ oz	1

ROY ROGERS

	GRAMS
Bacon Cheeseburger	31
Cheeseburger	34
Double-R-Bar Burger	34
Egg Sandwich	26
English Muffin	26
Bacon	0–1
Ham	0–1
Sausage	0–1
French Fries: 3-oz serving	29
French Fries, large: 4-oz serving	39
Fried Chicken	
Breasts: 8 oz	8
Drumsticks: 4 oz	2
Thighs: 6½ oz	7
Wings: 3½ oz	4
Hamburger	34
Hash Browns: 1 serving	17
Pancakes: 1 serving	36
Roast Beef Sandwich	34
Roast Beef Sandwich, Large	31
Roast Beef Sandwich w Cheese	35
Roast Beef Sandwich w Cheese, Large	31
Salad Bar and Fixins Bar Items	
Lettuce: 2 oz	2
Onions: 1 oz	3
Tomato: 2 oz	3
Cucumbers: ½ oz	0–1
Peppers: ¾ oz	1
Carrots: ¼ oz	0–1
Chick Peas: 1 oz	17
Radishes: ¾ oz	0–1
Red Beets: 1 oz	3
Bean Sprouts: 1 oz	2
Bacon Bits: ¼ oz	2
Parmesan Cheese: ¼ oz	0–1
Chow Mein Noodles: ½ oz	8
Potato Salad: 2 oz	8
Lo-cal Italian Dressing: 1 oz	2
Blue Cheese Dressing: 1 oz	2
French Dressing: 1 oz	5

	GRAMS
Diced Egg: ½ oz	0–1
Scrambled Eggs: 1 serving	1
Shake, Chocolate	60
Shake, Vanilla	53

TACO BELL

Bean Burrito	48
Beef Burrito	37
Beefy Tostado	21
Bellbeefer	23
Bellbeefer w Cheese	23
Burrito Supreme	43
Combination Burrito	43
Enchirito	42
Taco	14
Tostada	25

WENDY'S

Bacon: 2 strips	0–1
Bacon Cheeseburger on White Bun	23
Breakfast Sandwich	33
Chicken Sandwich on Multigrain Wheat Bun	31
Chili: 8 oz	26
Danish	44
French Fries, Regular: 1 serving	35
French Toast: 2 slices	45
Frosty: 12 fl oz	59
Garden Spot Salad Bar	
Alfalfa Sprouts: 2 oz	2
American Cheese, Imitation: 1 oz	1
Bacon Bits: ⅛ oz	0–1
Bell Peppers: ¼ cup	1
Blueberries: 1 tbsp	2
Breadsticks: 1	2
Broccoli: ½ cup	2
Cantaloupe: 2 pieces	1
Carrots: ¼ cup	3
Cauliflower: ½ cup	3
Cheddar Cheese, Imitation: 1 oz	1

GRAMS

	GRAMS
Chow Mein Noodles: ¼ cup	6
Cole slaw: ½ cup	3
Cottage Cheese: ½ cup	3
Croutons: 18	4
Cucumbers: ¼ cup	1
Eggs: 1 tbsp	0–1
Green Peas: ½ cup	9
Jalapeno Peppers: 1 tbsp	2
Lettuce, Iceberg: 1 cup	2
Lettuce, Romaine: 1 cup	2
Mild Pepperoncini or Banana Peppers: 1 tbsp	4
Mozzarella Cheese, Imitation: 1 oz	0–1
Mushrooms: ¼ cup	0–1
Oranges: 2 pieces	3
Pasta Salad: ½ cup	17
Peaches in Syrup: 2 pieces	4
Pineapple Chunks in Juice: ½ cup	20
Red Onions: 1 tbsp	0–1
Saltine Crackers: 4 pieces	8
Swiss Cheese, Imitation: 1 oz	0–1
Sunflower Seeds and Raisins: ¼ cup	12
Tomatoes: 1 oz	1
Turkey Ham: ¼ cup	1
Watermelon: 2 pieces	0–1
Dressings: 1 tbsp	
Blue Cheese	0–1
Celery Seed	3
Golden Italian	3
Oil	0–1
Ranch	0–1
Red French	5
Reduced Calorie Bacon & tomato	2
Reduced Calorie Creamy Cucumber	2
Reduced Calorie Italian	2
Reduced Calorie Thousand Island	2
Thousand Island	2
Wine Vinegar	0–1
Hamburger, Double, on White Bun	24
Hamburger, Single, on Multigrain Wheat Bun	20
Hamburger, Single, on White Bun	27
Home Fries: 1 serving	37

GRAMS

Hot Stuffed Baked Potatoes
    Bacon & Cheese   57
    Broccoli & Cheese   54
    Cheese   55
    Chicken à la King   59
    Chili & Cheese   63
    Plain   52
    Sour Cream & Chives   53
    Stroganoff & Sour Cream   60
Kids' Meal Hamburger   11
Light Menu
    Chicken Sandwich on Multigrain Wheat Bun   31
    Garden Spot Salad Bar *(see individual items)*
    Hamburger, Single, on Multigrain Wheat Bun   20
    Multigrain Wheat Bun   23
    Pick-up Window Side Salad   5
    Plain Baked Potato   52
Omelet #1—Ham & Cheese   6
Omelet #2—Ham, Cheese & Mushroom   7
Omelet #3—Ham, Cheese, Onion, Green Pepper   7
Omelet #4—Mushroom, Onion, Green Pepper   7
Pick-up Window Side Salad   5
Sausage: 1 patty   0–1
Scrambled Eggs: 1 serving   7
Taco Salad: 1 serving   36
Toast w Margarine: 2 slices   35

WHITE CASTLE

Cheeseburger   27
Fish (wo tartar sauce)   18
French fries   20
Hamburger   18

Index

283

ABOUT THE AUTHOR

JEAN CARPER is an independent writer and broadcaster, specializing in health, nutrition and consumer subjects. She has written numerous articles for national publications including *Reader's Digest* and the *Washington Post*. She is the author of eleven other books: *Stay Alive! Bitter Greetings: The Scandal of the Military Draft, The Dark Side of the Marketplace* (co-authored with Warren G. Magnuson), *Not With A Gun, Eating May Be Hazardous To Your Health* (co-authored with Jacqueline Verrett), *The All-In-One Carbohydrate Counter, The All-In-One Low Fat Gram Counter, The Revolutionary 7-Unit Low Fat Diet, The Brand Name Nutrition Counter, The National Medical Directory* and *Jean Carper's Total Nutrition Guide*. She was formerly a national consumer reporter for Westinghouse Broadcasting (Group W) and the Washington medical correspondent for Cable News Network (CNN). She lives in Washington, D.C.

BANTAM
SHOP·AT·HOME
C·A·T·A·L·O·G

Special Offer
Buy a Bantam Book
for only 50¢.

Now you can have Bantam's catalog filled with hundreds of titles plus take advantage of our unique and exciting bonus book offer. A special offer which gives you the opportunity to purchase a Bantam book for only 50¢. Here's how!

By ordering any five books at the regular price per order, you can also choose any other single book listed (up to a $4.95 value) for just 50¢. Some restrictions do apply, but for further details why not send for Bantam's catalog of titles today!

Just send us your name and address and we will send you a catalog!